INDUSTRIAL MARKETING:
an analytical approach to planning and execution

INDUSTRIAL MARKETING

*an analytical approach to
planning and execution*

Second Edition
LAWRENCE FISHER, PhD, MSc (Econ), AIS
*Principal Lecturer, School of Management Studies,
Polytechnic of Central London*

BUSINESS BOOKS LIMITED
London

First published 1969
Second edition 1976

ISBN 0 220 66292 4

*Printed in Great Britain by The Anchor Press Limited
and bound by Wm Brendon & Son Limited
both of Tiptree, Essex, for the publishers
Business Books Limited, 24 Highbury Crescent, London N5*

To K.L.F.

CONTENTS

LIST OF EXHIBITS

FOREWORD

There are many definitions of the word 'marketing', which is probably why it is one of the most confused of all the management disciplines in industry today. It is, however, vital in this era of rapidly changing technology that industrial companies have a detailed understanding of other markets to enable them to develop opportunities which may only present themselves for relatively short periods of time. There can be few decisions taken in a large industrial company which do not imply something about the future of the market and there is, therefore, a need for a continuous process of education in the field of marketing.

Marketing education and literature have developed in the last few years but at the same time there has been an increase in the demand from both the industrial and business schools for new ideas and more sophisticated techniques to develop marketing strategies. The subject of marketing is so diverse that there is a continual need for practitioners to be made aware of the latest developments and this can only be achieved by attendances at courses, seminars etc. or by reading published material.

The second edition of *Industrial Marketing* meets the requirements of both marketing and management students and like the first edition should become a standard work of great value to those engaged in business education and industrial marketing.

Lawrence Fisher is currently Principal Lecturer in the School of Management Studies at the Polytechnic of Central London with particular responsibilities for economics, marketing and business policy. Prior to his academic career, he had considerable practical experience in industrial marketing with companies engaged in the oil, plastics, rope

and wool industries. A founder member of the Industrial Marketing
Research Association, Lawrence Fisher has since 1963 played an active
part in the Association's affairs particularly with regard to education and
techniques.

R. GODDARD
Chairman
Industrial Marketing Research Association
August 1976

INTRODUCTION TO SECOND EDITION

Since the first edition of this book was published in 1969 ideas have moved forward and the general appreciation of the importance of the subject has much increased. The earlier book was a practical statement of the principles of industrial marketing which assumed no prior formal study of marketing.

When a new edition became an obvious need it was decided to bring the book up-to-date, to maintain the same philosophy and to keep the focus on the requirements of present and potential executives.

The second edition aims to give a clearly written, up-to-date and systematic coverage of current ideas on industrial marketing, together with new or revised material which will help to extend the frontiers of thought on its subject. The author hopes the practising executive can use this as a basis for checking and developing the background knowledge from which his own decisions germinate. The teacher will find a planned approach consistent with current thinking on marketing and management. He also seeks to offer a clear and concise book which many students will find easy to follow yet without loss of rigour.

These clearly include the students of industrial marketing. It should also fit well the needs of students of science or technology who attend courses which incorporate business management studies. To most of these industrial marketing is more relevant than consumer marketing.

In Chapter 1 the general philosophy of marketing is presented more concisely although the broader interpretation of marketing has been maintained together with the linkage to corporate strategy. More space is devoted later to a fresh approach to the study of buying behaviour, to planning and some other issues. The practical emphasis is maintained together with straightforward presentation.

In the first edition, acknowledgement was made to many skilled people who had generously advised and commented. The list is now too long for individual identification, but the author acknowledges his indebtedness to advisers in business, industry, public service and education and asks them to accept this as a token of his warm appreciation.

1 MARKETING IN AN INDUSTRIAL CONTEXT

In the year 1791 Matthew Boulton of Birmingham wrote to his partner, the Scots engineer James Watt, a letter which included the following:

> 'The people in London, Manchester and Birmingham are *steam mill* mad. I don't mean to hurry you but I think we should determine to take out a patent for certain methods of producing rotative motion from . . . the fire engine.'

Later he wrote again:

> '. . . the most likely line for the consumption of our engines is in the application of them to mills which is certainly an extensive field.'

Watt was an inventor, sometimes regarded as *the* inventor of the steam engine (then called the fire engine). His partner Boulton was a businessman of many talents. The partnership had already developed steam engines which had sold for pumping water from tin and copper mines in Cornwall. By the standards of Britain at the dawn of the industrial revolution these mines were important enterprises.

This market was nearing saturation. Boulton saw fresh opportunity in the vigorous development of textile and other new industries elsewhere. The steam engine which pumped out mines had however a major limitation: it provided only reciprocal motion. This was excellent for working pump rods up and down to raise water from the mines, but useless where rotating machinery needed to be driven. Boulton's correspondence urged Watt to adapt his invention to meet the needs of this untapped expanding market.

Watt did exactly this (although not without argument). He developed the sun-and-planet gearing to give rotative motion and incorporated other improvements. The new engine was a commercial as well as a technical success, orders exceeding expectations [1], and made a crucial contribution to the economic growth of Britain.

The relevance of this anecdote is that it shows in simple form the essence of what today is called marketing. There was identification of a need which the firm could reasonably expect to meet and the resources of the firm were directed to its satisfaction.

Nor is this the only example of the marketing attitude in the career of Boulton. He was aware of the importance of bringing his products to the attention of the public. For many years he showed visitors over his factory, which became a well-known attraction. The very first engine which the partnership ever sold was deliberately a big one for show purposes. When it was set to work two hundred years ago on 8 March 1776 it was introduced 'with much fanfare of trumpets'—and a long report in the Birmingham newspaper [1].

The suggestion sometimes made that marketing is a recent innovation is certainly open to question. In a limited sense it is coeval with business itself. No doubt at that early date it was crude and unsophisticated but the same could be said of Watt's steam engine.

Customer orientation

The key idea of marketing is that business thinking and planning start by considering customers, as they are now and as they will evolve in the future. A business whether private or state-owned exists by selling its products and services. By doing this it seeks to achieve its profit or other objectives. Where the customer has choice (for example whether to buy this or that product, whether to patronise this or that supplier) the successful sale and subsequent repeat sales depend upon the would-be supplier satisfying the prospective customer so that the choice is exercised in his favour.

Satisfying the customer can in fact be an elusive objective. In part it is a matter of providing the right piece of hardware with each detail fitted to the buying organisation's needs. In addition there may be many less tangible extras looked for in the supplier's offer: technical advice, after-sales service, credit, advice on selling at the next stage, and sometimes reassurance for the purchasing executive (on such issues as 'Am I wise in selecting this supplier?' and 'How shall I persuade my superior to accept my point of view?').

It is by no means easy in industrial marketing to decide exactly who should be regarded as 'the customer'. The marketing firm is selling to another company, which is a complex organisation of interacting individuals. That company is in turn selling to another customer—who may be an individual or an organisation. In later pages it will often be necessary to replace the concept of the customer by the more abstract concept of a group of individuals who influence the ultimate buying process. This group interacts within the boundary of the buying organisation with which the transaction is conducted and sometimes extends beyond the limits of that boundary. The industrial marketing man may find himself concerned not only with his immediate customer organisation but also with that customer's customer, and even beyond.

To urge the businessman to think about his customer more might seem presumptuous were it not for the evidence that customer orientation is not so easy as might at first appear.

A study of the reasons why Britain has had difficulty in expanding its exports by Prest and Coppock [2] includes the following comments:

> 'Export performance is not simply a matter of relative costs and prices. At a general level, behaviour in this field may be usefully interpreted in terms of the theory of monopolistic competition which stresses the importance of non-price factors where products are not homogeneous. One might, therefore, expect to find the volume of exports of manufacturers to be sensitive to factors like quality and design of products, the time between orders and deliveries, including the degree to which promised delivery dates are fulfilled in practice, the size and effectiveness of after-sales service, the degree to which manufacturers are prepared to cater for local market conditions, and the effectiveness and scale of their market research, advertising and sales promotion activities. Complaints that UK exporters have been negligent under all these headings have been numerous and seem endemic in the history of UK export performance.'

In the marketing firm the customer becomes the focus of the firm's operations, and a key task is understanding the customer and identifying the *need* that the marketing company seeks to meet, the *problem* it seeks to solve and the *benefit* it seeks to offer. For the industrial marketing firm a linked group of people replaces the simple concept of the customer and a constellation of related needs, problems, and benefits are involved.

Marketing and the changing environment

Customer orientation, basic as it is, must be related to the enterprise's need to satisfy its objectives in profit or other terms. It does not imply that the firm should seek to solve every need of every possible customer or move precipitately from one line of business to another without measuring the likely gains and counting the likely costs. A manager looking at the environment around him may see hosts of problems he might seek to solve and more customers he might seek to satisfy. His resources are limited in quantity and more or less specialised in type. He must therefore select.

How does he decide? Essentially this is a marketing decision for he is seeking the emerging opportunity which is likely over time to prove the most advantageous for his company. He must take account of the magnitude of the opportunity, the intensity of likely competition and constraints imposed by governmental action and other forces external to his own company. Having looked at these outside factors he turns his attention inwards to his own organisation and studies the inventory of its assets and skills to determine whether it is likely to operate successfully in this line of business.

Ideally the line selected should be that most likely to yield greatest success and should be determined after considering systematically feasible alternatives. This idea that the company should re-examine its policies in the light of anticipated changes in the external environment is common both to marketing and to the company's corporate strategy. These can both be viewed as aspects of the same fundamental idea: any difference turning on the fact that the corporate strategy is concerned with a longer time horizon and consideration of a wider class of environmental pressures. Marketing can well be defined as the total problem of the efficient adaptation of the firm to its environment—a matter further discussed in Chapter 19. Conversely the marketing decisions of the firm influence the environment. Often this influence is small, occasionally it is substantial. The marketing executive may be in the position of a change agent bringing innovation to a client system. He may well then call to mind the comment of Rogers with Shoemaker [3] in their classic work on innovation—'change agencies must be concerned with the consequences of innovation'.

Decision and action

The company having thus defined its strategic choice of business and markets systematically collects facts, figures, forecasts and indeed assumptions about customers, end-users, competitors, distributors and the constraints imposed by law and other institutions. Management now has to decide its own marketing action, that is to say how it will utilise the marketing instruments under its control.

It is normally in position to control the following marketing variables:

Products to be offered
Ancillary services to be provided
Price and other terms of sale
Communications with those who influence the purchase process
Channels of ownership and of physical distribution

Management has to select an appropriate mix, determining in what form and to what extent to use each variable. In addition it must make provision for the continuing process of collecting and interpreting market information.

The set of controllable variables above differs somewhat from that in other texts. Probably the best-know set is McCarthy's suggestion [51]:

Product
Place
Promotion
Price

The differences in the recommendation made here flow from the need to stress aspects of particular interest in an industrial marketing context, even at the sacrifice of the mnemonic quality of McCarthy's four P's.

Most writers define 'product' as including everything the customer receives in the transaction, whether goods or services, tangibles or intangibles. In industrial marketing the role of ancillary service is high and may be crucial. Yet there is little special discussion of services in marketing literature (save some notable exceptions). Identifying service as a separate variable directs attention to it.

The term 'communication' has also been preferred to 'promotion' because the marketing action which brings information before buying process influencers is wider than is commonly implied by promotion.

Distribution is used to include two related, but different, functions. The first is that aspect of distribution which is concerned with the chain of transactions through which rights in the goods are transferred. In this category comes a decision whether or not to use middlemen. The second meaning relates to the physical distribution of the goods: where and how they are transported, safeguarded and stored from point of production to point of usage. Physical distribution is outside the scope of the present book.

It should be stressed that making decisions about the form and extent of the deployment of the controllable marketing variables is not a process of making a series of unrelated decisions. On the contrary, the decisions should harmonise in an integrated marketing approach. This is sought by focus upon the customers in a particular market segment which is the unifying theme of the strategy.

This list of variables specifies major categories. Each is capable of further analysis and each is taken up later. Exhibit 1 illustrates the steps which have just been discussed by which the planning proceeds through the corporate stage to the determination of marketing action in the short and medium terms. The intended outcome is that at the final stage of execution all marketing activity is carried through in a manner consistent with the ultimate objectives of the firm.

There are few acts of the firm which do not ultimately to a lesser or greater degree impinge on some or all of its customers, and marketing management seeks to create a total company sensitivity to this fact. The company as a whole then works to achieve its objectives consistent with this customer orientation.

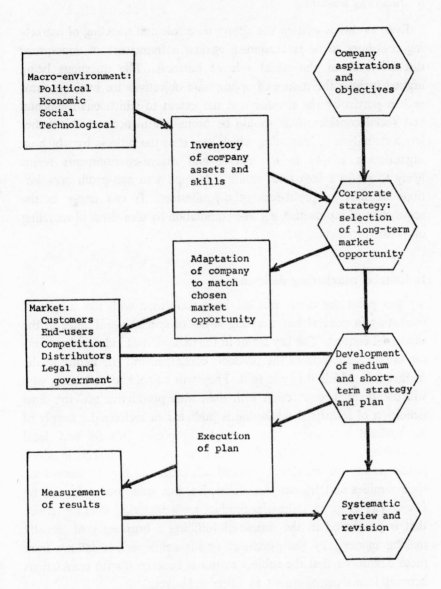

EXHIBIT 1 The firm and its environment

Even as this is written the appropriate role and meaning of marketing continues to be re-examined, against a framework of widespread discussion about the social role of business. The questions being argued include the nature of appropriate objectives for business firms and in particular the manner and the extent to which environmental and social considerations should be brought into account. Nevertheless a definition of marketing which sees it as the process by which an organisation adapts to its market and macro-environments seems likely to retain a long-term validity. It applies to non-profit organisations as well as profit-seeking organisations. It can apply to the acquisition of inputs also, e.g. the stimulation by user firms of recycling of 'waste' products.

Industrial marketing defined

To this point the discussion has been concerned with the subject of marketing in general but stressing issues of special significance in the industrial context. The key factor in the definition of industrial marketing is not the nature of the products concerned but the nature of the market into which they are sold. They will be sold to customers who will use them in connection with their own productive activity. This definition of industrial marketing is intended to include the supply of institutional customers (for example hospitals, prisons and local authorities). It distinguishes this area from consumer markets in which purchases are for the direct personal satisfaction of buyers themselves, their families and friends. An alternative, but analogous definition by Gisser [4] is of an industrial product as 'a material, item or service that is purchased in the course of fulfilling a business goal (usually making money), by the purchaser or his employer'. It follows from these definitions that the subject matter is concerned with transactions between formal organisations, as sellers and buyers.

Many goods will be in demand by both consumer and industrial customers, e.g. paint, motor spirit and typewriters. The dividing line between marketing approaches to the two classes of customer is not sharp and precise: differences are often a matter of degree and ideas are adapted from one sector to the other. Nevertheless, the difference of degree is quite considerable between typical industrial and typical consumer markets.

Achilladelis *et al.* [5] in a study of factors influencing success in innovating advanced products in the chemical and scientific instrument industries found that the more successful firms:

> 'understood user requirements better;
> employed greater sales efforts;
> devoted more efforts to educating users, and
> gave more publicity to the innovation.'

Somewhat similarly, a study by the National Economic Development Office [6] to identify marketing methods which have been found effective in the progress of the most successful machine tool firms reported that the marketing attitude was the most important factor—it was less important that marketing actions did not conform strictly to textbook standards. The report went on to say that within the various aspects of marketing attitudes, the most urgent improvement needed in the less successful firms was customer orientation.

Demand in industrial markets is derived: it is always linked ultimately to some demand for goods and services at the consumer level, if that term is interpreted to include purchase by public bodies for social consumption. The linkage may be short, direct and straightforward or it may be long, roundabout and difficult to identify because of the diverse route and loops through which it takes place.

Key definitions

Certain standard terms are adopted in this text to aid in describing market structure:

The *intermediate manufacturer* is a customer who buys from the marketing firm (which is the focus of this analysis) and uses the purchased items in his production process, reforming and adapting them, so that they form part of the products which he sells to a subsequent customer.

The *end-user* is the buying organisation or individual who physically retains possession of the goods and does not pass them on either as they are or in his own products. The typical examples of end-use are found in the purchase of consumables, of capital goods and of services. The consumer who buys goods for the benefit of himself and his family is also an end-user.

The term *customer* has been used freely and includes potential customers in the target market segments; it is not necessarily restricted to the current customers.

Institutions are organisations such as hospitals, prisons, charitable bodies, whose prime motive is not commercial business but the serving of some other purpose. Buying decisions cannot be related to commercial criteria such as expected profit, but the institutions commonly operate within budget constraints which may be more or less severe.

Analysis of the transaction

It is common to analyse the goods and services offered to industrial customers into a number of different classes. The list below is a typical analysis, but it is by no means the only or even necessarily the most important factor in developing the marketing strategy of a company. The *total* marketing situation has to be analysed and strategy fitted to it.

1   *Capital items*   These are items from which the customer will receive value over a period of time. Goods (such as production machinery) will commonly be capitalised in the accounts and written off over a number of years. Often they will involve significant expenditure and be a major decision for the buying company.

2   *Raw materials, processed materials, components, sub-assemblies* These items share the common feature that they enter directly into the customer's product, become physically part of it and in this way pass onwards incorporated in the goods he sells. Accordingly, they are often part of the customer's direct variable cost and affect the saleability of his product. Sometimes the customer's customer may be able to identify the qualities which they give in the product which he, in turn, buys. Raw materials commonly have a relatively wide range of applications, but as they

are processed into more advanced products, so they tend to be more closely adapted to a specific class of application. (Products which are marketed to a wide cross-section of industry are often referred to as being in horizontal demand; those marketed to a narrow market are referred to as being in vertical demand.) Items in this and the following class are *revenue* items.

3 *Consumables* These are items used up in a relatively short period without actually becoming part of the customer's product. They cover a considerable range, and include such items as lubricants, fuel and power, and stationery.

4 *Services* These cover a wide range from those services which provide a long-term benefit and are thus analogous to a capital item, although not treated as such in the accounts of the buying company (the services of a management consultant are an example of this), to other services such as those of banking, transport and insurance which are revenue items more analogous to a consumable product.

2 INDUSTRIAL MARKET BEHAVIOUR

The market is an arena in which each firm to some extent competes with others, to some extent cooperates with others and on occasions exercises control or influence over others (and conversely may be controlled or influenced by them). This arena is surrounded by the four areas of the wider environment: political action, economic change, social evolution and technological development. The firm over the years and decades must adapt to this evolving macro-environment, but this is a subject reserved for consideration in Chapter 19, in which the strategic adaptation of the firm is considered.

The first approach to understanding the behaviour of firms in the market was made by economists who studied the various ways in which supplier interaction in a market might be structured. The original approaches emphasised price behaviour but more recently the emphasis on this has been diluted. The study of these interactions was based largely upon 'ideal models' involving defined assumptions. These do not necessarily mirror precisely real-life circumstances but can help the executive infer what might happen in somewhat analagous situations.

Patterns of supply

Amongst natural products (sisal, wool, for example), where there are many suppliers, something like perfect competition might develop. The economist defines this as a situation in which there are many small firms and no one of them is sufficiently important that it can independently influence the market price by increasing or reducing the quantity of goods it offers to sell. Each has no alternative but to accept the going rate; the firm is a 'price taker'.

However, producers may not rest content with the fate to which this analysis abandons them. They may join together in partnership (perhaps under Government sponsorship) to promote the product, to improve its quality and to exercise some control over the volume of supply so that price may be influenced in their favour.

At the other extreme of the market spectrum from perfect competition is monopoly. In its strictest sense this implies control over total supply of a specific product by one supplier. Such a supplier would have great power to settle the level of price and gain better profits, subject to the limitations imposed by the amount which customers are willing to buy at different price levels.

For a monopoly to be maintained when profits are high there must also be barriers which make it difficult for new competitors to enter the business of supplying this product. Such barriers can include:

1   High cost of entering the business concerned.
2   Loyalty of customers to the existing supplier.
2   Need for special technological knowledge which is not easily obtained.
4   Control of important patents (this is becoming increasingly difficult to maintain).
5   Control of essential raw materials.
6   Government restrictions on entry (sometimes granted by Governments trying to promote the growth of an infant industry).

Supply situations approximating to monopoly often come under Government surveillance and most major countries have legislation to regulate the activities of firms which dominate individual industries. These differ in detail from one country to another. The United States and EEC law, for example, is largely based on the premise that competition is to be sustained. British law is less closely linked to this presumption; instead dominant firms providing 25 per cent or more of the supply of a product are liable to be investigated for the purpose of deciding whether they have been acting contrary to the public interest.

Restrictive trade practices in which a number of firms agree about, for example, prices to be charged or market shares, present some of the features of monopoly and may also be the subject of some form of regulation.

A special case of inter-firm cooperation is the formation of a consortium of firms to tender for a substantial contract. Such *ad hoc* arrangements are made when the resources required to meet the needs of the contract exceeds the capability of the firms individually. This may apply in relation to an extensive construction programme which is the subject of international competition.

Oligopoly, in which the supply of a product is concentrated in the hands of a few suppliers, is frequent; such products as industrial gases, baler twine and agricultural machinery have been found in this classification. In these circumstances a supplier in an oligopolistic market will in settling his selling price be heavily influenced by his expectations concerning the reaction of competing suppliers to that price. The direct effect of a price cut on the sales of a competitor may lead to sharp retaliation and a price war may follow. This is most likely in a capital intensive industry where variable costs are low and overheads high. If excess capacity arises in these conditions companies may be tempted to improve sales by cutting their prices, and these can fall to a level where fixed costs are not covered.

It is often argued that oligopoly is more likely to lead to implicit collaboration than to cut-throat competition. One firm may emerge as the leader in price setting. The price leader is likely to be the largest supplier but could be a smaller firm whose decisions are followed because of general respect for the judgment of its executives. If costs rise no other supplier is likely to raise its price until the price leader has done so. If costs fall, the price leader may well lead the way down, although in some cases smaller firms may find it advantageous to make minor concessions before the general drop. Similarly if there is a drop in demand the smaller firm may be the first to offer special discounts or price concessions, or a larger firm may lead the market to a new level.

Under the term 'monopolistic competition', product differentiation is introduced as a market factor. This refers to a situation in which product lines are generically similar, but differ by minor variations in technical features, ancillary service or supplier reputation. Products compete but each firm's offering is likely to be perceived as somewhat different by some segment of the market. Each firm has a monopoly of its own product yet remains in competition with other suppliers; hence 'monopolistic competition'. A supplier seeking a differential competitive advantage in this market may either offer a price concession or a product differentiation benefit or some balance between the two.

Patterns of demand

To some extent patterns of demand can be the mirror image of the supply side. One can have monopsonistic situations (only one buyer) or dominant purchasers, who may be very influential and seek keen terms. The US Robinson-Patman Act in general prohibits the giving of special discounts to favoured firms, except where justified by costs. The objective seems to be to prevent such firms using their bargaining power to gain advantages considered to be unfair.

In some countries monopsonistic buyers may be state-owned industries such as the British Post Office, responsible for all but a tiny part of the telephone system. The price problem of oligopolistic suppliers competing for business can be difficult.

It is in fact very common in industrial markets to find a large part of the demand coming from few buyers. That 80 per cent of the business comes from 20 per cent of the customers is a commonly heard phrase and is often not too far from the truth. On the other hand there are some markets in which the number of customers is high and much business comes in small orders; farmers, offices and small stores requirements.

Some users of a product may not purchase all their requirements through normal market transactions. Some may engage in reciprocity practices (trade relations). The basis of these practices is that firm A buys from firm B on condition that firm B buys other products from firm A. The net benefit from such deals needs to be carefully assessed. In these circumstances the demand is captive and not accessible to the outside supplier. A similar situation arises when a firm buys from a source in the same group of companies.

Indeed, customers may well be potential competitors when they are capable of taking the necessary steps to manufacture the product for themselves. Price rises or poor service cause careful thought about the relative economics of 'making' as opposed to 'buying'. Such a policy once put into effect may be difficult to reverse when specialised facilities have been established and staff employed for the purpose.

A supplier who finds the market does not respond to his offers is sometimes tempted to follow a policy of forward integration, and to take over one or more customer firms. While sometimes successful such a move must be set into the wider context of the long-term policy of the business. Taking over a customer brings with it a new set of problems from the customer's own business, and may antagonise other possible customers. Moreover if the takeover is built around the fact that the link between customer and supplier is technical linkage between the supplier's output and the customer's production, what happens if the evolution of technology or changes in relative prices destroys this link; if steel as a raw material is later replaced by plastics, for example? The original logic of the arrangement is then lost.

Market dimensions: Proximity and concentration

It has already been pointed out that the demand for all industrial goods (or producers' goods as some writers prefer to describe them) is a *derived* demand: it originates from an actual or (more generally) an anticipated final demand for goods and services. Demand derivation for the industrial product can vary along two major dimensions.

Proximity   This relates to the length of the chain of intermediate manufacturers which links the sale of the industrial product to demand in the final market. Some industrial goods sales are close to the final consumer and reaction to the consumer behaviour is therefore important in the short-term. This often requires that the product concerned be attuned to consumer preference not only on the technical level but also perhaps along the dimensions of taste and aesthetics. Sales will show short-term reaction to quantitative and qualitative changes in consumer behaviour and the firm concerned will design its information system to help anticipate these. There will be few 'pools' of inventory between the final and the industrial demand to absorb or exaggerate final demand changes. The converse applies when the chain is long. It will be noted that the consumer marketing situation is one of low proximity, and the subsistence producer of zero.

Examples of close proximity include: motor car components, consumer goods packaging and some building materials. Complex raw materials tend to have longer chains and some products will have different lengths of chains to different markets: crude oil which is used in the manufacture of petrochemicals has a longer chain than the same product used to fuel retail outlets. A characteristic of long-term capital item sales is that the link with the volume of final demand is not direct but broken and discontinuous.

Concentration This refers to the number of different final markets which are the sources of ultimate demand from which the industrial product demand derives. Where these are few (high concentration), demand can more easily be traced to its source and understood. Demand may even be promoted by advertising to the final customer on a generic or occasionally specific basis. Where there are many, demand is dispersed (low concentration) and market forecasts will tend to give more weight to model building based perhaps on macro-economic aggregates.

Concentration is to some extent related to the length of the chain. Where the chain is short (close proximity) the final demand will often be narrow or at least can often be segmented in a way which is relevant to the industrial producer's own marketing plan (as in packaging material). The smaller producer of a product with low concentration of final demand may however find marketing difficult to follow through beyond his immediate customer. Sometimes a chain of intermediate manufacturers may be 'led' by one major concern which is a substantial link in the chain and its commitment to the success of the chain is great. The object of such leadership is to harmonise relationships in order to maximise total chain efficiency. This has happened in, for example, synthetic fibres.

Patterns of interaction

The fact that industrial markets are often characterised by a limited number of potential buying firms and that these can have somewhat different needs has led Hokansson and Östberg [7] to suggest that 'the actual purchase transaction is . . . an interaction system between two active counterparts rather than merely a relationship between one active component and a passive market'. This leads (they argue) to a

power-dependence relationship. This relationship may well be progressively strengthened by mutual adaptation between the firms concerned: these adaptations involve coordination of, for example, technology and organisation to increase economic benefits from the
working together of the buyer and seller.

Relationships between firms often depend only to a limited extent upon
formal contracts. Mutual trust between the parties may be an ingredient
of greater practical importance, reducing the perceived uncertainty and
risk in the relationship. Social exchange between buyer and seller
develops and widens the area of interaction, contributes to the development of mutual trust and so influences this perception of risk and
uncertainty. Each side can accept in practice commitments well beyond
the documented contract (if there is one!).

This approach throws light on the stable long-term buyer/seller
relationships which sometimes exist between firms and the factors
which encourages these to grow and persist. The writers of the article
cited above quote examples of revenue items in support of their suggestion.

It was suggested earlier that marketing and corporate strategies may
be difficult to separate in industrial marketing and long-term customer/
supplier linkages are one factor fusing the two together.

The concept of market segmentation

No analysis of an industrial market would be complete without consideration of the way in which it could be segmented or broken down into 'sub-markets'. Market segmentation, which has been much discussed in the literature of consumer marketing in recent years, has long been an established feature of much industrial marketing. A clear understanding of the concept will, however, permit it to be used more systematically as a basis for a profitable and effective policy.

It is common to speak of 'the market' for nuts and bolts, or for oscilloscopes, or for plastics. In fact, different groups of buyers may have different market behaviour. Some may seek product features of no interest to others; some may be sensitive to price variation, and others relatively insensitive; some keen to take up new ideas, others more conservative; and some requiring a great deal of technical service, others having staff specialist to undertake this function.

A formal definition of a market segment is that it is 'a group of present or potential customers with some common characteristic which is relevant in explaining (and predicting) their response to a supplier's marketing stimuli' (Wind and Cardozo [8]). If the total market can be classified into such segments, within which buying organisations have similar reaction patterns, then it may be possible to devise different marketing strategies for different segments matching the special characteristics of each. This can gain a supplier a competitive advantage.

Market segmentation can be used to advantage in a number of different ways. In launching a new product which in its early marketing phase is likely to be expensive, the initial launch may be slanted towards a certain segment of the market comprising industries to which its offered advantages are particularly valuable. If the product resists corrosion, it may first be marketed to those industries where this problem is most serious. A marketing department may be organised so that specialists develop knowledge of particular segments and devise appropriately matched marketing strategies (as discussed in Chapter 18).

There are many ways of segmenting industrial markets. The com-

B

moner ways are discussed below, but this list should not be regarded as exhaustive. The imaginative marketing man will look out for other natural divisions between parts of his total market.

Industry segmentation using SIC categories is probably the commonest form of segmentation in industrial markets. Products are designed or adapted to meet the requirements of particular industries, and the marketing methods are adapted to meet the requirements of those industries.

Size of customer is another way in which analysis can be carried out. It may be an advantage to segment the market between large and small buyers of the product concerned. Thus a small manufacturer with low overheads may set out to deal with the low-volume customers whom the bigger company ignores. At the other extreme, one really big customer may be sufficiently important to be treated as a market segment on its own. If, for example, it was desired to develop the use of a particular product in the automobile industry, the supplier could prepare formulations suited to the needs of a particular company and analyse its models one by one to show where his product could be used to advantage. Alternatively 'size' may refer to the total size of the customer's business: a big firm/small firm division.

Applications for a product may also be a basis for segmentation. For example, equipment for R&D purposes may be made to finer tolerances, require more supplementary features, and command a higher price than the corresponding product for general plant use. The R&D market may justify attention as a separate segment. The electronic components market may be divided between computer applications, consumer durables applications and control applications.

Geographical segmentation is sometimes found. A small supplier may concentrate on supplying one part of the country only and thus be able to give prompt and individual service together with low transport costs. As some industries are regional in character, it may be possible to associate regional and industrial segmentation and to concentrate on supplying, for example, the West Riding textile industry in the UK. In international marketing, segmentation on a country or area basis may be essential to take account of differences in language, customs, climate, law and technological sophistication.

End-use segmentation relates to the final use of the product: end-uses in food, cosmetics and other high quality sectors may require different product characteristics (as compared with more run of the mill uses).

It has been suggested by Frank *et al*. [9] that it could be of value to adopt a two-stage model of segmentation. Stage 1 is the macro-segment as discussed above; Stage 2, the micro-segment based on the characteristics of the behaviour of the decision making units (DMUs) in the different buying companies. Thus, they argue, second-stage segmentation might distinguish between segments on the basis of the criteria used in evaluating alternative suppliers: one firm giving emphasis to prompt delivery and quality, another to lowest cost. There may also be between firms a differential willingness to accept innovative products.

Market segmentation recognises that different types of purchaser (and even the same purchasers on different occasions) have different needs. Identification of segments permits the marketing executive to focus his efforts more clearly and sharply on the needs of the segment and thus to match his offering to it with more precision. This reduces the size of the potential market to which each particular approach is apt, but it generally improves the possibility of marketing the product successfully. If a segment is identified which has not been satisfied by competitors' offerings, then a product appropriately adapted for that segment should command higher profit, and the attack on the segment should give better returns for a given marketing effort. On the other hand, the identified segment needs to be large enough to justify all the costs involved. In some industrial markets there is a continued process of 'fine tuning' market offers to shades of difference in the spectrum of market demand.

3 BUYER BEHAVIOUR

In the process of marketing, a firm is concerned to design products to meet its customers' needs as seen by those who influence buying in the target market, to provide services to help them and promotional 'messages' to move them towards a favourable buying decision. However before plans can be made to achieve this purpose the question 'how do these companies buy?' has to be answered.

Pressures on the firm

Within any organisation decisions are the result of an exchange of ideas and information between people. Nevertheless what these people do, say, decide, depends in part at least on the economic state of the firm. Not on this alone because the individuals have lives outside the organisation with their own sets of influences. Even within the organisation such factors as their professional status, their previous career and their personal relationships with other people, individually and as a group, influence the behaviour of employees.

Looking first then at the pressures on the customer-firm as a total system, the economic well-being of the firm, as it is and as it is expected to be in the near future, is clearly relevant to its type and quantity of purchase.

Purchases of revenue items (see page 11) are a function of the volume of sales, and these in turn are linked to the outgoing sales of the customer. Where the ultimate user markets are dispersed, the demand for the revenue items may be closely related to changes in national activity. Where ultimate markets are concentrated the demand will depend on supply, demand and competition in those markets.

The level of demand for customers' products is only one factor (important though it may well be). The current and potential profitability and liquidity of the customer is a second factor: potential profitability will encourage investment and demand for capital items. Capital items (such as machine tools) also react in an accentuated degree to changes in the level of final demand for their output products.

There can be a distinction between a firm being liquid (having ready cash or something like it) and being profitable. A firm which is short of liquid assets will be under pressure to take care in its current spending policy and may cut back on expenditure which does not yield an early return even though this might be a disadvantage in the long term. Advertising and training, for example, are tempting targets for cuts in such circumstances.

Principles of analysis

In examining what is implied in organisational purchasing, analysis can be along three dimensions:

1   *Process*   The pattern of information getting, information analysis, derivation of implications and decision-making which takes place as the purchasing organisation moves through a decision.
2   *Structure*   The way in which different members of the buying organisation and perhaps some people outside it are involved in the decision-making process.
3   *Content*   The factors which are taken into account at the different stages, including the personal pressures which bear on those participating.

Although this analysis is a convenient one, the three dimensions are to some degree linked and interact with each other.

An interesting study by Robinson *et al.* [10] suggests that there are three types of buying situation which may be conveniently distinguished for analytical purposes: the headings which he uses are given below, although the definitions here suggested have been modified from the original.

1   *The new task*—in which the organisation considering a purchase is for the first time seeking to meet a certain class of need.

2   *A straight rebuy*—in which the company is meeting a need which recurs so often that the process of purchase has become substantially routine.

3   *A modified rebuy*—which stands midway between (1) and (2), e.g. what was a new task is repeated and the purchase process is standardised somewhat without becoming routine *or* what would have been a straight rebuy is jolted from its routine by some unusual circumstance (perhaps the action of a marketing firm).

It may be convenient to think of these not as three separate states but as a continuum, from complete newness with the entire process to be determined at one extreme to total knowledge and complete routine at the other extreme.

For some of the following discussion the analysis is concerned with intrafirm behaviour under 'norms of rationality' to borrow a phrase from Thompson [11]. This means that it assumes that the purchase process is made in a way which is logically consistent with the formal goals of the company. There is however assumed to be a boundary or limit to this rationality (March and Simon [12]): the decision-making is not assumed to seek the best possible decision but one which is sufficiently 'satisfactory'. Once a certain level of result is achieved the search for a better decision is not pursued. Later in the discussion the implications of personal factors outside the norms of rationality, as here defined, will be discussed.

Process

The most complete attempt to describe the buying process is that of Robinson *et al.* [10] already referred to above. Exhibit 2 sets out in full the eight process stages of that model. This is worth careful study. The original authors emphasise that the process will not pass neatly and serially through these stages, more than one stage may be in operation at the same time. As with any attempt to describe by a general model a process which takes place in a wide range of different contexts, there is room for discussion as to the width of its applicability, the appropriateness of the stages which the authors have selected for

EXHIBIT 2 The buygrid analytic framework [10]

			BUYCLASSES		
			New task	Modified rebuy	Straight rebuy
B U Y P H A S E S	1	Anticipation or recognition of a problem (need) and a general solution			
	2	Determination of characteristics and quantity of needed item			
	3	Description of characteristics and quantity of needed item			
	4	Search for and qualification of potential sources			
	5	Acquisition and analysis of proposals			
	6	Evaluation of proposals and selection of supplier(s)			
	7	Selection of an order routine			
	8	Performance feedback and evaluation			

Notes

1 The most complex buying situations occur in the upper left portion of the BUYGRID matrix, when the largest number of decision makers and buying influences are involved. Thus, a New Task in its initial phase of problem recognition generally represents the greatest difficulty for management.

2 Clearly, a New Task may entail policy questions and special studies, whereas a Modified Rebuy may be more routine, and a Straight Rebuy essentially automatic.

3 As Buyphases are completed, moving from Phase 1 to Phase 8, the process of 'creeping commitment' occurs, and there is diminishing likelihood of new vendors gaining access to the buying situation.

definition and the adequacy of their description of the content of the stages.

The process starts with a stimulus which leads to identification of a need. Perception of this need has come about as a result of some pattern of pressures from within and without the organisation. In the simplest case of a repurchase of a simple component or raw material (which may even be decided by a model applied through a programmed computer) the stimulus may be that stock in hand has fallen below a certain level.

Many circumstances are more complex than this: as Becker and Whisler [13] have pointed out, in a state of slack (when a firm is generously endowed with resources) there may be an organisational mood to innovate on a broad front, and in a state of distress (when it is short of resources) executives may only look to innovations which will reduce processing costs. One might even go further and argue that in distress when ready money is the issue companies will try to cut back on activities which will release short-term liquidity even though the long-term effect may otherwise be a net disadvantage.

The model brackets together in Stage 1 the perception of need and broad identification of what will meet it. Yet there may be more than one way in which a particular class of need can be met, e.g. whether process control shall be by analogue or digital computer, whether a component shall be in metal or plastics. If those who influence the process lean in one direction rather than another at this early stage they may to some extent pre-empt the ultimate decision.

Even before Stage 1 there may be a prior disposition to perceive the need in one way rather than another way and to consider some products as providing a possible means to meet the need and implicitly excluding others. This predisposition which may be big or small, positive or negative, deserves attention and the marketing firm may have to build into its marketing plan actions to develop or maintain in its markets a particular level and quality of predisposition. It must also be aware that it cannot necessarily rely upon the prospect firm to identify the need and to see this particular supplier's class of product as a route to meeting it. The supplier may add to its job of maintaining the background level of predisposition that of taking specific catalytic action with certain firms to stimulate the process into motion when its information indicates that the time is ripe.

In the progress through later stages, it is difficult to see that the difference between determination of characteristics (Stage 2) and description (Stage 3) may commonly be so great as to justify separate stages. More crucial may be the Stage 4 listing of acceptable suppliers. A stage such as this seems to occur very commonly, sometimes explicitly and formally, sometimes implicitly and informally. Exceptionally a supplier may have established himself earlier in a strong position, e.g. by initially identifying the need, in which case there is a high probability that he will be chosen, and the progress towards formal placing of the order would follow in the absence of some later dislocating factor.

Even after a particular supplier is virtually selected (Stages 5 and 6) there may be further negotiations to determine details, especially if the product is complex. Packaging, payment, arrangements for calling forward supplies and other peripheral factors remain to be discussed (Stage 7). In many transactions one would expect a further stage after delivery of follow-up advice, service and, of course, feedback to the supplier company (Stage 8). It is a restricted view of the process to regard it solely as one of placing a specific order; it is more generally an aspect of a continuing relationship. Rejection of a product or supplier after initial purchases can destroy the relationship.

It will be noted that there are often two dimensions of authorisation: one *technical* concerning product characteristics and one *commercial* concerning the financial implications to the purchasing company. There are also two steps in supplier selection: the stage of listing a select panel from which the ultimate supplier is chosen and the final selection of the one firm (or more) to receive the business. Sometimes the panel may have only one name, and the second stage is redundant.

Structure

Process operates within the structure of relationship which binds the buying organisation together and which also on occasions overlaps what are normally considered the formal boundaries of the firm. Those concerned with the purchase interact formally or informally in a decision-making unit (DMU) and they are the buying process influencers (BPI). For analytical purposes it is possible to classify the elements of structure as in Exhibit 3. Examples only are cited in the Exhibit.

EXHIBIT 3   Typical elements in the buying structure

	Formal	Informal
Internal	Purchasing officer Executives directly affected Technical specialists	Operatives Secretaries
External	Consultants Government inspectorate Consultants	Suppliers' representatives Customers Distributors Fellow members of technical organisations Public opinion

The internal formal structure is rather like that laid down in company's organisation charts or what has become accepted in the firm as approved practice. The essence of what goes on is usually witnessed in internal memoranda and when researchers ask questions about the involvement of departments and of individuals within the organisation in the buying process it is the formal structure which is most readily mentioned.

The informal relationships, based more on personal affiliations and the logic of the adoption circumstance, may well be powerful. Sometimes their influence may not come forward until a late stage, perhaps after the product has been used for the first time in the purchasing firm. This late reaction may affect repeat purchases and long-term relationships.

One example illustrates such circumstances. A small company in dress manufacturing changed its supplier of threads and cottons. The new supplier's products satisfied the same standards as those of the previous supplier, but none the less very quickly came under criticism from machinists. Investigation showed that the sales representative of the former supplier used to spend time in the workroom cultivating good relations with the operators and adjusting machines to ensure that they were at proper settings. Lack of contact with the new supplier's representative created anxiety and distrust in the product. Machinists started to make too frequent and sometimes unwise adjustments to their machines, leading to more frequent breakages with an impact on production and costs.

Externally the formal elements of structure include people and organisations who can exercise some sanction over the company. Some of these sanctions stem from the need for the purchasing company to satisfy legal requirements in respect of safety, pollution, working conditions and other such matters. Clearance by organisations representing operatives of a purchase which affects operating conditions may be required by law or agreement between the parties.

The influence of the purchasing firm's customers, distributors and of final users also impinge upon its specifications or preferences: for example, clients may specify product or source explicitly by words or implicitly by behaviour (for example buying or not buying).

Purchases for use in research contexts may be influenced by information and attitudes communicated to the technologists and scientists therein by other members of their particular specialisation through the invisible college of conferences, journals or casual meetings. A supplier's salesman may be a substantial influence in the buying process throughout, thus intensifying linkage between the prospect firm and his own.

Who is involved in the internal formal structure in relation to a particular decisions process will vary according to a range of circumstances. The size of firm is one obvious factor. In a small firm the 'General Manager' will be involved in decisions which in a large firm will be delegated to a middle level executive.

To go beyond this to further general identification is difficult. However, an argument advanced in the previous edition of this book seems to have stood the test of time and is repeated, with modification in the light of comments by Hill [14] and other considerations.

There are two main dimensions to the prospect organisation's perception of the product interface. One is the perceived complexity of the product and its proposed application, the other is the commercial risk involved. Both of these are functions of a number of other variables and are probably somewhat related.

Product complexity (a term suggested by Lawyer [15]) depends upon a number of factors:

1   The inherent complexity of the product being purchased which is influenced by its technology, its newness and the extent to which there are differences between products meeting the same generic need.

2   The inherent complexity of the context in which the product is to be applied, such as the newness of the class of application, the related problems of installation and subsequent operation and service.

3   Perception of the product as technically complex depending upon the previous experience of the buying organisation in relation to this product and the sophistication of the firm's customary technological environment, i.e. its nature and level.

Commercial uncertainty depends upon:

1   The magnitude of the sums involved, this is partly the purchase cost and other initial outlays but also includes any possible consequential costs arising elsewhere in the buying firm, e.g. costs of a possible labour dispute if working practices are to be affected, and any long-term commitment, express or implied, e.g. the fact that a shift to a new raw material may involve dependence upon one source of supply or upon the supplier's ability to keep a production process in operation.

2   The extent to which the costs and benefits are predictable, where forecasts are of low reliability commercial uncertainty is increased.

These factors lead to the matrix suggested in Exhibit 4. When the purchase is low on both complexity and uncertainty the buyer tends to dominate the buying process. As it increases on either dimension appropriately specialised personnel are involved: for example, when possible raw material price fluctuation is significant, specialised commodity buyers are normal. As the need for technical knowledge increases, technical buyers come into the picture.

Gradually with intensification of the need for technical expertise the decision influence tends to fall under the dominance of the technologist, whereas if commercial uncertainty increases it is the policy maker who tends to take over.

EXHIBIT 4 The pattern of buying influences

Commercial uncertainty	Product complexity	
	Low	High
Low	Buyer emphasis	Technologist emphasis
High	Policy-maker emphasis	Total involvement

Finally, if there is both increase in complexity and commercial uncertainty more of the organisation's members become involved tending to the limit of total involvement of the organisation and perhaps even extending beyond the formal limits of the organisation. At the top left of Exhibit 4 would (in most firms) be the routine purchase of non-specialised stationery, at the bottom right is the purchase process on Concorde.

Content

Issues of content arise at many stages of the purchase process. The predisposition for example may be derived from regular experience and may lead through to the definition of supplier(s), products and quantity.

If however the supplier has a technological innovation to offer; can there then be predisposition? The answer can be 'yes'. Technologists in certain industries may be predisposed to try an innovative product because it is consistent with their own attitudes and the level of complexity to which they are accustomed. Moreover communication through appropriate channels can also help towards a willingness to adopt or at least to consider sympathetically the proposed innovation. Predisposition can be strong or weak, positive or negative.

The stimulus stage may arise in many ways, from the routine (especially for revenue products), to stimulus from a catalytic circumstance (plant expansion for example) or from a catalytic individual (the supplier's salesman or a staff member). Where it is the supplier's representative he is in a strong position to stay with the process and service the business.

The listing of qualified suppliers is also common either on informal or formal basis. The reputation of would-be suppliers is significant. If a supplier is not known and not discovered in the search process his chance to gain the business is lost. If his business and technical reputation is considered too low he is again in danger of not being listed. Sometimes Head Office may prescribe selection of suppliers from an authorised list, thus restricting Divisional decision.

In general, final discrimination is at the supplier choice stage, unless for some reason dissatisfaction arises when details are being finalised.

Let us make the following assumptions:

1   A number of discriminating criteria (by which the product/ supplier is judged).
2   Differences between each supplier's offering on each criteria.
3   The criteria being capable of ranking in a hierarchy of importance to the buyer.
4   Norms of rationality (as defined above).

It is then possible to outline a model in which comparison would be made on each criteria in descending order of importance until differences were found of relevance to the buying organisation. For example if criteria (in descending order) were : (1) delivery, (2) price, (3) preference for the salesman as an individual, then if differences between delivery offered by competing suppliers were trivial or non-existent, and the same applied to price, choice would be made on the personality of the salesman! This is the highest criteria which the relevant BPIs react to as a non-trivial difference.

In real life the model is more complex. There may be several discriminating criteria on which non-trivial differences exist. Sometimes these can be quantified on a common basis (usually financial), thus reducing the problem to a unique criteria. On other occasions even the most rational of decision-makers may have difficulty in arriving at a logical decision when the differences point in contrary directions. However, the model does indicate why important purchases may appear on occasion to be settled on minor factors.

Donnely and Holton [16] in a study of sales expenses which compared differentiated products with non-differentiated products, showed that hospitality and similar sales costs were far lower for differentiated products. This is consistent with the arguments above.

The discriminating criteria may also change in priority: perceived complexity of an innovatory purchase (the first purchase of a new technological product) may be such that the knowledge and expertise of the supplier will be the key factor in supplier choice. Later as customers' knowledge of the product builds up, suppliers' expertise is likely to decline in importance.

Formal criteria

These are criteria linked to the norms of rationality. The most obvious one is that the purchase will contribute to the greater profitability of the company or to some factor which is expected to be related to profitability such as risk reduction, cost reduction, improved technical efficiency, good relations with staff. The actual assessment is however not always easy and timing is affected by the pressures discussed earlier in this chapter.

To some extent therefore the buying process involves consideration by the DMU (which is not necessarily a pre-determined set of people but one which may change throughout the process) of criteria related to the organisations overall formal objectives. The criteria may be related to profit or cost improvement, but often they are more likely to be concerned with achieving a level considered satisfactory than searching for an ill-defined best.

Some of the more clear cut approaches are in relation to capital type purchases. Models have developed in recent years which take account of the cost, the return, the timing of the return and the uncertainties involved. The more sophisticated buying organisations will have adopted a discounted cash flow procedure (which discounts for time) and, bearing in mind the uncertainty of forecasts, will use decision analysis models to take account of the probability of different possible outcomes. They may test the robustness of their conclusions by sensitivity analysis. Less sophisticated firms may employ payback and return on investment as tests, or even argue by analogy that since a competitor has made a certain investment in plant or new technology they must follow (or the reverse if the competitor has cancelled a project).

On revenue products similarly delivery service which reduces the customer's need to hold inventory is a calculable benefit which can be brought into account.

An institution not oriented to profit can seek a certain level of benefit at minimum cost, but may trade-off benefit against cost. Thus in planning a new building an institution may be prepared to pay more than its original estimate for special benefits, e.g. better insulation and low maintenance finishes.

Some benefits are difficult to evaluate. What is the worth of better staff recreation facilities? This is hard to answer in anything like specific terms. In the adoption of new technology (for example the early adoption of computers for process control) it was difficult to assess what return would be and some adopting firms abandoned the attempt to make a specific financial calculation.

In non-profit-oriented organisations attempts are sometimes made to express so far as possible external social costs and benefits in 'money' terms. The objective is to achieve better judgment thereby, although there is controversy concerning the degree of success achieved. Often there will be several criteria, not all capable of measurement and difficult to reconcile.

It needs hardly saying that for raw materials and most other tangible revenue items purchased in the normal run of business there will be appropriate specifications and most buying firms will check these from time to time. Timely and prompt delivery may not always be checked in quite the same way, but deficiencies will gradually be observed.

Gisser [4] talks of the benefit/risk relationship at both the formal organisation level and at the personal level. The importance of this is such that the client firm may adopt purchasing policies oriented towards risk reduction, especially on products new to the firm. Supplier reputation may then outweigh cost differences and they will look for assistance on uncertain points. Initial purchases of a new product may be to gain experience.

Later as the uncertainty declines because of customer knowledge growth, selection may put more emphasis on price, quality, delivery which then move higher in the scale of importance amongst different criteria.

Decisions made under time pressure also have a special quality. The searching may well be reduced and along with it the period of negotiation: thus ease of identifying a source and of obtaining quick reaction both in quotation and delivery may be dominant considerations.

Finally in this section reciprocal purchasing policies find a place. If firm A buys from firm B and uses this factor to apply pressure on B to buy from A a situation of reciprocal purchasing arises. Such understandings are not uncommon but the true long-term and short-term economics need careful scrutiny especially by the partner under pressure.

Personal criteria

Personal criteria are those which are not linked to the formal objectives of the buying organisation but are more a function of the personal objectives of one or more BPIs. Donnely and Holton's study [16] mentioned above linked with the concept of a hierarchy of criteria is consistent with the view that if no clear basis for selection exists then personal criteria may have key importance. Sometimes the personal financial gain is a bigger factor, as illustrated by Lockheed's 1975 statement of large payments to individuals in many countries.

It is of course the personal element in the purchasing equation which often explains the importance of good personal relations between the salesman and the principle BPIs, and why the salesman seeks to establish personal links with the BPIs, to ease the way to a sale.

Risk/benefit relationships arise also at the personal level: the BPI in making a decision has to take account of the losses he personally would suffer in esteem, status, promotion prospects if the purchased product failed or caused harm, and compare this with the benefit he would receive if the product were satisfactory. If the size and probability of loss are high and those of benefit low, then he might well adopt a safety first policy. Benefit means an aid to fulfilling the normal aspirations of an individual—his desire to stand well with his superiors to develop his career and own self-interest, to satisfy his normal social and ego needs, to win the friendship and respect of others inside and outside the company, and to meet the standards which he sets for himself.

Purchasing Officers and other BPIs are of course concerned about their own careers. This can explain the existence of what has been called 'superior phobia' identified in a study by the NIAA Industrial Adverising Research Institute [17]: this may be defined as a high level of concern about what the boss may think, and a consequential concern not to stimulate undue questioning by him.

This in turn may throw light on the phenomenon identified by several researchers, that Purchasing Officers would not change sources of supply for a saving of 5 per cent on the cost of the item purchased. Any change of supplier involves risk both to the buying company and to the executive responsible for authorising the decision. A 5 per cent saving on a purchased item may represent a much smaller percentage saving in a firm's total cost. Such saving may easily be lost if for some unforeseen reason (delayed delivery, difference in quality or failure to render assistance or anticipate a problem as the established supplier would have done) unexpected problems arise and production is interrupted.

Individuals may also identify strongly with their department or other organisational unit—even putting departmental goals before the overall company goals. Situations of antagonism between departments can lead to departmental policies designed more to frustrate the competitor within the company than serve its overall goals.

The annual budget phenomenon also raises interesting issues of internal politics in some non-profit-oriented organisations, such as Government departments and educational establishments. Institutions may be required to work closely to annual budgets, over-spending of budget may be forbidden or at least subject to criticism. Underspending too has sometimes disadvantages as higher authority may take the view that this indicates an excessive budget figure—to be reduced next year!

Thus towards the end of the budget year the relevant BPI anxiously examines his organisation's financial position. Commonly careful house-keeping earlier in the year has left some funds in hand, and there is a prompt effort to spend this balance on items of recurring need.

It is worth noting that the purchase of new technology raises interesting and difficult issues. The newness means that the calculation of expected return on an objective basis is difficult, perhaps impossible, so that to some extent the purchase is an act of faith. Such decisions may well stem from a mixture of norms of rationality and personal attitudes of decision makers.

In some lines of business there seem to be individuals or firms who are opinion-leaders who adopt innovation early and are then followed by others. Rogers and Shoemaker [3] suggest that amongst individuals (farmers for example) there are commonly five types of adopter which can be distinguished: (1) innovators: venturesome; (2) early adopters: responsible; (3) early majority: deliberate; (4) late majority: sceptical; (5) laggards: traditional.

The BPI's perception of the product may at times not be objectively valid. An interesting example was described to the writer concerning such a simple product as cement. A large cement manufacturing company took over a small firm (with one plant only) but continued to supply its new subsidiary's traditional customers with cement packed in bags which carried the traditional supplier's name. On one occasion these bags were out-of-stock and cement was delivered in bags bearing the parent company's name. There was a sharp critical reaction; customers complained that the product delivered was inferior and rejected the supplier's explanation that it was still the same product made at the local plant.

Each BPI is a complete individual, subject to strains and stresses not only from his job, superiors, subordinates and colleagues but also from the outside world. He will be influenced by attitudes and emotions from current family, friends and the total macro-environment and will have been moulded by a host of pressures from the total culture in which he lives and sub-cultures of which he is a member (professional, religious and ethical, social, geographical, educational).

4 PREPARING A MARKETING PLAN

Planning is important in any field of business management, not least in marketing. The marketing plan is fundamental to virtually every other plan prepared within the business: from it flows the timing and volume of revenue, the demands on production, the development of the requisite technology, the number and type of work people employed and similarly for other aspects of the organisation. Together with its linked budget it should integrate and synthesise the business and synchronise it with the outside world. The plan is based on facts, forecasts and assumptions and is subject to review if these anticipations prove to be amiss.

Getting started

The executive embarking for the first time on preparing a marketing plan finds it will take from nine to twelve months, since it is apt to involve the collection of special data, company-wide consultation and much drafting and redrafting. Yet the plan offers many benefits:

1   The process of planning gives deeper insight into the operations of the business and frequently uncovers opportunities for improvements.
2   The plan itself coordinates the various departments behind company objectives.
3   It provides a basis for measuring progress in financial and other terms, thus facilitating control and correction.
4   Decisions are derived with a full appreciation of their implications for revenue and for current and capital costs.

5   It communicates to each department a statement of its role and shows how this role links with that of other departments.

6   It promotes an ability to see at an early stage external trends and shifts permitting logical adjustments to them.

7   In fact greater efficiency in general.

Types of plan

It seems to be well established and good practice to make the marketing plan in two parts, the first a longer-range plan for a period of five or more years ahead. The period of time which the planner chooses (the planning horizon) depends primarily on the length of time which it takes for the major marketing decisions to mature. What is the life-cycle of a product? How long does it take to establish a new product in the market? These are the sort of questions to be asked. If today's decisions will largely determine the future action of the company in major areas for nine or ten years, then this is the period of time to choose for the longer-range plan. The long-range plan is normally a rolling plan, that is to say it is reviewed annually, amended and extended forward one more year and the amount of detail is often limited.

Consistent with this plan, supporting it and set out more fully, is the shorter-term plan for a period of one or two years ahead. In great detail this will show the amounts of different products to be sold, through what channels, in what territories and by what dates, and will identify the nature and quantity of the marketing effort involved. In this chapter, the emphasis will be on this plan. The longer-ranging plan adheres to similar principles, except that the detail is less and the link to corporate strategy closer.

Sometimes it is desirable to reinforce the main plan with a 'project plan' dealing separately with some project of major importance. For example, the launch of a new range of products in a new market may involve substantial initial investment and it may be desirable to undertake detailed consideration in greater depth for a period of years of the implications of the project. Its oversight may therefore be more intensive and under separate control. The overall effect of the project will be incorporated in the main plan, but the separate project plan enables it to be controlled and executed separately.

Steps in the process

A plan is a complex array of interrelated ideas, detailing what action is to be taken, by whom, when and the desired effect. It is accompanied by an appropriate budget setting out its financial implications. It is not easy to identify the logical process by which the content is created, but Exhibit 5 suggests a sequence which is discussed more fully below.

Step 1   Inputs of information and policy

At the beginning there are three headings on which the total process is based:

The company's policy—partly its corporate strategy (see Chapter 19) defining the nature of its business, but more specifically the objectives set for growth and return in its different markets (which will be influenced by the longer-term objectives in the five or ten year plan as well as the need for current return). Objectives are rechecked and adapted if necessary as planning proceeds.

Market facts and forecasts describing the current market and expected future developments. Inevitably some assumptions are necessary. Where there are other important possible developments which cannot be ignored; for example, the possibility that an overseas competitor (which has been researching the market) may enter it. Reserve strategies may be devised and plans prepared against such contingencies. More market information may well be brought in later as needs appear.

Marketing audit—as well as looking outward it is also wise to look inward; the marketing audit checks the efficiency with which the current marketing tools are deployed. This may be an annual audit or carried out systematically over the year, but it does seem desirable to add this analysis of marketing efficiency to the regular control of opera-

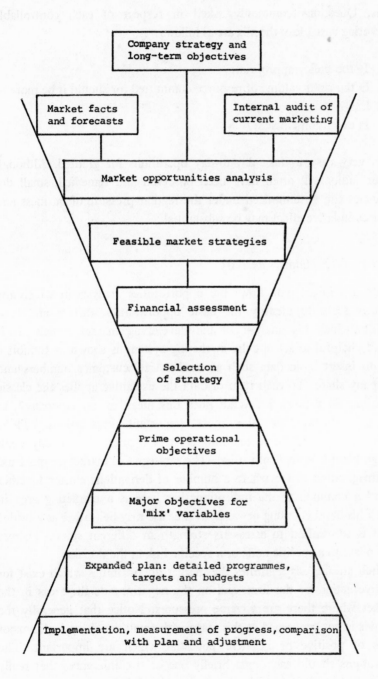

EXHIBIT 5 The planning process

tions. Questions commonly asked in respect of each controllable marketing variable of the mix are as follows:

Is the policy appropriate?
Is the right volume of resource committed (or should it be more or less)?
Is execution efficient?

It is very easy to take day-to-day operations for granted. Although major faults will often have been observed and remedied, small deficiencies can go unnoticed under the regular pressure of business and their cumulative effect may be substantial.

Step 2   *Opportunities analysis*

From this initial data flows the opportunities analysis in which the planner seeks to identify the basic opportunities, threats and constraints which his analysis of the developing market reveals. It is usually helpful to set out the marketing system as shown in Exhibit 6 and to insert basic data such as market size, customer numbers and company share. To each item of data the executive applies the classic question 'So what?', i.e. What does this mean to our company?, to derive and highlight the most important implications. These derivations are to be sorted into clusters (rather as a freshly dealt bridge hand is sorted into suits). The strategist in marketing must use his imagination to see where a number of derivations cluster together round a common theme indicating that here is a marketing area in which his hand is strong or weak, as the case may be (rather as a bridge hand is scrutinised to assess its strength in different suits). Themes may relate to a specific node or a specific link in the decision.

Such an analysis identifies the market opportunities which exist for positive action by the firm, and on the negative side the areas in the market where there are adverse pressures. Notice that generally the planner is not concerned at this stage with small details; it is the major areas of positive or negative potential which are important. The derivations should each state briefly one or two inferences that really matter from each item of data on each node of the marketing system.

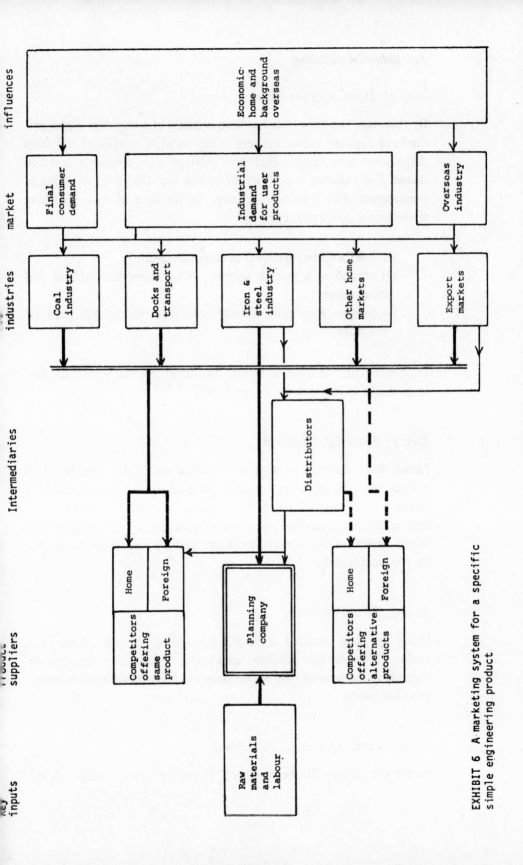

EXHIBIT 6 A marketing system for a specific
simple engineering product

Key inputs

Product suppliers

Intermediaries

industries

market

influences

Economic
home and
background
overseas

Final
consumer
demand

Industrial
demand
for user
products

Overseas
industry

Coal
industry

Docks and
transport

Iron &
steel
industry

Other home
markets

Export
markets

Distributors

Competitors
offering
same product

Home

Foreign

Planning
company

Competitors
offering
alternative
products

Home

Foreign

Raw
materials
and
labour

Step 3   Developing feasible strategies

By this stage the basic data has been reduced in a way that 'highlights' the brief derivations (the answers to the 'so what' questions) and these derivations have been sorted into clusters each around a common theme. Each cluster is now scrutinised to see what total messages of encouragement or warning it conveys. In the light of these, matching strategies are developed. For example:

> To 'hold' a declining market at minimum effort.
> To expand in a growth segment using improved products and more effort.
> To compete on a price/volume basis in a market with potential elasticity.

In essence the decision indicates the broad approach and the key instruments to implement this approach.

Step 4   Financial assessment

Ideally more than one strategy is developed and at this stage selection is made of the specific strategy to be adopted in each market. This involves a sales forecast and budget forecast to assess capital and current expenditure, revenue and net return, together with consideration of the likelihood of the successs of the strategy and its harmony with long-term objectives.

Step 5   Strategy selection

Using the data prepared at Step 4 the strategy is selected for each market. This in fact involves rather more stress than this phrase suggests as the forecast data is uncertain and it is often difficult to maintain objectively.

Step 6   Prime operational objectives

So far the process has been one of 'narrowing down': taking all the relevant available input data, identifying prime implications of related information, extracting the action implications from these clusters, finding matching strategies and electing the most promising. Now starts re-expansion: the objectives in each market in terms of volume, share, revenue, costs are identified and the role of each element of the mix outlined in general terms.

Step 7   Mix objectives

Further detail is filled in: the derived objectives for each mix element leads to their final budgets and detailed requirement. Linkages with production, engineering and finance are also confirmed.

Step 8   Detailed plan, programme and budget

Ideally each individual has a role and objectives derived systematically. Thus the firm is dealing with a defined market in such a way that the different executives' tasks are linked across the total mix, with timing, budget and responsibility defined.

After the usual final reviews and checks of plans and budgets this leads on to implementation. Then follows the normal control process of feed-back of measured information on results, for comparison with plans (at weekly or monthly intervals as appropriate). If necessary adjustment is made to offset adverse variances or to make the most of unexpected opportunities. Small adjustments are made continuously and with a concern for their impact on the plan as a whole.

Details of the mix

As strategy has been finalised, so the details for each element of the mix will have been studied and specified. They must be consistent with the strategy, of which they represent the development in depth, and this ensures that the elements harmonise with each other. They must also be consistent with the opportunities of the environment and with the resources of the company, and each should make its contribution in the most economical way.

In most industrial marketing plans, the following elements must be examined and decisions made on each—even if the decision is 'no change':

Product line
Products to be introduced.
Products to be withdrawn.
Products to be phased out.
Products to be modified.
Products to be 'pushed' intensively in present markets/applications.
Products to be 'pushed' extensively in new markets/applications.

Pricing
Changes in the general level of prices.
Differential changes, i.e. raising some and lowering others.
Discounts and credit terms.

Direct sales
Changes in number and organisation of sales force.
Remuneration, commission, expenses.
Recruitment, initial training.
Conferences, retraining.
Motivation and morale.

Advertising and sales promotion
Media advertising.
Direct mail.
Shows, exhibitions, films, symposia, seminars.
Public relations.
Literature.

Technical service
Pre-sale surveys, testing and advice.
Applications research.
Post-sale advice, maintenance, customer staff training.
Provision of spares.
Number and organisation of technical service force.
Remuneration, hiring, training.
Charges for service.

Physical distribution
Delivery time objectives.
Seasonal stock levels.
Location of stock.
Transport methods.

Distributors
Policy on distribution.
Discount structure.
Co-operation and motivation.

Market research
Special studies.
Continuing environmental desk research.
Continuous monitoring of company progress.

Marketing organisation and staff
Changes in organisation.
Staff recruitment, training.

Because the marketing plan guides the company as a whole, its implications for other departments—R&D, engineering, production—must be identified and examined in consultation with these departments. In this process, staff at all levels should be involved and it is becoming common to provide subordinate executives with information which permits them to determine their own objectives, which are then reviewed and discussed at a higher level. In this way the marketing plan leads naturally to a total company plan.

The detailed schedule above is, of course, only one way in which a plan may be drawn up. Each company's plan will show its own individual variations; for example, a company selling large items of capital equipment by tender would have to define the class or classes of customer from whom business would be sought, and the timing of business in order to 'balance' plant loading, but might not be concerned with seasonal stock levels and might have no separately defined sales force.

The detail of the plan will gradually be completed in a way consistent with the goals already set out. The process of analysis will often show that in certain parts of the plan there is more than one way of implementing the strategy, and each of these is examined for cost and effectiveness.

The strategy will be re-examined, moulded and developed in detail. The detailed goals will be modified as planning throws light on their feasibility until the marketing executive has a programme of expected sales month by month (or perhaps quarter by quarter in some industries), showing what is to be expected from each representative's area, from each product, from each market and so on. These month-by-month figures are the intermediate goals against which progress will be assessed.

Setting out the plan

The whole plan is now a substantial set of documents, and relevant parts of it are communicated to the different levels of operation in the company. The plan has, however, been built up by a long process of consultation and cooperation, so that its acceptance by major departments has been substantially ensured before its confirmation at board level.

The record of the plan comprises something on the following lines:

1   *Descriptive introduction* (i) Review of company progress in past periods and assessment of results achieved. (ii) Anticipated development in the economic environment, in customer and indirect customer behaviour, and in expected competitor reaction.

2   *Statement of marketing policies* A statement of the main goals in terms of sales, costs and profit (or contribution) and an outline of the strategy by which these goals are to be achieved, with particular reference to innovations.

3   *Detailed Plan* A statement of the elements under appropriate headings. The following layout has been suggested for consideration as the planner's record of the basis on which the plan is developed

(White [18]). The object is to show clearly the assumptions made about the future and their impact on each part of the plan:

Assumptions

Plan element	Economic environment	Customer behaviour	Competitive behaviour	Own ompany position	Supply of inputs
Product line					
Pricing					
Direct sales					
(and so on)					

Under 'Economic Environment' might be reference to inflationary trends, business activity and exchange rates. The next column might indicate assumptions that customers were illiquid and inclined to defer purchases that made demands on liquidity. Competitors might be expected to meet this by cutting margins or by delaying introduction of new products. The 'Own Company' situation might express comments on the domestic liquidity and profit situation, and any other matter reflecting on the company's resource availability (e.g. new plant coming on stream).

Changes under any of these headings would reflect on many of the elements in the left-hand column. Increases in prices of inputs might reflect not only on price but on resources locked up in stock-holding. Exchange rate variations might influence relative profitability of home/export markets.

4   *Budget*   From the elements of the plan flow the expected sales and prices, and concomitant revenue and cost forecasts, set out over months or other appropriate periods and broken down by responsibility centres. The budget figures also take account of cost trends and expected changes in efficiency.

5   *Control*   The budget is a key element of the control process. It makes it possible to assess progress month by month, as results are compared with expectations, and helps to localise the sources of departure from plan. A certain variation is naturally inevitable, but the amount of permissible variation should be predetermined, and if this is exceeded the variation should be the subject of analysis and appropriate action. Predetermination of permissible variation levels is of great value. The executive today

has so much paper flowing across his desk that he cannot scrutinise it all. If the amount of variation is predetermined, then he need only attend to those items for which the variance exceeds the norm. This 'management by exception' reduces the day-to-day load and permits more time for the more important issues. Results which are unexpectedly favourable also deserve attention, as exceptionally good performance may indicate that some opportunities capable of further exploitation have been missed.

Apart from overall costs and revenue, it is also desirable to identify other statistics or ratios which help to assess the efficiency of the marketing operation. What these may be will vary according to the detail of the plan, but such factors as new accounts opened, sales cost as percentage of sales, inquiries received, tenders submitted and tenders accepted may be indicators which in appropriate cases will show whether the company is on target and which may react before the financial accounts as a whole show any significant variation. They also indicate where in the organisation remedial action is needed.

The control system should also follow trends in the environment to check whether the basic assumptions and forecasts are correct. It is often more difficult to do this in precise terms, but assumptions about economic trends can be set out for comparison with appropriate published series (for example unemployment, price index numbers, the index of production, and so on). Assumptions which are less easy to quantify, such as those relating to competitors' behaviour, may be kept under systematic review. If there is a significant change, e.g. a new product introduced by competitors, this would normally be identified quickly, but the effect of small changes may not be noted for a very long while unless systematic procedures are adopted.

5 KNOWING YOUR MARKET

Executives in the marketing firm need information about what is happening 'out there' in the market environment in order to forecast and make plans to meet the expected future. This flows from the basic definition of marketing outlined in the first chapter. The knowledge required varies from one executive to another. The salesforce will require local, relatively short-term information, e.g. when customer's board will meet to decide on a particular contract. At the other extreme the corporate planner will need to know about trends in market demand and corporate technology which will influence his firm five to ten years in the future.

The search for information is a fundamental task. But information (and more particularly the forecasts which flow from it) is rarely completely accurate. It improves the *probability* of better decisions, it does not give certainty.

Moreover obtaining information involves cost: thus the economic test which has to be applied is whether the cost of getting the information is justified by the higher probability of a better decision. This is parallel with the test applied to other decisions on business expenditure, is the cost justified by a reasonable expectation of higher returns?

Information systems

A marketing information system can be defined as system whereby managers receive as a matter of course suitably analysed information which they require to deal with recurring management decisions. More ambitious proposals than this have been made, but this moderately stated proposal seems to be one which can be widely operated. It implies that the provision of this information is not only feasible but in

c

the sense already indicated useful enough to justify both the cost of providing it and the cost (in executive time) of scanning it at specified intervals.

It does have other implications: in particular it implies that each manager can identify the information which he needs and specify the priority and frequency with which he should give it attention. It is differentiated from that which he would *like* to see on a wider interest basis. This identification is not easy and requires each manager to review thoughtfully the information which is already being received and to assess whether it is genuinely useful. Redundant reports are then cancelled.

He must also review whether there is other information which he ought to receive by considering the occasions in the past on which he has requested special analyses. He can re-examine the trade and technical journals, checking with a list from a reference book to ensure that he has considered all likely to be relevant, and from his past experience that he has deleted those which have only served to clutter his in-tray. He should also ensure that appropriate Government and other published statistics are considered. To some extent he may be able to save his own time by delegating some of the scrutiny to a properly briefed assistant.

Internal sources

Much of the internal information is derived by the analysis of data generated in the course of the normal cycle of order-taking, production, delivery, invoicing and payment. Sales can be analysed by time (for example month or quarter), product class, region and sales territory. Comparison can be made with previous periods or with plans and forecasts. Some may be capable of comparison with data from other companies or for the whole industry. The problem of defining statistical terms to ensure proper comparison is a very real one and executives should be briefed about likely pitfalls and, where possible, standard terminology developed. The simple word 'sales' can for example be a source of difficulty. Does it refer to orders booked or deliveries made? Does it include inter-divisional transactions and if so (if the figures are in money terms) on what basis are the transactions valued?

The financial system is not the only source of useful information. Representatives' call records, customer complaints, rejects, service records may also be valuable. The staff market researcher is concerned to see that relevant data is extracted, analysed in useful classifications and, as far as possible, is comparable with data collected by Government and other outside bodies.

Secondary sources

This term refers to the use of statistical and related information collected by other organisations. In most countries the range and variety is considerable. It is produced by Government Departments, trade associations, universities, publishers, specialised journals and many other sources. The market research worker who specialises in a particular field comes to know what is available, the sources from which to obtain it, the pitfalls of definitions, how the statistics are collected and some idea of the margins of inaccuracy which may arise. The national government of a country will generally establish an export library which collects overseas trade and other statistics on a world-wide basis, and which is freely open to the information seekers.

The value of secondary data is often great, and can make available to the researcher information which has cost large sums to produce and which he could not obtain otherwise. Its limitations can also at times be strong: data may not exist or it may be on different definitions or in different units. Much work is continuing to improve data collected and to develop common bases of classification. Most major countries have standard classifications of industries, regions and commodities imported and exported.

Most company market researchers regularly file and index periodical and other published material, learn where information can be obtained and maintain contact with knowledgeable people in other industries. They are squirrels hoarding information as well as being ferrets who seek it out. Care must, however, be used in interpreting secondary information. Sometimes the analyst can be misled because the figures relate to only part of an industry and he mistakes them for the whole industry; also, such simple words as sales, exports and production are full of unexpected ambiguity. Occasionally figures from responsible sources have been found to be wrong. Cross-checking with other sources and with related series is essential. When using statistics from a particular source for the first time, it is desirable to examine the method by which the data is collected—sample design, response achieved and the questionnaire used. Sometimes widely quoted figures are based on small and unsatisfactory samples.

Primary sources

This implies the field collection of original information from customers, users, distributors, and others directly involved. This is generally a relatively expensive process. Some companies have their own market researchers capable of carrying out such work. Others will rely on specialised market research firms (even companies with their own staff will also employ specialist firms as well). The outside firm may serve primarily as data collector or may have a wider consultant role. Multi-client surveys which are sometimes offered by specialist firms can be an economical way of obtaining information. Joint participation of client and consultant is also sometimes possible.

Logically the market problem arises first, then the need for information to help solve the problem is identified. This leads on to an initial research brief specifying the market research need. These few steps turn out often to be none too easy to complete. Market research provides information, not normally ready-made solutions, and it will be the task of the marketing staff to turn the data generated into recommendations for action. Failure therefore to brief the market researcher adequately at the inception of the field research means that the information can be less useful than it should be.

A useful suggestion is for the marketing executive at the briefing stage to envisage the possible information which he might receive from the research. He then asks himself prior to research what action could be taken on such information. If he is not able to see how different results will indicate different marketing actions then the proposed research is not aiding him. He should examine further what information will better indicate the route management should take. He should try to gauge the financial benefit from better information, as an indicator as to how much should be invested in producing the information.

The practice of research

With an initial brief the researcher turns to the task of collecting information. He may need to start with a short period of familiarisation, unless already familiar with the subject-matter of the research. He must 'read himself in' to the problems, obtaining the necessary technical and general economic background. He reviews the information already in the company's files and records—there may even be previous studies in the same area.

This process may lead to a review of the research brief, and the general issues to be covered may be revised as the nature of the company's problems is more clearly understood. Indeed, the internal review can be as much part of the problem definition rather than part of the survey process.

There is also a period, often overlapping, of desk research on secondary sources before fieldwork is considered. The researcher may then finally determine fieldwork is necessary and develop an opinion about the form it might take (post, 'phone or personal interview or some combination of these), and population to be studied and the possible magnitude of cost. Sometimes desk research may prove to have provided so much information that fieldwork proves unnecessary.

Much of this early work may be carried out within the sponsoring company. Internal market research staff are nearer the marketing problem and should be able to assist in the identification of research needs, and help draw out the action implications of the ultimate findings.

When approaching a new market for the first time there is commonly a need for a report which will set out the structure of the market and the trends, rather on the following lines (so far as is relevant):

1   Estimated market size and potential, analysis by:
       product group,
       intermediate customer,
       end-use and/or end-user,
       region,
       captive or free, and/or
       other segments.
2   Description of buying decision procedures and influences.

3   Description of end-uses.
4   Schedule of major customers and end-users.
5   Schedule of major competitors, their size, share and policies.
6   Schedule and comparison of competing products,
7   Description of distribution channels, concentration, location, ownership, relevant Government policies.

If, however, desk research does not reveal the information—and although a valuable introduction, it may lack the detailed up-to-date information which is required—then the researcher may well consider fieldwork information. If a consultant is to be used it is at about this stage discussions develop, and terms of reference are prepared.

In planning a survey, 'who', 'what' and 'how' are the questions. Who is to be contacted? An appropriate selection of people who can help by providing information must be identified. Next the issues to be raised with them must be specified, and the researcher must decide whether and how to use 'phone, mail, personal interview, or some combination. The choice of method depends upon consideration of a wide variety of circumstances. Any consultant's proposal should incorporate a description of the proposed method, staff, sub-contracting (if any), date of submission of report, fees and other conditions of business.

Choosing the respondents

Whatever the method by which the study is to be carried out, it will often be necessary for the research worker to collect the information from only a sample of the companies in the market. Sometimes the relevant population is small and an attempt can be made to obtain information from all of them, subject to the necessary cooperation being obtained.

There are two main categories of respondent. The direct respondent speaks from the immediate experience of himself or his company. He is able to tell whether his company buys particular products, whether they are experimenting with new techniques, what type of equipment they operate, and so on. The indirect respondent speaks from his observation of knowledge of the experience of others. Intermediate manufacturers, for example, may express views on whether customers are likely to require particular qualities in a product, on the trends in manufacturing practice within the industry they serve and similar matters. Trade and research associations may offer analogous assistance.

In selecting direct respondents, the object is to select a sample from the market under study, such that from the information obtained inferences can be drawn about either the entire market or relevant segments.

Problems of sample selection are often of lesser consequence in many industrial studies. The total population of firms concerned may be small: sometimes less than 10 often less than 100. Moreover out of a population of 10 firms, most of the business may be in the hands of two; out of 100 it may be in the hands of 20. Thus the large firms are very important and the key skill may well be successfully obtaining good quality information from all (or as many as possible) of the large firms.

If the number of establishments in that industry is large (as, for example, in agriculture, building, or small offices), then it is possible to consider adopting sampling techniques rather like those used for consumer surveys. These techniques are described more fully in the basic textbooks on market research methods. They are based on probability theory or are quota samples, or some combination of the two.

Probability samples (often called random samples) have the theoretical advantage that the possible error from sampling in the accuracy of their results can be assessed if all the rules are followed. However, there are difficulties. Sampling frames (comprehensive lists of all the establishments in the population to be studied, required as a basis for selecting a sample), are often hard to obtain and may require special compilation from a number of sources. Reasons of economy or shortage of time make it impracticable to visit out of the way establishments inconveniently located. Selected sample companies may decline to cooperate and thus spoil the sample.

Quota sampling, the alternative basic idea from consumer research, usually has the advantage of economy and speed, but has not the same sound support from statistical theory as has the probability approach. Nevertheless, it is widely used in consumer studies and appears to give satisfaction. Defective sampling is only one source of error and not necessarily the most important. In quota sampling the population of firms is analysed into important groups, e.g. by industry, size, or country, and respondents selected to represent each group, the number selected being related to the importance and population of each group.

The sensible researcher will bear in mind the need for representation of all significant size-groups and all important or potentially important segments, and will adapt his sample to ensure a reasonable cross-representation. He will then seek to support his conclusions by cross-checking the information in other ways; he may, for example, compare information from suppliers of a product with that from users.

When the object of the survey is to try to foresee technological and other trends, it is sometimes desired to obtain high-quality opinions rather than 'facts'. In such cases the object may be to seek 'expert' individuals whose views have value, rather than a statistical sample of direct respondents.

Apart from the selection of the respondent company, there is a need to select the right individual to meet within the company. In theory, the right respondent is the executive most able to give an authoritative answer. In practice it may be desirable to contact first a sympathetic executive in the respondent organisation and obtain access to the authoritative sources (or sources) through the beneficient assistance of an introduction by this intermediary. Sometimes it is desirable to meet several respondents in order to obtain information on all the aspects of a problem.

Collecting the data

A great deal of information is collected by the three classic methods or some combination of them: telephone, post, personal interview. Combinations of methods involve, for example, postal survey to small users, personal visits to large; postal questionnaires with 'phone follow-up and so on. For larger surveys a pilot study will precede the full survey to test questionnaires and procedures.

The main advantages and disadvantages of the three classic methods are outlined below.

Postal surveys Apparently low cost, but this can be misleading as response rates are often poor, so that the true cost (in terms of real knowledge gained) can be higher. There are various devices which seek to raise the response level, and sometimes it may be possible to cross-check some results against nationally known data (special questions being inserted for this purpose). Clarity of questions, ease of answering, attractive layout, brevity, stamped reply envelopes and addressing respondents by name are all recommended. One does sometimes hear of long questionnaires achieving high response rates, so that the rules are only guidelines.

Personal interviews These can be expensive especially if in-depth with a senior respondent. They probably permit the highest level of response both in quantity and quality. Respondents frequently become very interested in the subject of the interview providing blueprints, samples, analyses and enlisting the aid of more expert colleagues.

Telephone Cost per contact can be low, especially if there are a number of interviewers situated in different parts of the country (thus keeping costs down). McFarlane-Smith [19] speaks of 'phone interviews from Britain with respondents in Holland, Belgium, France and Germany. The calls must be carefully planned and there seems to be a limit on the amount of information which can be obtained from an informant who is a stranger to the interviewer, although McFarlane-Smith mentions semi-structured interviews lasting 40–50 minutes.

In less formal situations where the interviewer is known to the respondents much can be obtained over the 'phone in a short period of time; small surveys have been carried out between 10.00 a.m. and 3.00 p.m. on the same day. Wilson [20] comments 'it is often the telephone interview which will provide the best time-cost-objective continuum'.

Group discussions An article by Ansell [21] indicates that these can be of value. Where the researcher is seeking ideas the interaction between informed people who perceive the problem area from different angles may well produce deeper insights. These may be checked by other methods.

Direct observation This is often possible and of value in seeking product improvements or adaptations. Much of what is done could be on a more formal basis.

Questionnaire design

There is considerable variation in the type of questionnaire which may be used in industrial market research studies. At the one extreme is a highly structured questionnaire in which the precise wording of questions to be asked is specified, their sequence laid down and even the range of possible answers formalised. At the other extreme a researcher may have only a list of discussion points on which he wishes to enlarge in the exchange with his respondent. A structured questionnaire is inevitable in mail surveys and may be used in other situations.

The structured form is indicated when the survey is large, with many respondents, a number of interviewers and will lead to information appropriately summarised in statistical form. It is of course widespread in consumer research. It does however mean that there must be in advance a grasp of the range of possible answers which respondents are likely to make (although some open-ended questions permitting freedom of reply may be included). Designing such questionnaires requires considerable skill and careful testing of the questionnaire before use to ensure that questions are appropriate and clear, the order logical and the whole structure (words and sequence) suited to producing unbiased answers.

Where the information sought is much more exploratory so that the interviewer is uncertain of the range of possible replies, and even the natural boundaries of the subject much less clear, such structure becomes difficult or impossible. Comments from a respondent may open up an unidentified aspect of the subject of real importance requiring exploration. Alternatively the respondent may wish to follow through a line of thought in his own way and a rigid questionnaire would prohibit this, or a general issue may require him to weigh pros and cons and mentally ramble around the issues involved turning up fresh aspects as they come to mind. There are also some interviews in which matters of a moderately confidential nature are discussed. This requires the building of a rapport between interviewer and respondent which could well be inhibited by a too rigid context. It may also be necessary to obtain information from a number of respondents' executives in each company visited to build up a full picture of a situation. Finally it may be noted that in some industries the number of respondent firms may be so few that they would be insufficient for a worthwhile pilot survey.

Submitting results

The final stage of the survey is the submission of the report which is generally directed to the commissioning firm's commercial directorate and staff. The following outline of content is suggested by Luck *et al.* [22]:

1 Brief statement of the research objectives.
2 Brief description of the sampling and other procedures, the data and persons who performed the work.
3 Highlights of the findings, the conclusions drawn from the data.
4 Recommendations stemming from the conclusions (if desired).
5 Detailed data and reasoning to support steps 3 and 4.
6 Restatement of conclusions or recommendations.
7 Appendix: data, forms, computations, and other essential materials omitted from step 5.

The whole report should be an easy-to-read document, suitably illustrated by simple graphs (although there are different views among executives as to the value of these), and appropriate statistics but in such a way that main issues come out clearly. If possible test it beforehand on a 'guinea pig'.

An opportunity to present the report to the relevant committee is helpful: appropriate visual aids can then be used to make quite sure that the main points are grasped and questions raised by the audience answered.

Ultimate responsibility for deriving from the data the inferences for marketing action in a formal sense lies with an executive of the Marketing Department but staff marketing researchers usually see this as a function in which they have an interest, for failure to draw proper inferences may reflect adversely on their work. The outside market research agency is sometimes more reserved since other factors than those in the commissioned survey may well be relevant to their client's decision. The consultant will usually make a formal verbal presentation at or before delivery of the report. He may also seek a subsequent review session and (where appropriate) offer to help in implementation.

Employing a consultant

Much industrial marketing research is contracted out to specialist research and consultancy organisations. This raises two major issues: what are the advantages of employing such an agent, and how can the client firm make most effective use of the agent? The following comments are largely based on a report by the Industrial Marketing Research Association [23]. The major criteria relevant to the choice between employing a consultant and undertaking the task with the client firm's own staff are (the report argues) the following:

Objectivity The outside consultant is free from the domestic pressures which afflict the client's employed staff and can thus form a more dispassionate view of the subject studied, either as an independent study or as a check on some earlier domestic study of a major problem.

Anonymity There are two primary parties to market research field studies: the one which seeks information (the originating company) and the one which has the information (the respondents). Either of these may prefer anonymity. The originator may wish its interest in the subject to be confidential (it may be exploring a possible new market or new product). A respondent may also not wish to have his own firm's data revealed but may be willing to provide information which is to be cloaked in the confidentiality of a statistical table based on data from many respondents.

Time The outside consultant with his resources may be able to start earlier and/or finish more quickly.

Skills The consultant may have specialised knowledge: of the industry to be studied, of a specialised technique, of local conditions or the local language.

The report stresses that once a contract is agreed the consultant should be regarded and treated as a temporary executive of the client organisation.

6 BUSINESS FORECASTING

Planning as discussed in Chapter 4 begins with forecasting. Every business decision whether it be to erect plant, recruit staff or purchase requirements, involves some assumptions about the future, even if these are not always explicitly stated. This chapter is concerned with the derivation and use of explicit quantitative, forecasts. In particular the concern is with forecasts relevant to the size and nature of the demand for a company's product.

Forecasts and plans

The results of a company in a market depend upon two classes of variable:

1   Those controlled by the company (notably its marketing mix).
2   Those outside the control of the company, which will be referred to as 'autonomous' variables.

Examples of long-term 'autonomous' variables whose trend could substantially influence a company's market are:

1   The level of industrial activity in the country concerned.
2   Demand for a specific final product, e.g. motor cars.
3   Activity of a specific user industry, e.g. coal mining.

The forecast of such statistical series is a necessary early step, as they set constraints on the feasible success level of a marketing company, and the company will need to take account of these in determining its own marketing effort. Note that more than one forecast is commonly necessary because of the number of series which may be relevant. The key series are those which impact most on the company's possible market size.

There are occasions where a direct forecast of the total market size for the company's product is valid. In the following circumstances, for example, it may be virtually autonomous:

1 The company concerned is a small part of the market.
2 Marketing strategy is very long term so that only previous action affects the relevant period.
3 The company's prime marketing decision is selecting the product because it has little other influence on long-term market size, and the product decision is already made.

It is also sometimes convenient to adopt assumptions which permit some other variables to be treated as autonomous. For example, it may be possible to treat the market size as autonomous by assuming at first that marketing policies remain unchanged, and to treat them as pre-determined, or to produce several forecasts based on different assumptions about feasible marketing strategies. The latter produces a range of results, but in view of the uncertainty of forecasting, a range is always more realistic. More sophisticated planning tools permit range forecasts to be used to advantage.

Initial forecasts are often produced by a forecaster not closely involved in direct marketing action, and thus (it is hoped) having a more dispassionate approach. Such forecasters when asked to produce a forecast for a product in which the company is a principal supplier, nevertheless have to make some assumptions about the effect of the company's activity: for example the extent to which research may uncover hitherto unknown applications. Thus he may change his role from a forecaster to what is virtually a target setter although this role change is unofficial and not perceived by others in the company (perhaps not even the forecaster himself).

The forecast of a company's own sales depends upon both autonomous externals and the company's planned marketing action. However, marketing and sales managers are not often cold-blooded analysts and the figures officially designated as 'sales forecasts' may be in truth targets. This implies that if there is a deficiency extra effort is likely to be deployed. The whole system of production having been geared up to match planned sales, any deficiency has widespread implications in the company and the identification of possible failure to reach targets can cause more activity and stimulate additional thinking towards closing the gap.

Implications of forecasting

The link between the forecast and the plan is not one way. Initially the plan is derived by consideration of possible marketing action within the constraints implied by the autonomous forecasts (accepting, as discussed above, that the autonomy may on occasions be somewhat spurious). There is also a reverse relationship which has its own special significance: the plan is now consistent with a particular view of the future contained in the forecast set. If as forecasts are reviewed annually, there are modifications (and there will be) than it is possible to adapt the plan in a logical and controlled way to match the new circumstances. This is not of course an argument for indifferences to accuracy. It is an argument for not rejecting forecasting because inaccuracy arises. Most forecasters retain a careful record of forecast revisions and the reason for them as an aid for the future avoidance of analogous deficiencies. Some senior management now prefer a range forecast rather than one specific figure: the market in ten years' time is indicated *not* as '100,000 tons' but '80,000 to 120,000 tons'.

This approach has much to commend it. It is more realistic. Although the forecaster may consider 100,000 tons the most probable outcome, the range gives an indication of the magnitude of possible error. In choosing between alternative strategies, executives can examine their implications in relation to the upper and lower limits of the range, as well as its central value.

A particular plan which may seem to be the best for the 'most probable' market may be so severely damaging at the lower figure that management may prefer a plan which is rather more defensive, giving reasonable protection in the poor market and a satisfactory (though perhaps not the theoretical optimum) result in the most probable situation. This type of sensitivity analysis is likely to be developed in the future, as the computer provides greater facility in calculating the implications of alternatives. It would be feasible to attach probabilities to different figures and to work out the most appropriate management decision on a probabilistic basis.

The growing interest in sensitivity analysis should be noted. Where a model is developed, the accuracy of the forecast will depend on the accuracy of the view of the independent variables' future behaviour. If the demand for a basic product depends upon the Gross National Product, then the question which a manager is tending to ask is 'If the GNP forecast is 5 per cent wrong, how far is our forecast astray?' In other words, how sensitive is the forecast to the assumption about the GNP? If the forecasting technique is very complex—and some models of increasing complexity are beginning to appear on the business scene—this is one way in which the manager can cut through the mathematical theory to identify the crucial assumptions to which he should give his own attention.

Forecasts should be as objective and as neutral as human ingenuity can make it, and the forecaster should not feel impelled to lean towards conservatism—or the other way. By permitting the forecaster to state a range, he is given a margin of protection and has no need to provide another hidden margin.

Building a forecast

Forecasting is hardly a science. Statistics generally play an important role—particularly for products such as basic materials which have a wide range of potential uses—but the judgment of individuals remains important. Judgment tends to be particularly important in industries with a high incidence of technological innovation and product obsolescence. Even in forecasts which are bespattered with mathematical formulae, there are often important judgments, perhaps introduced by such a phrase as 'it seems reasonable to suppose that . . .'.

Forecasters should support all their calculations by a wide and imaginative awareness of the implications of change. Such change may flow from technological developments (very important in industrial markets), from changes in consumer habits which at first sight may seem remote from the industrial market until deeply examined, from new discoveries of raw materials and fuel or from changes in economic or political circumstances. It often takes time before such developments are reflected in official statistics in such a way that they assist the long-term forecaster. One of the crucial problems in forecasting is attempting to identify those changes which represent 'turning points', either replacing growth by decline or introducing a new acceleration of growth.

The nature of forecasting is such that there is no unique technique. Forecasters adopt often several different approaches to any one problem, comparing results and attempting reconciliation.

The market which is the focus of the specific study should be clearly defined and it is wise, at least as a first step, to take account of all competition widely interpreted to include alternatives. An oil company, for example, may well first forecast the market for energy (including coal, natural gas, hydro-electricity and so on) before forecasting the oil share. A company operating in a local area may well forecast the total national market before turning to its own particular segment.

In a closely integrated long-term forecast most of the following elements may be found:

1   Background assumptions.
2   Past statistics and trend fitting.
3   Explanatory analyses or models (which may have a substantial statistical content).
4   Circumstantial and cross-checking evidence.
5   Personal judgment and intuition to modify and integrate.

Background assumptions are generally a major conditioning influence. Government policy on taxes, international monetary developments, policy decisions of key competitors may be crucial and the assumption given may make a great difference to the forecast. Such issues need clear identification in advance, and the assumptions made should be clearly specified. Other elements are discussed below.

There are three main approaches to the problem of making long-term forecasts, which may be combined or used in parallel to cross-check and buttress each other:

1   Treat the market as a whole and set out to forecast it as one entity without breaking it down further. Most weight is given to this approach when the market is diffuse and the product concerned is so fundamental that there is hardly any change in the pattern of consumer or investment demand which does not affect it.

2   Analyse the market into different major segments or different products which are then forecast separately. This approach is emphasised when the demand comes from a small number of major customer industries, end-uses or applications. It is also important when the demand pattern is changing because some parts of the market are developing faster than others, or because of changes in processes, or products of intermediate manufacturers. Sometimes this approach may be used for important parts of the total demand, with the residual demand treated as a whole. For segmented forecasts, the analyst must usually take the further step of forecasting the change of demand for the *output* of the customer industries. This may involve another cycle of forecasting.

3   Finally, there is the possibility of looking at each customer individually. As a systematic approach to long-term forecasting, this applies when demand is wholly or very substantially in the hands of a few big customers. The forecaster is then in the position of having to forecast the sales of each customer, the consequential volume of product demand and whether or not his company will win the business or some share of it.

It will be seen that each of the methods of calculation and estimation discussed in the following pages may be applied to any of these three classifications, but there will be differences in its importance and in the nature of the data to which it is applied. Note that the study of demand does not necessarily stop with study of the company's own product, but often goes forward to study the trend of end-use.

Trend fitting

The scrutiny of a past statistical series, the identification of a trend and the extension of that trend into the future is a common ingredient of a forecast. The data may be a statistical series dealing with any of the variables discusssed above.

Trend-fitting may best be described as a useful walking-stick but a bad crutch. Where past data exists, it is usually of value to attempt to identify the trend and to extend it forward. Extrapolation indicates what will emerge if the pattern of development which has operated in the past continues into the future. It thus offers at least a comparison with any alternative approach. Sometimes it is called a 'naive' method in that in its crudest form it involves no understanding of the forces at work which mould demand for the product. This is fair criticism. The present argument is that extrapolation is useful as one step, a first step, in building up a total forecast. Examples can also be quoted where the cold emotionless mathematics of 'naive' extrapolation have been more successful than the judgment of individuals.

Where the intention is to take past industry sales data and to extrapolate forward, the past data needs careful scrutiny. The figures are only relevant if they do in fact measure demand. This is different from sales if past demand has not been fully satisfied, as for example when power cuts have reduced sales of electricity below what customers were prepared to buy. Changes in definitions or in units of measurement must be identified and suitable adjustments made to convert them to an appropriate common basis; different nitrogenous fertilisers may have different percentage of nitrogen, and to measure the growth of consumption they must be converted to a common basis of nitrogen content. Trends may often be more clearly and logically defined when different major market segments are examined separately; how is demand developing in the coal industry? in steel? and so on.

This book is not primarily a statistical treatise, and therefore the present chapter treats statistical aspects of forecasting superficially. The reader is referred to the more specialised books for further reading.

Three main classes of trend are commonly distinguished by statisticians:

1 Linear trends show a pattern in which the series changes by the same *quantity* each year, as in the following total market sales statistics for imaginary product X which increase sales by 30 units each year.

Year	Units sold
1971	70
1972	100
1973	130
1974	160
1975	190

If drawn out on ordinary arithmetic graph paper such a series lies on a straight line. No genuine data would be as obligingly precise as this example, but a straight line is the simplest way of representing a series of this sort, and is therefore often used. There is seldom any good reason for the sales of a product to follow this trend and it is generally worth examining whether an alternative trend does not better match the data.

2   *Exponential trends* change by the same *percentage* each year as in the example below. If drawn on an ordinary scale graph paper the pattern of points traces out a curve, and on semi-log paper a straight line. The imaginary product Y below increases its sales by 30 per cent annually.

Year	Units sold
1971	77
1972	100
1973	130
1974	169
1975	220

Exponential trends seem to characterise the long-term pattern of total market sales of many basic products.

3   *S-trends* show a pattern of growth like an elongated S (as in Exhibit 7), as growth flattens off to an upper saturation ceiling. Several mathematical formulae are possible: noteably the logistic and Gompertz curves. It is sometimes possible to ease the problem by *separately* making an estimate of the saturation level.

The past histories of many products do not fit tightly to a mathematical formula. Most examples show rather vague variations: the effect of chance irregularities and uncertain incomplete cycles.

A simple way to approach trend identification is to calculate a simple moving average of the annual figures (a three- or five-year moving average is widely used) and to plot the trend and the original data on a graph. It is then often possible to see by inspection whether there is a reasonably well-defined trend and into which of the three categories above it may fall. More exact procedures can be found in the specialised literature. In principle to extrapolate into the future it

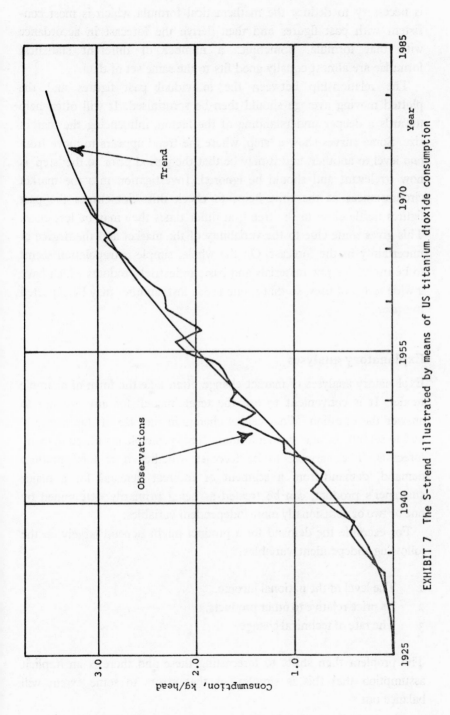

EXHIBIT 7   The S-trend illustrated by means of US titanium dioxide consumption

is necessary to deduce the mathematical formula which is most consistent with past figures and then derive the forecast in accordance with that formula. Sometimes a number of different statistical formulae are almost equally good fits to the same set of data.

The relationship between the individual past figures and the plotted moving average should then be scrutinised. It will often help towards a deeper understanding of the factors influencing the market size. Some curves show a 'step' where the trend appears to move from one level to another, and it may be that the period prior to the 'step' is now irrelevant and should be ignored. Investigation into the market circumstances at the time helps to check this. Sometimes the past figures nestle close to the trend; at other times they may be less close. This gives some clue to the variability of the market and the degree of uncertainty in the forecast. On the whole, simple extrapolation seems to be useful for raw materials and basic industrial products which have a wide range of uses, so that if one use is lost, another may be expected to arise.

Explanatory analyses

Explanatory analyses of market change often take the form of a simple model. It is convenient to use the term 'model' for any attempt to answer the question 'What causes change in the size of this market?' and to set out the answer in a formula. This principle is utilised in many forecasts. The variable to be forecast, whether it is total product demand, demand from a segment or indirect demand for a major customer's product, can be treated as being primarily determined by one or two or occasionally more independent variables.

For example the demand for a product might depend largely on the following independent variables:

1   The level of the national income.
2   Its price relative to other products.
3   The rate of technical change.

The problem then shifts to forecasting these and there is an implicit assumption that this is simpler, or that errors to some extent will balance out.

The national income is commonly forecast by considering its past trend and the comments of various specialised organisations (governmental, academic and business): prices by studies of the cost structure, trends in the cost of various inputs and the possible effect of improved efficiency. Technological advance cannot usually be measured directly, but if development is reasonably continuous and smooth it may be possible to treat it as if it advanced by more-or-less regular annual increments, and use time (the number of years) as a substitute for direct measurement. (Alternatively special allowances made by technical calculation for identified advances can be added or subtracted.)

Thus the forecaster can set up an equation expressing demand as a function of these independent variables, and by the fairly simple statistical technique of regression analysis deduce a relationship which he assumes to continue throughout the forecasting period. This equation is applied to the separate forecasts for the independent variables, and thus provides a forecast for the product under review. Where a special technical allowance is made (as suggested above) this is incorporated separately after the regression on the other variables.

When studying demand as a whole for a basic material it is common to relate the trend of demand in a country with the national income or some other measure of economic activity. Exhibit 8 shows the relationship between the British index of industrial production and sulphuric acid consumption over a number of years.

The approach discussed above considers the market for the product as an aggregate. Better forecasts are sometimes achieved by a segment-by-segment study when, for example, technological and social changes affect major industries [49].

The researcher accordingly studies each end-use separately seeking to forecast the future development of the end-use concerned, e.g. motor cars, machine tools, agricultural machinery. Change in the size of the end-use market has then to be converted to an estimate of change in demand for the product under study. The conversion is effected by multiplying by a coefficient which indicates the extra demand for the forecast product which arises from a unit change in output of the end-use product. The resulting estimates of demand from the different end-uses in total provide the market forecast. Maclean [24] has drawn attention to the need to take account of changes in these coefficients which can arise both from technical causes, e.g. more economic designs

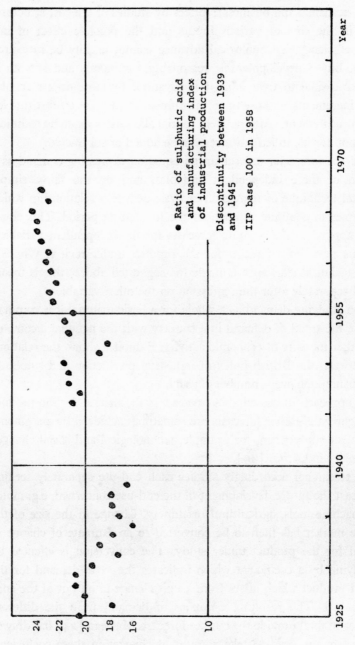

EXHIBIT 8 The link between materials consumption and industrial activity illustrated by means of the sulphuric acid manufacturing index of industrial production

• Ratio of sulphuric acid and manufacturing index of industrial production

Discontinuity between 1939 and 1945

IIP base 100 in 1958

or more efficient processes, and from economic causes (relative changes in prices of alternative materials or other inputs).

Major categories of capital goods often show a long-run trend which moves with national income. They may react very strongly to shorter-term fluctuations in the rate of national growth. A particular type of capital good may be affected in part by this general pattern and in part by a longer trend reflecting technological change peculiar to the product concerned. The demand for consumable goods and minor items of capital equipment will be affected by development of the different industries served and it may be necessary to study separately the trends of sales to these major customer segments as described in the previous paragraph and then treat the balance of demand as moving with the Gross National Product.

Thus the general principle behind model-building in the present context is to find a small number of factors which are thought to explain most of the market variation and for which some reasonable forecast is feasible, and then to fit them to the dependent variable (the series which is being forecast) by a simple equation.

Sometimes the formula is derived by technical considerations rather than by statistics. If it is known or anticipated that on average the demand for brickwork for houses and bungalows will be 6500 bricks per 1000 square feet of floor area, then a forecast of the number of houses and bungalows which will be built can be turned in a forecast for bricks. Here a technical coefficient has been used to obtain a measure of demand for one product from a forecast of the demand for the product which incorporates it.

Such procedures are used because sufficient data for a reliable regression analysis is not available, and a better technical coefficient can therefore be derived from the knowledge of engineers or technologists. It is also appropriate when it is known that a change in products or processes is occurring which will noticeably alter past relationships so that historic statistical coefficients will no longer be relevant.

Circumstantial and crosschecking evidence

Technical change of this type is the only one of the circumstances where the assistance offered by statistics may be limited. Sometimes the statistics do not exist—no one has bothered to collect them. Sometimes the product is new, or new to the country.

There are various lines of thought which prove of value in limiting the range within which the forecast lies. One is to 'ask your customers' —either major ones, the best informed or a cross-section of them. Not all customers make good forecasts of course. Sometimes it is possible to work with them to explore the factors which affect their demand and with their aid to build up a view of their market. Where capital equipment is concerned, some customers will reveal their future plans, although even these are liable to change as a result of economic or other developments.

The forecaster may seek to obtain supplementary information in order to modify a forecast undertaken by methods mentioned above. In almost every forecast it is necessary to consider the question 'Is technological change likely to affect the size of my market?' The more sophisticated customers may help to answer such questions as 'To what extent is demand for industrial lubricants likely to be reduced because improved products last longer?' The customer is not always the only or necessarily the best source. It may be that a research association or an end-user can be of more help.

With new products it is sometimes possible to carry out a techno-economic study in conjunction with customers to ascertain what bene-fit the new product offers in comparison with existing methods in different industries and applications, and thus to make an approximate assessment of the potential market segment by segment. Sometimes this has been done in such a way that a view was formed of the possible sales at different price levels.

International comparison can be helpful, largely as a check, or perhaps in desperation. When, as a basis for forecasting, a comparison is made between the Gross National Product and domestic consumption of a product in one country, the cautious forecaster wonders whether this calculated relationship holds for other countries. If a multi-national regression is encouraging, he considers his forecast that much stronger.

In certain areas of technology, some UK executives seem to have developed a working rule that the UK is always a more-or-less fixed number of years behind the United States in adopting new technology. The time-lag is a subject of dispute, and the relevance of the principle would vary between countries and between industries. It does represent a possible line of approach when there is little else on which to form a judgment. In making inter-country comparisons, geographical, climatic and cultural backgrounds need to be considered to decide whether inference is reasonable.

In forecasting new products, unless they clearly replace products which have become obsolete and are to be withdrawn, there is a period of time which inevitably elapses before the bulk of potential users adopt the product. Even if the product offers benefits, unless these are abundantly self-evident, and clearly advantageous, there will be a period of consideration and assessment. For capital goods, existing assets may be required to yield at least a reasonable working life before new improved equipment is installed. These are factors in the forecast.

Personal judgment and intuition

When statistics prove of limited avail, personal judgment takes over. In some cases the role of personal judgment is substantial, and it becomes extremely important that it should be objective and dispassionate. There is much to be said for placing the long-term forecasting operation in the hands of an individual detached from the day-to-day battle for order-winning. He is less likely in times of boom to take the view that the sky's the limit and in times of setback to forget that this too can be temporary. It is no easy task to distinguish significant longer-term developments from the continual short-term to-and-fro of the tides of business.

A common first step is for the opinion of well-informed specialists to be consulted and these views to be assessed bearing in mind the knowledge and attitudes of respondents.

A number of interesting methods have been developed for technological forecasting. These include the Delphi technique: an attempt to use human intuition in such a manner that behavioural influences are minimised. In this method, the forecaster seeks advice from experts by questionnaire. Information returned is then passed back to respondents (anonymously) and they are then asked for their opinions again after review in the light of the feedback. This gives an opportunity for them to take account of new information without an embarrassing recantation of publicity stated opinions and without being under pressure to go along with the majority or being overimpressed by some expert.

The information fed back to respondents anonymously can include:

1   Other respondents reasons for their forecast (especially for extreme views).
2   Other respondents criticisms of these reasons.
3   Summary statistics—median and spread of opinions.

There are a number of variations of the method discussed in more specialised literature.

Short-term forecasting

In short-term forecasting, some matters which are of little significance in the longer term come to the fore. Short-term forecasting is concerned with the months and quarters immediately ahead; seasonal variations in product demand and the cyclical variation of the economy have thus to be reflected.

Valuable statistical techniques have been developed. The traditional method of calculating a moving average of demand month by month over a series of years, extending this forward, building in seasonal variation factors, and garnishing the result with market knowledge still has much to commend it. It is in almost every introductory textbook on statistics.

For products that sell in bulk (as opposed to major capital goods), a technique honoured with the rather horrifying name of exponentially weighted smoothing averages is increasingly used and has been widely adopted. Despite the forbidding name and the mathematics needed to substantiate it, practical application is simple. The basic rule for making the forecast for a month ahead is:

1   Take the forecast made earlier for the latest month for which actual figures are available.
2   Calculate the size of the error, i.e. latest month's actual sales minus the forecast.
3   Adjust the former forecast by adding a proportion of the error

if it is positive (or subtracting if it is negative) to give the new forecast for the following month.

Additional allowance needs to be made for any trend in the data and for seasonal variation, but this too is straightforward. The proportion of the error to be added needs to be established by experience, but figures in the region of 0.2 to 0.3 seem to be commonly used. Where many hundreds of forecasts need to be made each month to cover all of a company's products, a computer can produce all the necessary information very quickly.

The alternative approach is the 'grass roots' approach in which individual members of the sales force are asked from their own contact with customers what they expect their customers' purchases to be for the coming month. This is still a valuable method even when statistical forecasts (as mentioned above) are used the sales staff should be asked to comment on the figures produced. They may know, for example, that a particular company is at that very moment finalising decision on a new purchase. Where the purchase pattern is 'lumpy' so that there are extreme variations from month to month in the value of orders booked, statistical methods offer less. This can apply to large capital equipment. Forecasts then still depend heavily on close knowledge and contact with the customer company, modified by some awareness of the pressures on the customer, for example changes in the state of the economy which can lead to changes in customers' best thought out plans.

In using the 'grass roots' approach it is sometimes found that individual salesmen tend consistently either to over or to under estimate future sales. Allowance can be made for this by simple adjustment to correct for the amount of 'normal' discrepancy for each individual.

7 PRODUCT PLANNING

Product planning has become in recent years one of the most crucial areas in determining the success or failure of an enterprise. Technological advance, new methods in industry and more rapid change in the patterns of final consumer behaviour have reacted on industrial markets, and products have become obsolete at a faster rate than ever before. Yet, at the same time, many companies have been unsuccessful in launching new products to replace the old.

Thus the problem of the business executive in product planning is like the classic problem of Odysseus trying to navigate the narrow passage between the whirlpool of Charybdis and the monster Scylla. Too far in one direction, and profits are sucked down by the Charybdis of product obsolescence; too far the other, and the profits are snatched away by the Scylla of new product failures.

From a great deal of discussion on this subject certain common lines of thought have emerged. There is disagreement on detail and some confusion of terminology, but the main core of ideas has achieved a wide measure of acceptance. Nevertheless, detailed application of these ideas must differ from one company to another. It will depend upon the type of customer and structure of the market, upon the technology of the industry, upon the economics and other characteristics of the production process, and upon the traditions and attitudes of the people in the company concerned.

The overall purpose of product planning is to ensure that the product range is composed of those products which make most profitable use of the resources of the company in relation to the opportunities of the environment. It is this which brings it within the basic concept of marketing on which this book is based.

To maintain an appropriate product line over time, it is necessary both to adopt new products and to drop old ones. The process of developing new products means searching out ideas, examining them for their suitability, and developing from such embryonic ideas as are suitable, products which will achieve success in the market-place. There must also be review of the product range to examine whether current products are pulling their weight or whether the company is struggling along, committing to low-profitability products financial resources and executives' time which could be used elsewhere to greater advantage.

What is a product?

The marketing man views the product not as a piece of hardware, but as a device by which the resources of a company are turned into customer-satisfying benefits. It is useful, but not easy, to try to analyse the customer implications of the product by dissecting it into more fundamental elements.

The following is a suggested approach to the problem of product analysis. It divides the product concept into five elements which can often be distinguished from each other:

The basic core of the product concept is the statement of the generic need which it satisfies and the service which it supplies to customers. It indicates the way in which this particular product sets out to serve the buying company. Thus a fork-lift truck might be described as a materials-handling device for relatively small loads. There are, however, often other alternative products, technically different but serving the same general purpose.

Primary differentiation will distinguish the different ways in which various products satisfy the same class of need. How does the fork-lift truck differ from the conveyor and from overhead handling equipment? Considerations such as load-carrying, flexibility and ease of control come to the fore here. Different products also make different demands on a customer in terms of staff skills required, ancillary equipment and investment. In industrial marketing primary differentiation is associated with fundamental technical differences.

Secondary differentiation separates one model from another. Technical specifications are a relevant basis for secondary differentiation of products—capacity, mode of holding the load, turning circle and so on. Differentiation can also be achieved by variations in certain additional features (optional extras) which offer benefits required in some applications but not others.

Tertiary differentiations and matters which do not affect the applications to which the product is suited. They may make its use more convenient to the customer e.g. ergonomic considerations in engineering products, or they may make it easier to open, measure or dispense. They can relate to the external appearance of the product, e.g. aesthetic features, packaging and labelling. For instance, in disposable surgical instruments the aesthetic aspects may be considered a significant marketing characteristic. Even in industrial marketing such factors can help to create confidence in BPIs, and help give an edge over competition.

Ancillary service Both commercial and technical services, although not part of the hardware, add extra value to the product (see Chapter 12).

This analysis is probably best suited to an engineering or other fabricated product; for other types of product it may require modification. The basis is the idea that the product is specified implicitly or explicitly by the market and the customer. As the product concept is elaborated in detail, so is it focused more sharply on particular applications by particular classes of customers. In turn the customers' own requirements are better understood and reflected back with increasing sharpness to define the product ever more precisely. The ability to provide what the customer wants on acceptable terms depends to some extent on the state of technology at the time, and advances in technology increasingly make it possible to offer better value.

Sometimes finding out what product innovation the customer wants is not difficult. These can be sources of dissatisfaction with existing products which can well be remedied, resulting in an improved product. It becomes more difficult to identify customer needs which can be expected to emerge in the future but which the customer has not yet recognised. The marketing man must then try to stand in the shoes of the customer of tomorrow and to think through the problems he will face so that his needs may be anticipated even before they have become clear to the customer. This requires information, thought and insight penetrating through the intermediate manufacturer and subsequent customers to the end-user and the background macro-environment.

The product life cycle

A familiar and very valuable tool in developing an effective product policy is the idea of the product life cycle. The underlying hypothesis is that products are in the market for a span of years, during which total market sales pass through the successive phases illustrated in Exhibit 9. These are initiation, growth, maturity, saturation and decline.

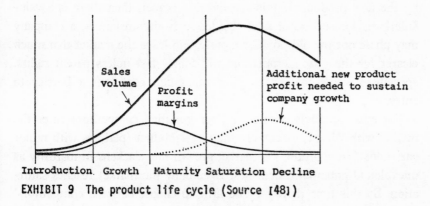

EXHIBIT 9 The product life cycle (Source [48])

This may not be applicable to all products in all industries, but it is certainly widespread. The length of the cycle varies from industry to industry, and the tendency over the last quarter of a century or so has been for this cycle to shorten. It may be that those industries which do not appear to be affected by this phenomenon either have no life cycle, or else that the cycle is of such a length that it stretches beyond the time-span of even the longest of corporate plans. Nevertheless, let the producer beware! Advances in technology and the reaction of changes

D

in consumer habits and fashions are increasingly dethroning well-established products in the most unexpected way.

Essentially, the hypothesis is this. In its early days after the product is launched into the market, growth of sales proceeds gradually. This is a difficult time, and if not carefully handled can be long drawn out. A high proportion of the products which are launched fail to achieve success at this stage and this is one of the problems of product policy.

If the product survives through introduction, the growth of the market accelerates. Expansion comes about as a result of such factors as awareness of the product by potential customers, and a widening of markets from the discovery of additional applications. The marketing effort of the innovating company operates to promote market growth, and price reductions may support this effort.

A product may grow very fast in the early stages of the cycle, because the users of the product which it supersedes have been consciously dissatisfied. Explicit complaints about an existing product contribute to a clear specification of customer requirements to be met by the new product. If this specification is met, then there is a valuable basis for successful sales. Under such circumstances, a company may phase out the old product rapidly, and leave the market that much clearer for the new. Competitors will follow fast unless patent rights, specialised know-how or supplier reputation represent a barrier to entry.

For most products, sooner or later imitating competitors enter the market with what is essentially the same product (perhaps with minor variations). In addition, the market growth rate slackens in maturity as unexploited potential diminishes. Eventually the market reaches saturation. By this time there may be little to choose between competitors' products. A new product may now enter the market, and the original product, now obsolescent, will begin to decline.

Life-cycle variations

Not every product has a life cycle exactly like Exhibit 9. There are variants, some important.

The foothills   One feature which is not uncommon in industrial markets is the phenomenon of a 'foothill' in the early stage of the cycle, i.e.

a small spurt in demand, followed by a limited decline. After the foothill, the main pattern of the cycle reasserts itself if the product is successful. This foothill probably arises from the fact that potential customers make limited purchases for the purpose of evaluating the product and gaining experience—thus causing the spurt—and there is then a lull while they form an opinion of the product.

The plateau At the saturation stage, if there is no better product forthcoming, the product demand may well rest on a plateau for a while, perhaps growing with the growth of the economy as a whole, but not capturing new markets. However, there are some instances in which, even after reaching apparent saturation, renewed expansion has been achieved by giving fresh thought to the product. This phenomenon of 'regeneration' is discussed more fully later in this chapter.

The redoubt When decay does set in, the product does not necessarily lose its entire market at the same time. While the later innovating product may gain the main markets, there may remain a redoubt of resistance in which the existing product is still preferred and may continue to offer profitable sales for some time. This may not be of much interest to the bigger company, but may suit the smaller 'follower' company.

Fresh heights In certain markets, the growth of sales follows a wavelike pattern: a surge of sales, followed by a slowing down before a new surge. This would match a market in which growth depends on finding new applications; each surge represents a new segment opened up, perhaps induced by the discovery of new applications and matched product variations.

The profit cycle

Associated with the cycle of demand is the change in financial returns from the product, illustrated by the cycle of net profit in Exhibit 9. On introduction of the product's life cycle, the net profit margin is commonly low despite the favourable price. This is a result of high costs, low volume, perhaps initial teething troubles in production, relatively heavy demands on technical service and initial publicity. Later, moving towards maturity with extra volume, increased experience, a decline in initial expenses and thus lower costs give a wider margin despite possible price falls.

Price reductions to help market growth and to meet competitive pressures are common over the life cycle. As cost reductions taper off, falling prices force down the profit margin. This often happens in maturity before total market sales decline, and at this stage an innovating company may seek to bring out a further new product to maintain and expand sales and profits.

The net profit margin thus signals decline in advance of the fall of sales. The concept of net profit is, however, somewhat unsatisfactory for this purpose, because the margin may well turn upon the convention which the company's accountant has adopted in allocating the initial capital investment and the overheads of the company.

Alternatively, therefore, it is suggested that if no new capital investment is called for, the assessment of the product's return should emphasise the 'contribution' which is being made (see page 90 for a discussion of this term), or if fresh capital investment is required it should stress the net cash flow. The executive should regularly review the contribution from the product, and a decline in contribution is an early warning of the time when the introduction of a new product will become necessary.

Strategy and the life cycle

As the product develops over its life cycle, changes in strategy become necessary. Some of these changes are sufficiently common (but not universal) to justify special comment here.

When the product is launched, the company has usually spent heavily on development and perhaps on research also, and the future of the product is somewhat problematical. Capacity too may be relatively limited. In general this leads to the company seeking a relatively high price, which implies it must find a market segment which obtains an appropriate benefit. (Other approaches are possible, but rare in industrial marketing—this is discussed in Chapter 16.)

At the same time, the fact that the product is new implies widespread ignorance in customer companies, and perhaps some prejudice. The communication task of the innovating company is therefore to educate, through press relations (often very successful with new products), the sales and service force, and different forms of advertising and publicity. Sometimes, even before the product is formally on the market, it may be tested with customers and the success of these tests may enable sales to be made to the 'guinea-pigs' and provide information to help sell the product elsewhere.

As sales rise and competitors follow with the same or similar products (as commonly happens unless effective patents or other barriers keep them out), prices may well fall in real terms. ('In real terms' means after discounting the effect of any decline in the value of money which may have taken place. Here and elsewhere in this book, the term 'price' or 'price change' is to be interpreted in this way, unless the contest makes it clear that the contrary is intended.) Sometimes greater secondary differentiation develops and the combined effect of these adaptations and price decline is to aid the market expansion into fresh applications.

Promotional efforts tend to emphasise more the supplier or the supplier's brand, and the educational effort of the early phase fades away. The need for technical service may also be less as customers are now well informed about the product. Expansion of production capacity can run beyond the growth of the market as demand moves towards saturation. Regeneration policies seek to maximise the market and to extend product life by offering variants.

This is the point where an innovating firm may bring out a newer product. This further reduces the demand for the ageing product and intensifies pressure on price. By this time there will often be defined standards current for the product to the level of secondary differentiation, or major buyers may determine their own specifications. It is sometimes said that at this stage the product tends to become like a 'commodity', with customers buying against specifications and emphasising price. For some products this point is never reached, but the pressures are frequently in this direction. More firms may by now introduce new products and de-emphasise or withdraw the old one, but suppliers with low overheads may be inclined to continue even at low prices.

Product decisions

If the view is accepted that for most products (except perhaps a favoured and diminishing minority) the life-cycle is limited, then this has implications for management action.

Clearly, it is necessary to carry out a policy of planned readiness to introduce a new product as the old one becomes obsolete. In fact, a planned product policy will aim to achieve a balance between:

1   Products in the pipeline of development.
2   New products not yet making much contribution.
3   Developing and mature products making the main contribution and carrying a deficiency on others.
4   Decaying products which are candidates for withdrawal from the range in the near future.
5   Complementary products, low volume, to provide a full line.

This is a planning task of no mean difficulty and a challenge to the skill of the manager. It requires forecasts of the length of cycle of the product to anticipate the date on which it will be timely to introduce the next new product. The profits of the company are maintained and expanded by introducing new products when the profits from the present ones decline, and this involves maintaining a sort of 'product calendar' to show when new products must be ready. All departments are then geared to match their work with this requirement.

Extending the life cycle

Apart from developing new products (discussed in the next chapter), a successful product policy requires a regular and systematic review of existing products. If the product is prospering, then it is necessary to consider whether it should be developed more fully. If the product is not so successful, then the company may be concerned either to regenerate or eliminate the product.

With the prospering product, the company may wish to reinforce success by cultivating the present market more intensively, by allocating more resources to those areas of the market which have unrealised potential, or be seeking new applications. This may require more active market research, more market development, more prospecting, and modification of the product's characteristics to match particular applications.

Inevitably there comes a stage when the regular analysis of product results shows that the return from some is beginning to flag. These products have survived the agonies of product launch, and have been successful in the market; now comes the first hint that they will not be earning their keep much longer. Can such products be regenerated and given a further boost to sales and returns?

Clues that regeneration may be possible include such symptoms as: declining product sales when no more advanced product has entered the market, competitors increasing their market share, information that potential customers are deterred by price or unsatisfactory features of the product, and undeveloped markets which are likely to respond to modifications/variations.

In such circumstances, there is a chance that the product may be given a further lease of profitable life. It may be modified to give it a boost across the full span of the market, or it may be adapted in a way which strengthens it in a particular market segment in which there is still opportunity.

Regeneration can be achieved in a number of ways, separately or in combination. Market research, sales, distributors, customers, service, may suggest ideas for improving the product for existing customers, or identify areas for further exploitation. Ideas from an industrial designer have helped to revive sales for a fabricated product in a surprising way. Value analysis has an important role: it may show how costs can be reduced without loss of product efficiency or appearance.

Product regeneration must be handled with care. It is not a substitute for new product policy, but a complement to it, and care is necessary that it does not become an excuse for keeping in the range products which have become obsolete but which no one has had the courage to drop. This requires clear target figures in the market plan against which results can be checked.

Product retirement

This brings into focus the next major issue in product planning—the retirement of obsolescent products. This can cause strong emotional reactions in a company. There is almost always some objection to any proposal to drop a product, and dealing with this requires judgment, courage and determination from management. It is remarkable how often a company in difficulties is taken over by a successful bidder or calls in a 'company doctor' and one of his first steps is to eliminate products offering little return. Obsolescent products distract from the worthwhile products, and tie up capital and other resources which could be spent on digging out new and better products.

The contribution test

The test of whether to keep a product in the range must depend very much on its financial return—not only today's return, but the return which is to be expected over the next few years. The starting point of the calculation is the 'contribution to overheads and profit' which the product is making at present, or in the latest period for which figures are available. On this basis, and a realistic appreciation of trends in development, a view is formed of its likely contribution in the years ahead. The meaning of 'contribution' is discussed below, and it is as well to make it quite clear that the contribution would be interpreted differently if the question were one of *adding* new products or incurring capital expenditure on current products. What is suggested here is that, in considering whether *existing* products should be kept in the range or dropped, a key financial calculation is the product's contribution. This figure is then to be interpreted by the executive responsible, who will also take account of other factors, such as the effect on other products in the line or range.

The product's contribution is calculated as the difference between its net sales revenue and those incremental costs which arise from manufacturing and marketing the product and which would *not* arise if the product were dropped. These costs are commonly regarded as including direct wages and related costs, materials, variable selling costs (salesmen's commission), and other variables such as royalties, stockholding costs, and freight. Fixed costs traceable to the product concerned may also sometimes be relevant.

What is incremental can only be decided by a study of the particular circumstances. In practice, some companies find it sufficient to approximate to the contribution by deducting as incremental only direct labour and materials. Other extra costs may be small and make little difference to the final decision after marketing 'imponderables' have been taken into account. The wage bill, on the other hand, may include a fixed element.

It should be noted that for the purpose of calculating the contribution, general administrative overheads are not charged to each product because they are not affected. Contribution is an important concept, and is considered in depth in more specialised textbooks.

Note that if a whole line of products is under review, then sales, service, clerical and administrative staff may be reduced if it is dropped. These costs accordingly become incremental and are also deducted in arriving at the contribution. There may also be policy fixed costs which are incurred for a particular line by management decision: attendance at an exhibition relevant to that line but not to others, literature, or market and product development costs. Table 1 sets out details for an imaginary company manufacturing and marketing five products. It will be seen that although product A provides one-third of the revenue, its share of total contribution is only 25 per cent. Product B provides less than one-third of revenue but over half the contribution. B has the highest unit contribution, but even for C the contribution ratio is higher than it is for A. E is not covering its vari-

TABLE 1 Comparative contribution analysis

1 Product	2 Price £	3 Unit sales 000's	4 Revenue £'000s	5 Variable costs £'000s	6 Contribution £'000s	7 Contribution £ per unit	8 Ratio*
A	120	5	600	450	150	30	0.25
B	90	6	540	200	340	57	0.63
C	80	3	240	150	90	30	0.37
D	60	5	300	250	50	10	0.17
E	60	2	120	150	-30	-15	-0.25
TOTAL			1800	1200	600		0.33
Less General overheads					400		
PROFIT					200		

*Contribution as a proportion of revenue (also sometimes described as price/volume ratio)

able costs and its future comes into question. Finally D is not doing well, and on most common methods of allocating overheads D would be showing a loss.

Questions immediately suggest themselves. For example, can B be pushed more strongly and can resources allocated to other products be diverted to making and marketing it? This possibility should be explored.

Product E is a strong candidate for phasing out (although some further comments are made later in this chapter). D is making a contribution to overheads, but a low one. If there is nothing else upon which the resources used for D can be employed, then on financial grounds alone D is worth keeping in the line. If it is dropped without a replacement, £50,000 in contribution is lost but general overheads are unchanged.

One word of caution is necessary. If a common facility used by several products creates a 'bottleneck', it may be necessary to consider contribution in relation to the use of that scarce facility. For example if A, B, C, D and E are made on the same machine their demand on that scarce resource is competitive. The position may be analysed as shown in Table 2.

TABLE 2   Comparative contributions under a constraint

1 Product	2 Revenue per tonne Price, £	3 Contribution ratio*	4 Contribution (£) per unit	5 Units of machine time to produce 1 unit	6 Contribution per unit of machine time**
A	120	0.25	30	1	30
B	90	0.63	57	3	19
C	80	0.37	30	2	15
D	60	0.17	10	2.5	4
E	60	-0.25	-15	0.5	Negative

*As in Table 1
**Column 4 divided by column 5

As machine time is therefore a bottleneck, a useful test of the value of each of the products is to see how much contribution is generated for each unit of machine time which it utilises. In this case A has a clear margin over the others and therefore is given priority. However, if the price level of A was to fall as a result of this policy (or for some other reason) the issue would need to be reviewed. There are also other considerations relating to the balance between products in the same line. Note that B and C produce very similar contributions, but D is well down the scale and E is negative. Clearly both of these latter are open to question. Such an example as this is very simplified but illustrates the role of numbers in a review of product policy and prices. In complex problems where there are more constraints linear programming and related techniques have been used to find an answer. Extreme instances arise in, for example, the chemical industry where a continuous process is able to produce a different mix of product output proportions; the choice of mix depends in part on the price level of the different output products and the costs and qualities of the different feedstocks. In such circumstances a complex mathematical model may provide the basis of the solution and an on-line computer may be needed to calculate the optimum policy.

A company as a whole must, of course, cover its full overheads and yield a surplus if it is to trade and be profitable in the long run. If this is not happening, there are many other matters to be examined, such as the need to reduce costs or to identify and bring into the line more profitable products. When, however, the company is engaged in a systematic re-examination of its individual products and not actually contemplating additional investment, then the contribution is the item to be scrutinised. Where the contribution is negligible or nil, the first presumption is that the product should be phased out. Where the contribution is low, then the possibility of replacing it with more profitable products should be considered.

Other considerations

Under what circumstances, if any, should a product which is not expected to make a contribution be retained in the range? Clearly, if its contribution can be improved by regeneration or by some other means (perhaps by the simple process of raising the price!), then the product may be saved at least for the time being. Moreover, a new product will often not contribute at the beginning of its career, and this may have to be accepted for a while, if its future return has been assessed and will justify present losses.

The relationship between products in the same line needs consideration. These products may be competitive (if one is bought then another is not), they may be complementary (a buyer requiring one product is likely to require another), or they may be neutral. For example, different grades/sizes and finishes of photographic paper may be competitive up to a point, so long as a reasonable range is provided. In providing minor hand-tools a line may have to provide all sizes within certain limits in order to satisfy buyers. A range of laminates of different colours presents a similar dilemma.

These factors must be evaluated and an attempt made to quantify them. A salesman may well be selling non-contributing products when he could be selling contributing ones (perhaps with little more effort). Every non-contributing product sold means that the other products must recover the resulting shortfall even *before anything is available towards overheads*, let alone profit. The difficulty is that salesmen's successes are generally measured by turnover, but marketing results should be measured on an operating basis by contribution and on the longer-term basis by profit or cash flow.

The analysis can be carried further and contribution measured for different markets and different customers. It may be that a company is keeping a non-contributing product in its line to maintain the goodwill and therefore the business of a particular customer. Yet analysis may show that the customer's *entire business* is not contributing.

If the salesman is provided with sufficient motivation and shown how other products will serve his customer better, he will often, when it comes to the crunch, be able to sell alternative products to the customer. In one instance, a company ceased to manufacture certain products but continued to supply them by acting as a distributor for another supplier.

Finally, there is often one product in the line which makes no contribution but is supposed to support the company's image. If it does do this, any loss should be charged to the public relations budget and the public relations staff can then decide whether it supports the image to a sufficient extent to justify this cost.

A non-contributing product may sometimes be justly regarded as an 'investment' in long-term market or customer development. The danger is that this view may too easily be adopted as a way of avoiding unpalatable decisions. If it is considered, a serious attempt should be made to evaluate future returns and to discount these to current values: discounting takes account of the time before returns mature and helps assess whether any time lag involved is justified by the size of the ultimate pay-off.

The marketing man should be cautious in the extreme about carrying products and customers making no present contribution and little prospect of any in the near future, and none too keen on those making low contributions. The more poor relatives there are in the family, the harder do the other members have to work. The policy should be to ensure that the company devotes its resources to those products which, over their lifetime, give the best contribution, and that additions and deletions should work to this purpose.

8 DEVELOPING NEW PRODUCTS

What is a new product? Newness is a relative term and it is as difficult to define the difference between a 'new' product and a variation on an old one as it is to define the difference between hot and cold. The extremes are obvious, but there is no border line. Very few products represent a fundamental departure from the past. Perhaps the most substantial changes are exemplified by technological advances such as the development of the first wholly synthetic fibres, or of the transistor. From the customer's point of view, these largely represent better ways of doing something which has already been done before, by offering improved or additional qualities. Nylon is a textile used in clothes with its functions of warmth, propriety and adornment, to mention one primary end-use. The transistor superseded the thermionic valve and made electronic equipment cheaper, compact and more versatile, with advantages to ultimate users seeking to satisfy their needs for entertainment, for communication and for more efficient industrial operation.

These new products represented major technological advances. Far more commonly, new products involve the use of established technological knowledge to produce a product which is 'new' in the customer's terms. New models of typewriters over the years have offered additional or different features without a substantial change in the basic machine; even the biggest change, the electric typewriter, has not involved a technological advance comparable with those mentioned above. Nevertheless, to the customer it was a new product offering advantages not available before. It must also have involved the manufacturer in considerable development and production problems.

Many products are only minor variations of existing products to improve operational efficiency, or to overcome difficulties which have been found in use, or adaptations for a new application. For example, a maker of a commercial vehicle might alter the type or location of switches or handles. Many companies would not regard minor variations as creating a new product and would delegate authority for them to a product manager or other appropriate middle executive. This is a convenient arrangement, although such delegation needs to be clearly defined and controlled.

Nevertheless, an attempt must be made to give at least a broad indication of what is implied by the concept of newness in the present discussions. A useful approach to this is suggested by the analysis of the product in the preceding chapter.

Firstly, any product with a basic core differing from those of established products in the company is new to that company. In fact, this change in the core of the product concept is what is commonly implied by the term 'diversification' in business discussions. The product is so different from existing products that it represents a change in the business of the company. Most companies also certainly treat the introduction of a product with different primary characteristics as 'new', but there would probably be less agreement on whether this term should be applied to secondary variations. In companies where such changes involve considerable costs in capital investment, retraining staff and so on, the safest policy is to treat secondary product variation as 'new product development' and to handle it in accordance with the general company arrangements for new products.

Tertiary differentiation would not normally be regarded as new product introduction, and the authority to deal with these may be decentralised. However, it is essential that some record be kept of them, and some simplified basis for centralised approval should be adopted within the company. Moreover, if these small changes are not introduced in a co-ordinated way, there can be problems in keeping catalogues up-to-date, in ensuring that distributors have the right replacements and so on. However, as long as these changes have been carefully checked, do not require significant capital expenditure and have been the subject of proper interdepartmental consultation, the benefits to be obtained from more complex procedures are probably outweighed by the cost involved and the clogging of communication channels.

New products, for the purpose of this chapter, can include products new to the company, even if they may be already established in the market by another company. A company which for the first time brings out a certain product in the market is referred to as an innovator, and the companies which follow it are imitators.

The fact that one company is already manufacturing and selling the product apparently successfully does not *necessarily* mean that another company which imitates it will be able to do the same. There may be differences between the skills or the established markets of the two companies which make the comparison a misleading one. To succeed it may be desirable for the imitator company to offer a product which incorporates advantages that the innovating company's product does not have, or to concentrate on a special market segment. The role of an imitator can often be an advantageous one, particularly for the smaller firm, but it still requires management skill in its application.

The basic approach

How then is a businessman to devise and carry through successfully a policy of new product development? Any systematic approach must have certain elements which have to be applied in different ways according to circumstances:

1   *Product guidelines*   A broad indication of the general class of products which is considered to be appropriate to the company's long-term strategy and present market situation.

2   *Search procedure*   Arrangements for the seeking of product ideas which are consistent with these guidelines.

3   *Screening and development procedure*   A formalised and controlled system by which ideas are developed, screened from time to time, and if found satisfactory are carried forward until they are ultimately marketed.

Product guidelines

If a company had to examine every possible product before it selected one, the problem of deciding which was the best product for it to launch would become impossible. So from the very beginning of thinking about new products, a company will find it necessary to indicate in broad terms those categories of products which have a reasonable probability of being suited to market needs and to its own capabilities in the years immediately ahead. This ensures that even at the earliest stage, when expenditure on the development of the product is lowest, time and money is allocated only to products which have some justification for consideration. Moreover, when the company is actively searching for new product ideas, the establishment of guidelines which answer the question 'What sort of product are we seeking?' is essential to direct the executives concerned.

The use of product guidelines is sometimes criticised on the grounds that it may exclude products which the company could in fact market with success. This is possible, but it is unlikely if the guidelines are drawn up after careful study. Moreover, the object of new product development is not only to seek products which are profitable in themselves, but to sort out the few which are the best, in terms of profit and risk, and which also contribute to the long-term development of the company.

The value of product guidelines is illustrated by the story of one group of companies in which it was customary to establish such guidelines for each member company. The objection that this unduly restricted these companies was met by allowing each managing director to spend up to a certain maximum sum annually on products of his own choosing outside the guidelines. Experience of these discretionary products was such that the authorised expenditure became known within the group as the 'managing directors' folly'.

The guidelines themselves must be consistent with the overall corporate strategy of the company concerned. This strategy is the starting point from which they are developed. They may be broad, leaving a wide field for exploration, or narrow and precise. Some companies have very strict and exact ideas of their product needs at a particular time, for example when it is necessary to replace obsolete items in the product line. On other occasions the guidelines may be very wide because of difficulty in defining what precisely will be most compatible with the company's logical development. Wider guidelines permit more product ideas to qualify but consequently involve more cost in developing accepted ideas and in the stricter screening required later.

The following paragraphs indicate some of the factors that may be relevant to the determination of product guidelines.

Corporate objectives The corporate objectives discussed in the final chapter will have indicated what business the company wishes to be in and whether products are to be directed towards diversification or otherwise. They will also indicate the status which that company seeks to have within that industry—to emphasise innovation and pioneer new ideas, or to emphasise imitation and adapt existing ideas to limited segments of the market or producing cheaper versions. If these points are not in corporate objectives, then they must be considered for the purpose of the guidelines.

Market considerations Even if it wishes to remain in the same business, the company may have reasons for wishing to develop certain markets and avoiding others. If present markets are growing and have much untapped potential, then the aim will be to exploit this opportunity. On the contrary, if the present market is unattractive, then the need to develop alternatives must be specified. One company which suffered severely from loss of markets when a major defence project was cancelled specified that, in order to spread its risk, new products should be suited to general industrial purposes rather than defence. Similarly, a company which has become heavily reliant upon one customer may seek products which will offset this.

Marketing skills will also be relevant to the specification of product guidelines. If the present sales force can carry more products without loss of effort on present lines, then it might be desired to develop products which are of interest to the company's present customers. The company may also have an 'image' or name in the market which it is anxious to preserve or develop, and this may influence its choice of product.

Production considerations Here again many points may arise. Is the product to be based on the use of present skills and equipment? Or is the company keen to develop new skills? Is there some plant which is under-utilized, the capacity of which the company should wish to exploit? Has it control over supplies of certain raw materials? Some companies are best able to produce standardised products which are made in bulk, others are by past skills and experience better placed to make smaller quantities to customer specification.

R&D factors Particular skill in certain aspects of R&D and a high efficiency in developing products of technical originality and sophistication within the field of their experience is another characteristic which it may be worth while exploiting. Another company had recently taken on a number of science graduates as part of their longer-term planning and was anxious to employ their skills at as early a date as possible. Other companies may have little skill in this field, and may therefore be interested in products which have already had all the R&D problems solved, or in minor variations of these.

Service considerations This is a consideration which has probably not been given all the attention in industrial marketing which it deserves. A reputation for giving trustworthy service in certain lines of business is an asset that may be worth exploiting.

Financial and risk factors At this very early stage it is difficult to be precise in defining desirable risk levels and the financial return which is sought, for the simple reason that until some study has been given to the product, it is not normally possible to evaluate the risk involved and the return to be expected. Nevertheless, some companies indicate the turnover level which the product may be required to achieve. Large companies with heavy overheads may require a reasonable probability of achieving a certain minimum figure. A small company may set an upper limit in order to concentrate on markets in which larger companies are not likely to compete. Alternatively, the financial guidelines may set a limit on the amount of new capital investment required. Other companies prefer products which are patentable and therefore somewhat protected from competition.

Considerations of time Sometimes a company—which has perhaps been slow to awake to the importance of product planning—may require new products urgently. With no time to develop a product, there is an immediate need for a 'ready-made' product, perhaps through a licensing agreement for a product which is successfully marketed in another country. This may need to be backed up by the longer-term development of products for the future.

The product search

The product guidelines have now indicated the general class of product that is required and thus opened the way for a search for suitable products. The product search seeks to bring forward as many eligible products as possible so that, by a process of sifting, the best may be determined. Much searching is continuous, sometimes supplemented by intensified search in depth when circumstances require. In the latter case it is usual to take extra care to direct the search by specifying relatively restrictive guidelines.

The basic concept of marketing is that ideas come forward from insight into the market. This does not mean that the task of identifying new product possibilities can be put on the shoulders of the customer. The innovating company seeks to anticipate his needs. Nor does it exclude seeking ideas from other indirect sources and examining their suitability for the markets with which the company is concerned.

Many product ideas are devised from the study of evolutionary growth and change in the company's established markets and its natural extensions. Existing products are progressively modified to exploit technological advance, to meet changes in customers' markets, technology and products, and to develop new applications. A somewhat different situation arises when a company seeks to change direction and switch from its traditional product mission because of prospective market decline.

In the evolutionary situation the company will look first to its contacts with the market for ideas about changing requirements: the sales force, the service force, formal market research, distributors and others. Its internal departments—R&D, engineering, design— will be familiar with its market and contribute to the pool of ideas with suggestions arising from their own work. Indeed, ideas can come from employees at all levels.

However, no one organisation can assume that its own staff will have the monopoly of ideas, and the search will extend outside the company, particularly when the guidelines stress diversification or change in the primary characteristics of the product. Nor is it easy to develop feasible ideas which match both the market and the company concerned. Trade and technical literature, scientific journals, research organisations, universities will justify continuous attention. Patents —new, established, or expiring—can be examined with a view to acquiring licences, and the search can be extended overseas to the USA, Europe, the USSR and Japan through specialised consultants.

The search then produces a large number of product ideas—and it is surprising how many ideas can come forward from a conscientious search. But at this stage many are often more than rudimentary concepts of what the products should offer.

The concepts should be expressed as precisely and clearly as possible. From the point of view of the marketing man the question 'What are the principal additional benefits which we propose to offer to potential customers that they are not already enjoying?' should be clearly answered. Sometimes at this stage this may in fact be all there is of the product concept.

The concept may describe specific modifications of existing products: a variation of a lubricant, or a plastic to offer advantages under a certain range of conditions (for example, conditions of heat, cold, atmospheric pollution or fungal growth), in certain markets or applications.

The screening process

Once a product concept has qualified by satisfying the guidelines, the company begins spending money and allocating resources to its development and examination. Yet at this stage it may have less than a 1 per cent chance of becoming a successful product. The next steps are designed to build up information about the proposed product, and use this information to decide whether or not to continue with it. Evidently, it is an advantage to eliminate unsuitable ideas as early as possible before any substantial expense has been involved.

The company has also to move from the concept to a fully developed product. There may be occasions when this is a simple task, as when the company plans to produce under licence a product which has already proved itself elsewhere. There are, however, many occasions when the product has to go through stages of refining the concept, developing the specification, adding to its definition and planning production and marketing. These can involve years of time and trouble.

The object of the screening process is to permit all the developments to take place in a controlled way. At certain predetermined stages in the development of the product, all the information must be brought together in order that a decision should be made about its future. This decision may be:

1   To authorise the commencement of the next stage of development.
2   To drop the product.
3   To refer the product back for further consideration.

The number of times a product is screened during its development and the exact point at which those screens are inserted will vary with the type of business. The example below suggests four screenings, but it is clear that some companies operate with fewer, and other companies with more. More screenings are probably justified when development time is long and costs are high.

The process of screening is illustrated in Exhibit 10, which also shows the two main lines of development: within the firm (perhaps involving R&D, production, engineering and design) working on problems of developing the physical product, and outside obtaining market information and planning marketing.

The four stages are:

1   Preliminary analysis.
2   Commercial analysis.
3   Development.
4   Testing.

Preliminary analysis   The first stage is a brief and inexpensive review. The market assessment indicated is based on desk research, with perhaps some telephone inquiries among informed opinion. The object is to obtain a view on such points as:

1   How significant to the customers is the benefit offered by the proposed product?

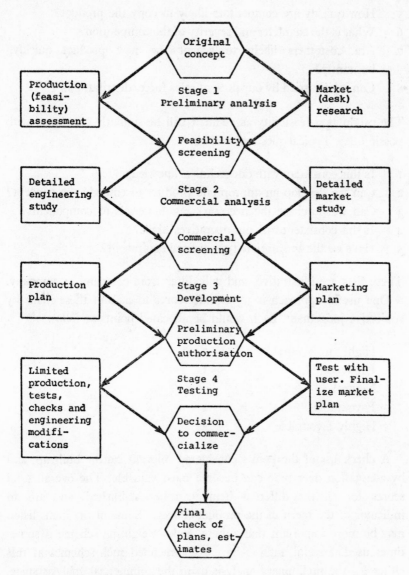

EXHIBIT 10 Screening new products

2   Within what range is market size likely to be?
3   Is it growing/about the same/declining?
4   Is the market difficult to enter?
5   How quickly are competitors likely to copy the product?
6   What is the character and severity of the competition?
7   Are customers likely to accept the new product quickly/hesitantly?
8   Can it be carried by our present sales force/distributors?

The production feasibility assessment will be similarly concerned with possibilities. Typical questions will be:

1   Is this consistent with our technical knowledge?
2   Can we develop an appropriate product to embody the concept?
3   Can we purchase the necessary raw materials or components?
4   Is this consistent with our operatives' skills?
5   Have we the appropriate type of fixed equipment?

These lists are illustrative, and will differ from company to company.
One useful approach is to allocate scores to each of these items by subjective judgement. Each would be allocated points as follows:

Highly unfavourable	− 2
Unfavourable	− 1
Neutral	0
Favourable	1
Highly favourable	2

A check list of the points considered relevant can be built up, and by adaptation over time can become most valuable. The overall total scores for all the different items can be established, and are an indicator of the merit of the product concept. Some of the items listed may be more important than others, and a weighting scheme is sometimes used. Several authors have recommended such schemes as this either for the preliminary analysis or in the commercial analysis stage.

The overall score is useful as a guide, but sometimes the information on a particular point will be such as to preclude the product completely, if, for example, it is likely to require an expertise which the company does not have and might find difficulty in obtaining.

Experience will show where the cut-off point between acceptable and non-acceptable ideas should be, and products falling below this will be excluded. Assuming that a satisfactory flow of initial product ideas has been achieved, as many as two-thirds of them may be eliminated at this stage.

Commercial analysis Products which pass the first stage satisfactorily will now go forward for more detailed treatment, and the expenditure on them begins to mount sharply. This stage is one of the most important, and many companies may wish to subdivide it. The objective is to move from a 'concept' of the product in broad terms to a fully developed and detailed specification, supported by forecasts of expenditure and revenue in considerable detail, an assessment of the risk involved and a calculation of expected return on a discounted cash flow basis.

Market research has a very important task to perform here. It must evaluate the market, segment by segment, to produce a detailed 'customer specification', setting out performance characteristics which this product should meet. By examining the value of the product to each segment, market research will prepare estimates of possible sales at different price levels. It must form an opinion of the speed at which demand is likely to build up and the possibility of competitors copying the product or reacting in some other way. A rough marketing plan may now be prepared, together with supporting costs.

Those responsible for production are also examining their problems, and preparing details of costs and investment requirements. Together with the marketing department's calculation, these are the basis for the view of expected commercial results on which authorisation for the next stage is decided. Where products involve considerable basic research, an analysis such as this is recommended prior to any major expenditure.

Development and testing The number of products which reach this stage is now a modest figure—perhaps 10 to 15 per cent of the number of starters. Many different departments of the company are now involved in some way or other. The production department is involved in the detailed plan of the process by which the product is to be made: blueprints are prepared, sources of supply for equipment, components and raw materials are explored. Prototypes may now be produced. The marketing department develops its marketing plan, with literature and other promotional material being designed, arrangements for recruiting and training new salesmen or retraining existing salesmen, the training of servicemen, settling of discount arrangements and the outlining of other marketing details. Careful management control is needed to ensure that this stage is completed smoothly and expeditiously.

By the end of this stage, the commercial assessment will be reviewed in the light of this considerable volume of work. Estimates are now much firmer.

The design of the product is now frozen, that is to say no material alteration can be introduced after this date (although engineering modifications are, of course, still possible). Freezing the design is an important step; instances have been reported where product development has dragged on interminably because there always seemed room for improvement. In one company, a certain product was first devised for mechanical operation, then electrical operation was considered better and seemed an idea worth adopting, until somebody else had the even better idea of an electronic product. After seven years there was still no new product, and the existing product was becoming increasingly obsolete and sales were sharply declining. This should be avoided by writing a 'freezing point' into the product-planning system, after which point the product must stand or fall on its frozen merits. Further bright ideas can be the starting point for the next new product.

By the end of the development stage the field has narrowed considerably. In the next stage—that of testing—prototypes are tested and checked, and engineering modifications made. In consumer products this would be the point for test marketing. This is not normally possible for industrial goods, but it may be possible to place first samples then larger quantities with users to give experience of practical problems which may arise in the transference of the product from the control of the makers to the control of the users.

Following this stage, estimates and plans will be checked and the decision whether or not to commercialise is made. Sometimes this is a very gradual process. Phased marketing, whereby the most promising market sectors are attacked first and subsequent extension of the marketing programme is based on review of results, leaves considerable flexibility in the hands of the marketing manager.

Commercialisation The final decision to commercialise or not is made after a satisfactory check of the eventual estimates or plans. Commercialisation can be gradual: phased marketing whereby the most promising segments based on the review of results. The marketing manager has thus flexibility and can adjust to the feedback. At other times there is a more well-defined launch date accompanied by press relations and advertising action. Such a public release is a turning point.

Speaking of the decision to launch, Gisser [4] stresses the advantages of being first when there are several companies on the same trail. There are promotional advantages in being 'new' which followers miss, and the new product moves first to revenue earning in the best markets (if thought out). There are risks in being first—many new products fail and a delicate balance is involved.

The same author stresses the need for adequate 'launch funds' to penetrate the market and accelerate revenue earning. He argues that the probability of growing at 'maximum achievable' rate is increased. Moreover should the product then fail this is clearly not due to inadequate funding but the fault is to be found in the product itself.

Follow-up Systematic arrangements will be made for monitoring the sales and contribution from the product, so that any necessary action can be taken. It will also involve the collection of feedback on the product, service and relative price from customers, users and distributors, and watching the marketing behaviour of competing firms.

Organisation of the product function

The importance of product planning to the company as a whole needs little emphasis. Indeed, it is often in the long run the key factor in success or failure in industrial marketing. The right new product opens up new applications, new customers, new markets; the obsolete product loses the present ones.

The life-cycle concept, discussed in Chapter 7, implies that a company must plan for its new products while current products are still prosperous and must try to foresee when current products will require replacement. There will be a timetable indicating approximately when such a product will be required.

Co-ordination and control are therefore essential, and a common device is to establish a special new product or product planning section which is responsible for the entire product programme of the company. In smaller companies the new product function may fall on the shoulders of one executive specially designated for this purpose. His task is to keep the range of products up to date by bringing in the new and dropping the obsolete.

For a major new product, once the preliminary stage of screening is complete, the actual process of development is controlled by a special task force (or working party or project team, according to the terminology preferred). This is responsible for screening at each stage and for authorising budget and timetable for the next stage. The working party may vary in composition, with different departments being represented as the product progresses through the various stages. At first the product planning section may lead the working party, but as the final stages near, the product manager or other line executive will have increased responsibility, and will take over when the working party is wound up.

Radically new products

In some industries where technological advance is particularly rapid, 'among the characteristics of successful innovation are the capacity of the innovator to *couple* efficient R&D with knowledge of the market requirements' (Freeman [26]). The same author goes on to distinguish innovation strategy between 'offensive' innovation designed to achieve technical and market leadership from others described respectively as defensive, imitative, dependent, traditional and opportunist.

Relatively few firms can carry out an offensive strategy and normally in-house R&D has a key role, and may often undertake fundamental research oriented towards the firms' background interests. Such firms may also have a substantial communication job educating and training customers and their own staff.

Briefly, Freeman's defensive firm may still be active in R&D but does not wish to be first (hoping to learn from the mistakes of innovators) or may not have the capacity for original innovation. He may still have an education and training task.

The *imitative* firms (as the term implies) follows behind, perhaps far behind, and according to Freeman 'must enjoy certain advantage to enter the market in competition with the established innovating firms', for example a captive market or a decisive cost advantage.

A *dependent* strategy involves a satellite or subordinate role in relation to other stronger firms: innovating at their requests. Traditionalist firms operate under severe competition or other disadvantages in traditional industries and scientific inputs are minimal. The *opportunist* spots an ecological niche in a changing market by identifying some new opportunity not requiring in-house R&D or complex design.

It has been suggested that when radically new products are desired, a 'venture' team approach can be adopted with advantage. This possibility is discussed further on page 248.

9 THE COMMUNICATION MATRIX

However good the product, however excellent the technical service, however prompt the delivery, the world outside the company will remain indifferent until these advantages are brought to its attention. And even when they are brought to the notice of prospect companies, their claims compete with a host of rival claims for the attention of busy executives. The average decision-maker has an established set of ideas, knowledge, opinions and prejudices which affect the way in which he will react to information put to him. The message must reach him with credibility and impact. It is not a passive supply of information but a force designed to modify his ways of thinking and move him to a positive appreciation of the offering.

This is the task of communication. The term 'communication' is used because it is more comprehensive than such words as 'promotion', 'advertising' or 'salesmanship'. Its definition includes 'all the procedures by which one mind may affect another' (Shannon and Weaver [27]), and it opens up a wider range of possibilities for original thinking about how a company may put forward its ideas in the industrial market. Buying decision-makers and influencers build up their ideas about a company and its products, logically or otherwise, by messages through a wide range of media. Research and careful thought may well produce original, economic and effective communication plans, identifying and using media which might otherwise have been overlooked.

Personal representation is very often the centre-piece of the communication strategy, with other methods supporting it. These other methods seek to make personal selling more effective, efficient and economical.

The concept advanced here is one of a total communication

strategy, designed not only to provide a natural path to sales, but to help the customer make the right purchase, obtain full benefit from his purchase and to develop and nurture an enduring relationship between supplier and customer. Such a strategy requires an approximate blend selection of target audience, message, media and timing.

Deriving communication objectives

Overall objectives will often flow in a straightforward way from a clearly defined strategy. They will be subordinate to marketing objectives and perhaps limited by the resources which the company is able to devote to communication.

If a campaign is concerned with introducing certain innovative products, then the communication objectives must be directed towards executives concerned with decisions of this nature. It may be designed to at first create a predisposition to adopt a particular solution to a business problem by educating in the benefits the new product offers. It must also, at appropriate stages, educate in the use of the product, help overcome technical problems of adoption and installation, and support at customer board level the awareness of the supplier. Later, as the product matures, emphasis may well switch to unexploited opportunities in new markets and new applications and may give more weight to increasing company or brand awareness to meet competitive pressure.

In the short term, objectives may include:

Developing a new application.
Introducing a product variation.
Widening the market for existing products.
Exploiting seasonal or other short-term possibilities.
Promoting inquiries and creating interest.
Reminding to buy, stock and use.

In the somewhat longer term objectives: may include:

Developing understanding of the problems which the product
  aims to solve, and widening markets and applications.
Educating customer's staff to get full benefit from the product

(by better maintenance, more efficient usage or improved marketing to *their* customers).

Correcting false impressions.

Strengthening links with customers in the current market.

Projecting the company's image and developing confidence in its commercial and technical standards.

Building links outside its immediate market.

Making known new products.

Having decided on the general purpose of the communication strategy further questions arise. These can be classified under the four basic headings:

Men To whom should we communicate? The answer to this will flow from the analysis of buying behaviour, discussed earlier, in which the different buying decision-makers and influencers have been identified. These are target audiences. Some of these will have key roles deserving considerable attention, others may require less attention. This is taken up later in this chapter.

Message What effect do we wish to achieve? This is based on the understanding of the present knowledge and attitudes of the target audiences coupled with an identification of desired knowledge and attitudes; this indicates the direction and intensity of the shift being sought.

Media Through what channels shall the messages be conveyed? Usually the sales force plays a large part but there are many supporting media available. In the consumer field mass advertising can be compared to an artist working on a large canvas with a broad brush. The industrial marketing man is frequently working like a miniaturist with tiny painstaking strokes on small areas. His target may be only one important firm, but the buying decision may result from a process involving pressures from numerous people. The total effect sought may require a number of communications, differing in nature, through several media.

Sequence and timing Given the need for multiperson, multi-message, multimedia plans there follows a need for sequence and timing to be considered. Who is to know first? Must the technical manager be aware before the Board lest he be antagonised should discussion develop in which he cannot play his proper role? And when the time comes for the customers' salesmen to sell *their* consequential products, what should be done to help them?

Choosing the target

The first issue is simply—to whom? Analysis of the buying process is the first step. The promotion manager must however seek maximum leverage from his communication expenditure, that is to say the most favourable relationship between outlay and benefit. He may therefore concentrate most expenditure on key targets who have decisive influence. Key targets are a small number of executives whose views predominate over others in making the buying decision. This predominance comes about from one of three sources:

1   *Formal appointment*, e.g. in a line capacity, perhaps as director or senior manager.
2   *Specialised knowledge*, e.g. a technologist in specifying a complex product or a commodity buyer on price movements.
3   *The logic of circumstances*, as for example when operatives are reluctant to use a proposed new product.

Some key targets may be outside the prospect company: the authority of an official inspectorate is an example. They may change from time to time: as one group accepts a product or supplier another may move into a key role. For example, a customer incorporates a new material or component in his product: now his salesmen move to a key role as they have to sell their employer's product.

The choice of message

An approach to this aspect of communication policy can be adapted from the principles of a well-known book on advertising by Colley [28], who writes:

E

'All commercial communications that aim at the ultimate objective of a sale must carry a prospect through four levels of understanding—from unawareness to:

Awareness: The prospect must first be *aware* of the existence of a brand or a company.

Comprehension: He must have a *comprehension* of what the product is and what it will do for him.

Conviction: He must arrive at a mental disposition or *conviction* to buy the product.

Action: Finally he must stir himself to *action*.'

It has sometimes been suggested that for many purposes of consumer marketing this procedure is too logical, and that there are other routes by which the consumer arrives at the action point. This question is outside the present field. In industrial marketing, it is certainly helpful to widen the analysis quoted above.

A domestic company may expect not to be completely unknown to customers in its own home market. Nevertheless, it may not be sufficiently known that the company manufactures certain lines of products, or it may not be known or appreciated that the product is capable of use for certain purposes.

A product may claim to solve a problem, but customer executives may not even be aware that the problem matters. For example, they may never have thought about the effect of noise on efficiency and the loss which it might involve, yet an understanding of this may be a prerequisite of purchasing products which deaden noise.

Market ignorance may be of a large number of different things, for example:

The company which is marketing the product.
The need that the product aims to meet.
The existence of the product.
The fact that the company makes the product.
Applications for the product within the prospect company.
How the product is used to best advantage.
Changes in the product or in supplier service.

But if ignorance of these matters gives a zero score, existing predisposition can sometimes justify negative scores. Having become aware, perhaps only somewhat vaguely, of the product and of what it offers, executives may have overrated the problems and difficulties of obtaining the benefits of the product, or have wrongly assessed those benefits in relation to those of competing products, or they may wrongly consider that the benefits are insufficient to justify the cost and financial risk implications of using the product.

At any point of time the marketing man will be faced with a set of existing attitudes in his audiences. Yet each of these audiences has a part in the complex procedure determining the purchase of the product. To play that part in a proper way, each must have the 'right' information and the 'right' attitude. What 'right' means has to be determined by the marketing executive from knowledge of how the buying decision is made. The task of persuasive communication is to shift these individuals from their present knowledge and attitudes to the 'right' ones—those appropriate to the buying behaviour sought.

This may involve one message only, for example a mail shot to small builders with an offer on special terms of some well-known item of equipment. More commonly, there is a series of messages required to carry the target audience to the requisite state of mind. Consider the example of an imaginary new product to control or reduce noise in factories. One decision-making group is the directors of companies engaged in an identified 'noisy' industry. Information gathered prior to the campaign indicates that few of this group are aware that this is a problem deserving consideration, and fewer still have heard of the product. If they become aware of the problem, it is likely that they may find it hard to appreciate that it has the substantial effects on productivity which the suppliers of the product claim.

The first step must be to bring home the basic problem of its economic implications. This may require a campaign of an 'educational' nature directed to this group and to informed opinion generally. Secondly, gradually developing in emphasis, the work of XYZ in this field is to be brought out. Thirdly, the campaign is to show the value of XYZ's new product in reducing noise, and finally to win approval of a study of the costs and benefits through a survey of the plan of specific customers.

It may be objected that not all directors in the target market segment will have the same attitudes and ideas. This is true. If it were possible to quantify precisely, one would like to specify as shown in Table 3. Similar analyses are desirable for other buying influences.

TABLE 3 Attitudes analysis: attitudes of directors/senior executives in target industries

	Present attitude, %	Required attitude, %*
Aware of problem	10	75
Aware of XYZ's work	8	60
Aware of XYZ's product	5	50
Would approve survey by XYZ	4	40
Could be expected to approve installation after survey	?	20

*This is the target to be achieved at the end of the campaign

It may be premature to expect that as fully quantified an approach as this can often be obtained at present. Discussion shows that some approximation to this principle increasingly underlies many efficient approaches to marketing communication.

The company image

Many of the tools of marketing communication are 'passive' rather than 'active' in relation to the marketing process. That is to say, they are not directly concerned with influencing buying behaviour in relation to specific purchases, but provide a background against which the more active tools of advertising, sales promotion and personal selling can positively motivate buyers and users. What is active and what is passive can vary, and it is sometimes possible to convert a tool which is commonly passive to an active role in a particular set of circumstances. Such matters as the company's letter-heading, its vans, and certain types of Press work (to quote a few examples) are commonly background communications to the company's general public relations concern with the 'image' of the company.

The word 'image' occurs often in marketing discussions. It has been defined as the complex of 'knowledge, feelings, ideas and beliefs' about a company which are commonly associated with its name in the minds of customers or other groups of individuals (Gunther [29]). It is the personality which the company is seen to possess. Different groups of individuals may have different images for the same company; buyers, the trade unions, the Government, all may see the company in different ways from each other. It can affect the relationship between employees and management, the ability of the company to attract the right type and quality of recruits, and it may have political significance or affect the company's valuation on the stock market.

Levitt [30] has indicated in an experiment carried out on purchasing executives and others how the reaction to a salesman's presentation can be influenced by these initial ideas about a company, a favourable image creating a more receptive customer. The same experiment also indicated that this advantage could be lost if the salesman's presentation was poor. This example not only illustrates the benefit of a good image, but also the importance of integrating all aspects of the company's communications scheme into an efficient whole. The 'image' may have especial importance to firms whose product is an intangible service, especially a 'capital' service such as management consultancy. There is then no physical artefact to see, measure, or test. The purchaser without previous experience of the supplier has little else but reputation to guide him.

Channels of communication

Clearly the development of the necessary attitudes and understanding can be a substantial task. To carry it out, the industrial marketing man has a rich variety of communication channels available to him. Very rarely will any one channel be used to the exclusion of all others. It will be necessary to use a variety of channels not only because of the different decision-makers and influences who have to be contacted, but because frequently it will be advantageous to address the same group of individuals through different channels. The different channels have a different quality of impact, and thus will reinforce each other, and the variety of approaches will give a freshness to the message.

The total concept of communication which is here advanced is designed not only to promote sales in the limited sense, but, applying the 'service' concept of Chapter 1, to help the customer to benefit from his purchase and thus re-purchase the same and other products from the same supplier.

A company is constantly 'communicating' with its market in a wide variety of ways, if communication is used to refer not only to an oral or written message in its everyday sense, but to any symbol or act of behaviour from which the market may draw inferences about the company or its products, or its service, or any other matter relating to it. Some of the communications which pass between the firm and the market may never be consciously considered as having marketing implications by the originating company. Yet they may well have such an effect, if not in the short term, then cumulatively over time. Under the total communication concept, the company aims to bring all its communications under conscious control, to organise them so that they are mutually reinforcing and to ensure that all messages shall be consistent with the marketing needs of the company—or at least not antagonistic to them!

Table 4 gives a checklist of possible channels and is reasonably comprehensive. Some are obviously particularly suited to the short- and medium-term objectives of the company. Others are appropriate to the longer-term objective of projecting the company image.

The roles of the main channels are discussed in later chapters. It will be noted that the table includes more than is commonly included in the 'promotional' approach to marketing communication. It aims to include virtually all the sources from which inferences may be drawn, in accordance with the definition of 'communication' adopted. Some of the items listed may be regarded as more important in consumer than in industrial marketing. For example, the name of the product, the design of the pack, the name of the company and the appearance of the product are sometimes regarded as having implications only in consumer marketing. Nevertheless, there have been occasions when each of these has had an important role in the industrial field.

A product designed to be used as a material in putty manufacture was developed on a base of polybutadiene rubber. Experience with the product has been described as follows:

> 'To say that we met sales resistance from putty manufacturers is an understatement. Many, even the biggest manufacturers, told us our putty was no good and they had no intention of changing their formulations which had remained unaltered since great-grandfather started the business.

TABLE 4 Checklist of communication channels

Personal communication:	Sales force and technical representatives High-level contacts Technical service force Switchboard operators Distributor sales force Customer sales force
Media advertising:	Television Radio General Press Posters Trade and technical Press
Direct advertising:	Direct mail, including letter-writing Sales literature Technical literature and reference material Price lists and catalogues Calendars and diaries External house journal (prestige or technological)
Exhibition or similar occasions:	Trade exhibitions Distributor-sponsored exhibitions Company exhibitions Demonstartion visits to company plant and laboratories Sampling by customer Films Showroom and window display
The product:	Physical appearance Name Packaging and labelling
Public relations:	Press releases and relations Speeches and writings by company executives Symposia and seminars
Background material:	Company's name Letter-heading Vans Staff uniforms

'So, once again, we decided that marketing and technical pressure must be kept up in order to bring this project to a profitable conclusion. It was now realised that maybe the thought of incorporating a "rubber" was not acceptable to the putty manufacturer. "Rubber" is an unfortunate word to use in many contexts since the layman thinks of it in terms of an elastic insoluble black lump. Rubber to the putty manufacturer also meant "Thiokol" which was expensive or "Butyl" which gave very difficult mixing and a tough unworkable putty. Our new approach was to sell an oil-modified polybutadiene in attractive

kegs and call it Unipol 31. In this form it did not resemble
rubber. The material eased many of the mixing problems of the
putty manufacturer. Unipol 31 in this form has attracted quite a
demand . . .' (Duck [31]).

Because communication is also concerned with the effective use of
the product, it is often helpful to include instructions on or enclosed
with the pack. This particularly concerns minor maintenance goods
which may be used by inexperienced workers. Packaging can assist
ease of identification by the storeman, thus facilitating the use of the
product and consequently helping sales. In an experiment in the USA
products normally enclosed in brown kraft cartons were sent in white
packs. It was found that this resulted in greater care in handling and
unpacking [32].

In the product itself aesthetic qualities may encourage engineers to
spend more time at the supplier's stand at an exhibition. These
matters may sound trivial. It is however often difficult to put one's
finger on all the factors which influence sales. Attention to these small
matters will often cost relatively little and may make that slight difference in securing useful marginal sales. They reinforce main selling
tools, or at least do not run counter to them, as they may do if
neglected.

The communication grid

As this is brought together the entire scheme can be laid out as a matrix,
as shown in the abbreviated Exhibit 11. This brings together the four
key dimensions of the communication plan:

> Man (target audience).
> Message (what is to be communicated).
> Media (or methods of communication).
> Sequence.

Each row deals with a message/media combination. At the top is the
target audience. The number in each cell indicates the sequence in
which messages are being sent, that is to say the order of the steps in
the plan. This is a systematic procedure for laying out this total com-

munication plan and involves setting out and interrelating all the planned messages.

The entire process can be listed as follows:

1   Determining market strategy and targets.
2   Deriving broad communication objectives.
3   Schedule of groups who make or influence the buying process, with particular identification of key targets.
4   Schedule of current and desired attitudes and knowledge.
5   Selection of targets ('Men').
6   Specification of specific message purpose ('Message').
7   Choice of channels ('Media') and identification of inter-relationships ('Sequence').
8   Harmonising Men, Message, Media, Sequence as in illustrated communication grid.
9   Detailed development of copy, salesmen's brief, etc.
10 Carrying through campaign.
11 Review of results.

Although this order is logical, there will usually be feedback at different stages which can lead to review of some early stages. For example, when relative cost of channels is examined it may lead to a review of the 'Men' targets. Finally there is review during implementation.

Parallel to the plan may be certain background 'messages' which are available for continuous selling support, such as technical literature. Even with this there may be special tasks to be fulfilled at particular times which should be built into the systematic matrix.

Sometimes the company may achieve promotional leverage by promoting to a customer's customer, or to the final consumer. Manufacturers of synthetic fibres have on occasion carried through such a policy of back-pressure selling, so that the final consumers' demands for products incorporating a particular synthetic have helped to 'pull' that fibre through intermediate manufacturers. The cost of communicating to final consumers may often be disproportionate. Even when it is not disproportionate it may be difficult to ensure that the consumer demand generated is passed back to the company responsible. Only if the specific material promoted can be wholly (or almost so)

EXHIBIT 11 The matrix of men, messages and media

MESSAGE	MEN (Target decision-makers and influences)							MEDIA
	Customer				User & distributor			
	Board	Technical specifier	Marketing manager	Purchasing officer	Distribution management	Sales and service force	User	
Awareness of problem	1							PR - professional press
Technical background		2 3						Symposia / Technical journals
Specific advantages			4					Trade press
Price/delivery				5	5			Sales force
Technical details		6			6			Mail shot
(Details omitted)								
Maintenance techniques			20		20	20		Specialised house journal
Ultimate user benefits (backselling)							21 21	Display advertising / PR National press
Merchandising of ultimate user advertising			22		22			Mail shot

related to the marketing firm is this approach normally economic. In some instances an industry wide back-selling campaign may be possible where local legislation permits or facilitates it.

Sometimes leverage may be enhanced by focusing on a group of executives for whom the product is particularly appealing. For example, packaging which adds sales appeal may attract marketing executives. Conversely there may be points of resistance, e.g. specialists who consider the new proposal may affect them adversely may need special consideration.

While different channels are discussed in subsequent chapters, their cost and availability may be relevant in target selection. The fact that effective communication is feasible on attractive terms enhances the cost/benefit ratio of a particular section of audience.

Thus the factors relevant to target group selection can be summarised as follows:

1   The influence of the target group in supporting or resisting progress towards a favourable decision on product or supplier.
2   The extent to which their knowledge and attitudes require modifying to facilitate desired buying behaviour.
3   The probability of such modification, bearing in mind:
    a   their degree of commitment to other products/suppliers;
    b   the additional benefits being offered.
4   The cost and feasibility of communicating with them with credibility and impact.

During the campaign, the emphasis may shift from one target to another. It may first be necessary to persuade top management that there is a problem to be solved, next to show technical specifiers that the proposed solution is feasible and similarly for other target audiences. The analysis is subject to review as the market situation changes and as competitors react.

10 PERSONAL COMMUNICATION

Personal communication is a key area in industrial marketing. The heading 'personal communication' is preferred at this point to 'selling' or 'salesmanship' because it emphasises the wide range of face-to-face contact between supplier and customer, and the fact that this relationship usually involves much more than achieving a sale in the short term. It often involves cementing and maintaining a long-term relationship between the two parties, and the representative who forgets that his object is to serve the customer may well harm a relationship which can be as valuable an asset to his firm as a major item of capital equipment.

To the customer the salesman is often the representative of the supplying company in a very full sense. He is the prime contact between his firm and the customer—sometimes almost the only one— and he is apt to be charged with the faults of the company, and the company with the faults of its representative. The actual placing of some orders is not through the salesman at all, but by phone or by post. However, if the company has done its marketing correctly, and the salesman his work to the same standard, then the actual order which follows is a direct consequence of these efforts.

The variety of contact

There are some situations in industrial marketing where a formal sales force is only part of a wider network of personal communication between the two companies. This applies particularly where the purchase of the product has implications of product complexity and commercial risk for the buying company. New and additional capital equipment can involve not only heavy expenditure, but a change in the way in which the company operates. It may mean replanning production, retraining staff (perhaps making some present skills obsolete), even reorganising the management structure. Something similar may be involved when a component which represents an important technological advance is to be adopted as standard by an original equipment manufacturer.

This is the total involvement section of Exhibit 4. These purchases imply high cost, high risk and high innovation. There are therefore many people involved in the buying decision, many questions raised and many problems to be solved. The product will require careful adaptation to match the buying company's vector of needs, and ample service to accompany it. Selling and marketing become fused together. At appropriate stages in the negotiations, many different members of the staff of the supplying company will make contact with their opposite numbers in the prospect company and selling is multi-level.

At the other extreme is the salesman who calls on many customers to make small sales of a standardised product, e.g. a man calling on small builders to sell paint brushes. Here the product and its brand name are well known, the sum involved in the average purchase is modest, no service is required and the degree of innovation and risk to the purchaser is nil. The time required to complete the sale is small, there will only be one person involved in the buying decision and he meets only one salesman from the company for a short period.

It is not hard to identify further circumstances which are different again from both of these—the representative calling on architects to seek specification of a product, or calling on retail shops to seek the right to survey and tender for an illuminated sign. In neither case does the sale automatically follow from the call, but in both the representative's task is an essential prerequisite to securing the order, and the link is close.

With this range of circumstances, there corresponds a range of titles for the man whose prime job it is to be the focus for commercial contacts with the customer: salesman, sales engineer, technical representative, marketing engineer, account executive and others. Each company must analyse its own particular market to decide the role of the sales force and the key ingredients to success in building sales. This determines the type of individual required for the job, and what his technical knowledge, intellectual ability and general background must be in order to carry out his task effectively. The cost of the representative must also be consistent with the amount of business he can be expected to generate.

Personal selling is in many ways the most efficient, and certainly the most flexible, of the means of communication available to the industrial marketing manager. The salesman can and often must help the buyer and other executives of the prospect company to clarify their problems, and from the armoury of products and services which his company has to offer he can identify that combination which most aptly meets the needs of the customer. He can adjust the appeals which he makes to the problems of the company he is dealing with and to the personal attitudes of the people he is meeting. He can identify not only the present needs of his customers, but will seek to anticipate future needs and when they will arise. As a result, he will plan to call on the customer at the right time and feed back information to his own company to assist in the development of new products to satisfy the need which, from his observation, he anticipates will emerge in the future.

Representatives are, however, expensive. There is not only the cost of the salary, and commission where paid, but also the cost of super-annuation and other benefits, and of travelling and expenses. These can add as much again to the cost of the salesman. Finally, there are the overhead costs of recruiting, managing, training and administering the sales force.

The sales task

Like the other members of the staff of the company, the representative should have a written job description which will make clear what he is supposed to do, to whom he is responsible, and the extent of his own authority. While the nature of his job may at first sight seem self-evident, there are a large number of details which need specifying. For example, what is the responsibility of the salesman in such things as credit control, prospecting, service, dealing with complaints, making returns to head office, agreeing allowances for defective items, collecting market intelligence and so on? Many of these points are not always sharply defined, and by default may not receive the attention they deserve, or may receive too much so that other matters are neglected.

The basis of the job description is an analysis of what the salesman is required to do in the course of his duties, and his relationship with the rest of the company's organisation. Commonly such factors as the following may be covered in the course of this analysis:

Selling functions
Classes of products to be sold.
Classes of companies to be called upon.
People to be seen (functions, knowledge, status, whether individual or group presentations).
Nature of 'sale' (e.g. is it a straight sale, request for survey, specification, negotiations?).
Degree of authority with salesman. (May he vary price, or agree allowances for below-standard products?)
Assistance to distributors.

Technical functions
Keeping customers informed of new products.
Assisting customers to define requirements (e.g. by survey).
After-sales service. (To what extent does the salesman need to analyse technical problems himself and perhaps make minor adjustments?)
Training and instructing customer's staff.

Commercial functions
Informal market intelligence on customer plans and competitors' actions.
Identifying need for new or improved products.
Checking credit status.
Planning or recommending marketing action within his territory.
Attending exhibitions, tying in mail shots, organizing film shows, seminars.

Administrative responsibilities
Filling out orders.
Training new representatives.
Planning his activities for coverage of territory.
Requesting specialised service for customers.

Preparing a job description for the sales force requires a careful scrutiny of what is done and what should be done. It will be carried out in consultation with the sales staff, but it may be worth seeking specialised advice so that the analysis is objective and not restricted by preconceived ideas. Once the analysis is complete, it should lead on to a written description of the job. From this follows the specification of the person to fill the job. What specialised knowledge, intellectual qualities, emotional and physical requirements, education (both general and vocational) and experience are required? What age, family, background, mobility and status are preferred? In selling, personal qualities are of great importance, and the individual's own motivation, enthusiasm and determination are key factors.

In most industrial marketing situations, four considerations come to the front in the work of the representative. These may be described as:

1   Selling and human relations skills.
2   Diagnostic skill.
3   Technical background.
4   Organising ability.

Selling skills have not always been regarded as important by companies concerned with industrial marketing. This point of view has been consistent with a general attitude towards marketing which is now passing. There is increasing awareness of the value of skills in understanding and dealing with people which lead to efficient, economical and successful selling. This may need to be supported by some technical background, although the value of technical knowledge has sometimes been overrated and the value of sales ability underrated. Sometimes new men, less talented technically, but better equipped in selling skills, have moved products which the existing sales force had found hard to sell. Even in high-level selling, when director meets director, or a group of executives negotiate around a table, a key factor in success is the ability to understand the natural human reactions of the man on the other side and to match arguments and presentation to them. The importance of mutual trust has already been stressed in Chapter 2.

Diagnostic skill is the ability of the representative to assist the customer in identifying and analysing his problems, so that suitable products may be recommended. The customer himself may not have identified the problems clearly and sharply, or may even have misunderstood them. The representative may carry out a survey to identify the customer's needs for his products and to recommend what grades, qualities or types of product should be used. Often this will show how a more advanced or better selected product will give greater efficiency. The analysis may go further and identify trends in the customer's market and anticipate the nature of his market requirements in the future. If the salesman passes such information back to his company, it will help in the identification of new products. The salesman's diagnostic skill may be the trigger which sets the buying-process in motion in the prospect firm and improves the match between what the customer wants and what the firm offers.

The need for technical background in selling some products is self-evident. This may not mean that every man in the sales force needs to meet this requirement. It may be that there should be different classes of representative with different levels of skill and advanced technical support should be available on request.

The need for technical skill takes many forms. It may be part of the diagnosis which permits the salesman to make the correct prescription. Where products are made or modified to individual customer's needs the salesman must work with the customer's technical and marketing staff to determine the specification. The technical ability required will aim to assist the customer to develop *his* product idea, prototype, pre-production and save commercialisation 'bugs'. This work will be different in emphasis from that of the technician employed elsewhere in the company.

A product which is complex to design and make need not always be technically complex to sell, install and use. When the customer organisation is not accustomed to advanced technology the selling firm may seek a product form which reduces its complexity to the customer.

Finally, administrative and organizational ability is necessary. The representative must be aware that his time is expensive and be able to organise his work to ensure proper contact with his customers and economic use of his time. Even the less well paid, making regular calls on customers in a market where most orders are small, must plan to maximise call time and reduce travelling time. He should ensure that the time in social exchanges is not disproportionate, make proper reports and keep efficient records.

Selection

Selection is a matter of finding the right person to match the specification. When the emphasis is on personal characteristics, the task of finding the right person is difficult enough, but when it requires both selling potential and some technical background it is even more difficult.

Applications may be sought from outside the company through the general or technical Press, through agents or through personal introduction. Where a specific technical qualification is necessary, professional societies may circulate vacancy notices to their members.

Many companies welcome applications from salesmen of competitors, distributors or other companies selling to the same market but in some industries this policy is considered unfair and 'no poaching' is the norm. There also seems to be interest in recruiting salesmen who have been trained by well-known consumer-goods manufacturers, and this seems a reasonable step where empathy is the key to sales success.

In industries where the technical content of the sale is high, it will often be necessary to recruit staff from elsewhere in the company, or outside, with a degree or appropriate technical qualifications and to train them for the sales force. Some firms who consider they require technical background rather than technical expertise seek people who, having started technical training, have felt the appeal of a commercial career. These can have sufficient technical knowledge plus the necessary personal qualities.

Not everyone has the potential to become a good salesman, any more than everyone is suited for accountancy, or law. It is important that the individuals concerned are keen (and suited) to sell. They must be commercially minded and adept at understanding and dealing with people. Sometimes a suitable person too young to enter the sales force may be taken on and employed in some other capacity before becoming a salesman. This can be a useful device to match personal qualities with the necessary background. In larger companies, sales force recruitment is regarded as a continuous process and the company is always interested in suitable applicants, even though there is no current vacancy.

The personal qualities needed in selling are difficult to assess and whereas for many occupations selection is largely by 'selection tests', in industrial selling such tests are less used. The interview as a method of selection is more justified in selling than in other occupations, for the 'interview' situation is, in fact, the one in which the prospective candidate will work. Selling oneself is the first part of the total job of making a sale, and this is a skill which should be shown at an interview. It is also an opportunity to explore the value of previous experience and to check qualifications for the post. There is both good and bad interviewing, and any executive who undertakes the responsibility of selection by this method should ensure that he is well acquainted with the principles of interviewing.

Most companies require two interviews: a preliminary short-listing by a middle manager (perhaps the field sales manager in the area concerned); then, for those short-listed, a second interview at a more senior level. Some companies require more interviews.

While the development of selection tests for industrial salesmen is still in its infancy, there are signs that such tests may have more to contribute in the future. They will not take the responsibility of selection off the shoulders of the sales manager, but will provide additional information.

The appropriateness of any test for a particular industrial market needs to be checked when it is brought into use.

It is often said that salesmen should have 'empathy', an understanding of how people feel—and 'drive' and determination to achieve and product results. There is some question whether 'drive' is the key consideration when the sales task involves long-term development of customer relations before the sale is made. In such cases the salesman's motivation may better be affiliative, i.e. he may find personal fulfilment in good social relations with the customers. The achievement-oriented salesman may not stay and succeed in these long-term situations.

Sales training

Whereas at one time there was little formal training in selling and personal relations for industrial salesmen, recent years have seen a rapid growth. Larger companies can devise schemes of training specially adapted to their own needs, either using their own specialised staff or employing consultants. Introduction is preceded by a careful study of the training needs for that particular company's sales task. Smaller companies may send staff on external courses, where they will work with people from other companies. This is not necessarily a bad thing so long as the interests of the participants in the course are not too widely diffused and so long as the methods used give each individual time to examine the problem of adapting the techniques taught to his own context. Such outside courses cannot, however, focus as sharply on the needs of specific companies as can custom-tailored courses. Moreover, they commonly deal only with the selling skills and not with other aspects, such as knowledge of the particular market, particular competitors or particular products.

Sales training is, however, a continuous, not a once-for-all, process. The opening stages may well be a period of classroom work, associated with planned field training, but later stages will often put more responsibility on the shoulders of the sales manager or field sales manager whose regular supervision of the sales force involves an element of built-in training. This is not restricted to the regular sales conference with its opportunities for case-study work, role-playing, films and other learning aids. It is day-by-day on the job, and the executives who have to undertake this responsibility may well be given some training in the art of training—not to make them specialists but to provide some background.

In addition to selling skills, salesmen's training includes product and applications knowledge, customer and market knowledge, the planning of the salesman's work, and company policy and procedures. It is also usually worth giving wider insight into the principles of marketing so that he understands better and sympathises with the company's policy decisions about, for example, the introduction of new products. Training and re-training is now recognised as important in all branches of industry and at all levels. The sale is the point at which all the previous operations of the company reach fulfilment. The introduction of sales training in a firm is a recognition of this fact and not a criticism of past sales efforts. Almost all representatives will gain from systematic training; the best may gain only a little, but others will gain more.

Salaries and incentives

The variation in salesmen's earnings is considerable. Sometimes the higher earnings are for men with special technical qualifications, but high earnings are also sometimes achieved by salesmen working mainly on commission whose results come from their own skill in dealing with customers and putting over the product. Some managements fear that the relationship between the representative and his customer can be so strong that if the representative leaves, customers go too.

Industrial marketing companies today often pay entirely by salary. They do this for a combination of reasons. Partly they find it the way to attract the right class of individual—often a man with high professional qualifications who seeks a career in the industry and may well, in due course, move into a higher managerial post. From his viewpoint, rewards by career development are more appropriate than commission. He seeks a post with prospects, superannuation and similar rights. Mortgages are more easily obtained against salary than against commission, and he is guarded against fortuitous fluctuations in income arising from cause outside his control.

A salary only is also often logical. The 'sale' may be made by the combined efforts of a group of people and not that of a lone individual. It may well be difficult or impossible to decide what part of the success in achieving a sale is attributable to one or other person. Conversely, a representative may do his job well, yet no sale is completed. For example, he may successfully obtain the right to tender, but the company's tender is not successful. The representative must also spend his time cultivating new accounts for future business. He must not seek short-term increases in sales which could damage relations with a customer who might afterwards feel the victim of a 'hard sell'. The representative's function is very often to create a durable relationship with the customer to the benefit of both parties. He is a consultant to the customer as much as he is a salesman.

Other companies consider that absence of commission blunts incentive. When sales depend more specifically on the efforts of the salesman and where the order is placed after a short period of negotiation, the case for some financial incentive is strong. Usually this is only a small part of total remuneration, between 5 and 15 per cent.

Larger proportions usually apply for short-term sales, where the salesman is more a lone wolf offering a speciality outside the usual run of business purchases.

Where a commission element is appropriate there are many systems to consider. The simplest is to pay a certain small percentage on all sales. An alternative is to pay commission on all sales over quota. This 'bites' at the point where the effort required in getting sales is greatest, and on those marginal sales the percentage rate can be made attractive.

A sharper incentive is provided by paying a lump sum when the quota is exceeded; but once the lump sum has been achieved, there is then no more incentive. This is suitable if the company can clearly identify an appropriate feasible quota, but having achieved that wishes the salesman to spend his time prospecting or advising present customers. Group commission (whereby all sales—and perhaps other staff—in an area share in commission or bonus payments) is a way of recognising and encouraging team work.

The arrangements suggested above all imply that the test of success for the salesman is the volume of sales. This may not be so. It may be that the correct test is the volume of profit or contribution generated. This may not vary directly in proportion to sales, because some products contribute more than others, or because the saleman has some authority to vary price and may be tempted to cut prices too quickly if sales volume is the crucial test.

Often the sales manager may have a series of tasks which the salesman is required to work towards. There may be some products, perhaps new products, on which a certain level of sale is specially required to meet the company plan, or it may be desired to achieve a balance of sales between different parts of the range. It is difficult to reflect all these variables in an incentive scheme. Point systems can be operated in order to encourage a balanced pattern of achievement, the salesman being rewarded according to the total accumulated. These more complex schemes can raise greater difficulty in implementation.

Commissions and similar incentive schemes must be substantially accepted by the sales force to be successful. This means they must be carefully discussed before introduction and the salesmen satisfied of their fairness. Difficult problems—such as arise when representatives in different territories both have a hand in producing business—need to be clarified. The scheme should be well understood, and the salesman should be able to assess what he will receive from a sale. It must, of course, be administered efficiently and commission paid promptly.

Some companies are now experimenting with the use of competitions as short-term incentives. These appear less acceptable in industrial marketing than in consumer marketing, particularly for older or highly qualified salesmen. There may be some areas in which suitably planned competitions have something to offer, or some particular short-term achievement to reward. A competition or contest can be used for a short-term incentive and then withdrawn without creating protest. This is more difficult with monetary incentives. The absence of a sales-linked incentive scheme implies that the salesman's work is recognised financially at the regular review of his salary. In order that this appraisal be fair, there should be a clear understanding of what the salesman is expected to achieve, and understanding of the bases by which achievement is to be assessed.

Whatever remuneration method is adopted, it should seek to attract and keep salesmen of appropriate quality, provide sufficient incentive to encourage them to carry out the tasks required of them with skill and diligence, and be consistent with the economic use of the sales force.

Material and monetary awards are not the only incentives, and sometimes not the most important. Some individuals appear to have a limit beyond which financial incentives seem to have little effect. Motivation can be reinforced from other sources. The average representative spends only a small proportion of his time in the office meeting his colleagues in the sales force and in the company generally. He can easily feel that he is not part of the team, that his efforts are not adequately supported and his problems not fully appreciated. This can have a demoralising effect, leading to loss of drive and perhaps to unnecessary staff turnover. It is, in fact, very easy for the salesman to find himself in the position that many of the communications from his head office are queries open to the interpretation that something has not gone too well and that he is being called on for an explanation—'This account is lost', 'That customer has complained' and so on. The good work which he has done may often not seem to call for specific action from head office, so he hears little about it.

Regular contact and recognition seems to be a method by which interest and motivation can be raised and maintained. With smaller sales forces, the sales manager can regularly spend some time in the field with his men, as part of the normal routine, not only to improve selling efficiency but to promote mutual understanding. If the sales force is too large for him to do this personally, the work must be delegated to field sales supervisors. The general sales manager works closely with them and treats attendance at local sales meetings as an important part of his functions.

Regular 'newsletters' to salesmen, if well done, have been found to be of value not only in passing on routine information about organisation and marketing changes, but also in reporting sales successes of individual members of the sales force and their contribution in other ways to the company's work. Where the representatives are requested to pass back information about new and competing products, then it is useful if they can be told how some of this information has been applied in practice. This underlines the value to the company of a task which some salesmen find irksome. Sales conferences can also be given a democratic atmosphere when common problems of the salesmen are discussed. Individual salesmen are encouraged to express their views on their problems and how they are approached and to discuss how they make their presentations and demonstrations. This passes good ideas from one to another and generates team spirit and co-operation in the sales force.

Finally, the need for informal contact between the sales force and other staff in the company can easily be overlooked. Good relations with other departments (R&D, Engineering, Production, Finance) can lubricate the operation of the company and help to ease the problem of interdepartmental difficulties which inevitably arise from time to time. Suitable social occasions can bring together staff from different departments and contribute to this result.

Other contacts with the customer

The salesman will rarely be the only contact with an important customer, although he will be the prime one. Where the product represents major innovation in the customer firm, there will be continual close contact with a large number of people meeting on both sides (called 'total involvement' in Chapter 3). In any company, senior management will often find it profitable to facilitate arrangements for personal contact with customers' senior staff, at least in the case of major customers and those with good potential. This may be used to enlarge the representative's circle of contacts in the buying company and to help him to meet decision-makers whom he might otherwise find it difficult to reach. Such meetings serve to show customers the interest which is taken in them and to improve relationships on a broad basis with the companies visited. The meeting may be a formal visit to the customer's office, at an exhibition or some other venue of interest to the customer's executive. Where a company is supplying a customer regularly with components or parts on a long-term basis, there may be regular contact between a plant or factory manager of the supplier and senior executives of the customer which are an important link in maintaining the long-term relationship.

The service force, the sales office staff, the switchboard operator and others will also have to deal with customers and prospects from time to time. They need guidance and training. Service can be a valuable link with the customer, reinforcing the salesman, meeting other people in the company and often being in a position to identify a customer's need for replacement equipment and to make recommendations about the replacement which might be selected.

Delay or lack of consideration at the switchboard can also lose orders and even customers. In the sales office, too, any member of the staff (particularly in the small firm) may deal with a customer or a prospect on the 'phone or face to face. Even if not an expert salesman, staff members should be commercially minded, keen to facilitate sales and aware of the importance of tact, consideration and need for accurate recording of details and quick action by follow-up.

11 SALES FORCE ECONOMICS

Where the market for a product is concentrated in a small number of companies, each representing a large amount of business, the personal contact with the buying companies is conducted through a few executives. Each of these is, in effect if not in name, an account executive in the best sense of the word, combining and consolidating the promotional work of his company and directing it towards the executives of the target companies. He will call in other members of the staff of his company to work with him and to cooperate in making presentations to clients, as necessary. Where, however, the market is more dispersed, the 'sales force' in its traditional sense appears. Even if this is only small—perhaps six members—the question immediately arises: 'How shall the force be organised?' This requires careful consideration so that the sales force approximates to the optimum relationship between increasing marketing 'push' and keeping costs down.

Ideas on organisation

There are, in fact, four main approaches to the problem of organisation, and it may well be possible and desirable as the sales force increases in size to combine more than one of these in order to achieve the best results. The four approaches are:

1   Specialisation by class of customer.
2   Specialisation by type of product.
3   Specialisation by territory.
4   Specialisation by function.

The basic principles of marketing immediately suggest that, other things being equal, the first approach deserves most careful consideration. Each representative specialises in serving a particular class of customer (or other market segment), and thus gains expert knowledge of the industry concerned, its technology, the way in which the buying decision is made, its growth prospects, its customers and all other matters which throw light on its present and future needs. This type of specialisation may well be regarded as the ideal form for the sales force handling industrial products. The representative becomes personally acquainted with a large number of individual decision-makers in customer companies and can explore their particular problems in subtlety and depth. He knows not only who makes what decision, but also what influences him, and when the decision is made. The salesman is able to provide his company with information which enables its management to adapt and improve its products, and to permit better planning of advertising and promotion generally.

One writer speaks of this system with great enthusiasm [33]. He cites its advantages as:

1 'The salesman lines up his calls by industry or trade channel, rather than territory; a practice to which we have given the name "industry marketing".'

2 'By thus specialising in an industry, the salesman becomes virtually a "partner" of the customer, so much so that he can quite literally forecast the future sales and marketing strategies both of his customers and of his own company.'

3 'With that close relationship, the salesman deals with the top customer-management levels where basic company policy is made.'

There are, however, certain problems which the industry approach presents. The representative concerned has to be acquainted with all his company's products, and where they differ in type of technology this may require a width of knowledge which is not obtainable at a cost proportionate to the potential business.

Specialisation by product is most appropriate where the products concerned are diverse and require different technical knowledge, and where the key decision-makers in the prospect companies differ from one class of product to another. Under these circumstances, the sales force will be organised according to the class of product, or (which is analogous) there will be separate sales forces for different products. This type of organisation is very common—in fact it sometimes exists where there does not seem to be adequate reason for it. It perhaps originates from the fact that in many companies different plants produce different products and the tendency, therefore, has been to develop distinct sales forces for each class of product, without serious examination of the alternatives. Sometimes its roots are historic: companies with independent sales forces have merged but the former selling arrangements have continued. It can mean that one buying firm will have two or even more representatives for the same company calling. This is not necessarily a disadvantage. They may have different people to see. In any case even if they both see the same purchasing officer, he may prefer this to one prolonged interview with the same man.

The industry approach is also less valuable where competing products concerned are undifferentiated and technically fairly simple. Buying firms are well aware of possible applications, and understanding the individual industry does less to advance sales. Sometimes there are only one or two people involved in making the buying decision, and the potential business from each customer is small. This points to a territory organisation to reduce the amount of travelling between calls and maximise the face-to-face time. The representatives concerned may need little specialised technical knowledge, but should be good at dealing with people.

The territory form of organisation is widespread. The major advantage is that the area to be covered by the representative is geographically smaller and this reduces travelling between calls. If there is need to visit an account urgently, the representative can quickly be on the spot. From the representative's point of view, not only is travelling time less but nights away from home are also often reduced.

When the sales force is large territory organisation may well be coordinated with one of the two forms mentioned above. For example, the sales force may be divided first into sections concerned with different industries (or products) and subsequently these sections are subdivided into territories.

Where industries are localised in a particular area, the salesman responsible for that area in any case automatically tends to become a specialist in the local industry, and this can provide a convenient amalgamation of the industry and territory principles—always provided that the other industries in that area, including new and developing industries, are not thereby neglected.

Finally, it is worth considering the possibility of specialisation by function. This is a more controversial issue and less widely adopted. The principle is that a total selling job may require a different type of representative at different stages. For example, specialisation may be achieved by separating out development work from the regular work of the representative and placing this in the hands of a specialised representative. Development work here means something beyond the normal job of prospecting; it is concerned with developing the market for new products or for new applications of established products. This may mean that a few major customers have to be introduced to the product, and considerable time may be required for working with each of these few companies to overcome technical, production and commercial difficulties. In addition, there may be a problem of price negotiation which is not within the responsibility and competence of the regular representative in many sales forces. For this reason some companies will place this work in the hands of a very small number of specialists with special status. Once the initial development work is done, the selling operation for what is now a standard product passes over to the main sales force. The existence of a separate force such as this may sometimes cause resentment among the other sales staff. It may be possible alternatively to build small teams in which different classes of salesmen work together.

In other cases, the negotiation may pass through a series of stages which involve a number of meetings over several months and at different levels. For example, a particular market may be such that it is necessary to make a large number of calls to identify a genuine 'prospect', using this word to mean a company which at the particular time has a need for the product concerned. Once prospects are identified, then there is a further meeting or series of meetings, and at a certain stage technical advice is required.

This situation might be met by a sales 'team' of a senior representative, technical representative and junior representative. The junior has the prime task of identifying prospects. Once they have been identified, the senior representative is available to provide reinforcement, perhaps at a higher level. The technical representative is called in when required and may be concerned in supplementary discussions with the technical staff of the prospect. Finally, there may be a major meeting to complete the transaction, which may involve a number of executives.

The ratio of technical to non-technical representatives varies according to the requirement of the market concerned. The team is coordinated by a senior representative or, if it becomes larger, by a field sales manager. Such arrangements make the best use of the time of the more costly representatives by delegating work which does not require their attention to subordinates.

Economic models

Many of the more fully worked-out ideas about the economics of the field sales force were developed in connection with the selling of mass consumer goods to retailers. This means that the ideas as they stand initially can be out of line with what is feasible in a large number of industrial selling situations. They require adapting, to a lesser or greater degree. The scalpel-sharp calculations of the leading mass-selling consumer-goods manufacturer must be replaced by a more flexible and rather more rough-hewn approach to match the realities of the industrial market where sales patterns show lower predictability and higher variation.

Nevertheless, the basic problem of deciding how to obtain value for the money spent on the sales force remains, as do the consequent questions, such as: 'How many salesmen should we have?' 'How often shall they call?' 'How much time shall we spend with this customer?' These underlie all well-founded approaches to sales.

The ideas described in the following pages apply most effectively to those products which are standardised and are sold to a reasonably predictable demand in a horizontal market. The salesman has then to cover the territory regularly and efficiently. Where the market is partly like this, but also contain a few large customers, the ideas are capable of adaptation as will be discussed later.

As a simple hypothesis (which can be modified for more complex markets) the amount of business produced by a salesman depends upon the following variables:

The number of calls made.

The proportion of calls identified as current prospects, i.e. potential buyers at the time.

The number of prospects who place an order.

The size of the order.

If the above description forms a reasonable 'model' of the market, then it suggests some interesting lines of thought about the direction in which increased efficiency might be sought. For example, suppose that in one standard period of four weeks a salesman

Makes eighty calls.

Identifies 75 per cent as current prospects.

Successfully makes a sale to 60 per cent of these.

Achieves an average order size of £300.

The total value of the sales obtained is therefore £10,800.

However, if small improvements can be made under each heading, sales will be increased provided that improvements in one item are not offset by decline elsewhere. This is important; for example, extra calls must not be sought by unreasonably reducing the length of calls with important customers and losing business as a result. If the number of calls rises to 85, identified current prospects to 78 per cent, conversion of prospects to 63 per cent, and the average sale to £320, then the total sales are now £13,366.

The increase under each heading is moderate, but the total overall improvement is great. The sales manager may decide at a particular time that one of these variables promises more potential improvement than the others, and will focus sales effort accordingly. He can do this by a combination of methods; comparing the performance of different salesmen, from market analysis which pinpoints prospects more accurately, special presentations or from a work study type of approach. Thought on these lines may help to focus on priorities which offer the quickest possibilities of improvement.

Other markets may require somewhat different models. If, for example, the sale consists of negotiations involving several calls, the model will need to reflect this.

The general point is that progress is most likely to be achieved by analysing the total selling task into its elements, measuring each of these, studying their possibilities, focusing on those elements which offer most opportunity for improvements on a cost/return calculation and then measuring market reaction to assess progress.

Systematic planning

The object of operations planning is to ensure that all worthwhile customers are called upon regularly at proper intervals of time and with minimum travelling and other costs. This has been brought to a fine art by some of the larger consumer-goods companies selling mass consumption branded products which meet a more regular and predictable order pattern. The problems in industrial marketing are different, but this does not mean that it is never possible to learn anything from those companies. Something can often be learned, provided proper adaptation is made to the more flexible approach required in industrial markets. It is first necessary to outline briefly the principles which are used in consumer goods, and then discuss the problems of adapting these ideas. The following is adapted from O'Shaughnessy [34].

The accounts to be called on are classified into three (or perhaps more) groups according to the frequency at which they should be visited. This frequency is a function of the expectation of business volume:

A   Accounts to be called on weekly (these are large accounts).
B   Accounts to be called on fortnightly (medium accounts).
C   Accounts to be called on monthly (small accounts).

There may be some smaller than C accounts which are not called on at all as the amount of business does not warrant the cost involved. These are supplied through distributors, who may be serviced by specialist salesmen.

The next stage is to draw up a plan which will ensure that the salesman covers the entire territory over (for example) the twenty working days in a lunar month, calling on each customer the correct number of times. The territory size itself is matched to the feasible work-load.

As a first step, each salesman's territory is divided into five segments (see Exhibit 12), each of which has in it one-fifth of the sales work-load for that territory. These segments may not be of equal area, but the time involved for the representative in covering them (including travelling and time with the customer) is equalised as far as is possible. Each segment is then to be visited on a particular day of

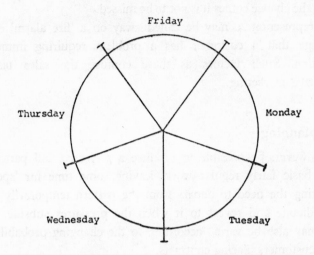

EXHIBIT 12 Territory planning. For predictable products segments have equal work-loads, and four overlapping routes to visit accounts with appropriate frequency

the week, segment A on Mondays, segment B on Tuesdays, and so on. This is the first step in balancing the work-load over the twenty days. As there are four Mondays in the lunar month during which the whole cycle of work is to be covered, the next step is to consider segment A and to split up the work in this segment over four days. This means that all the A accounts in that segment are to be visited every Monday (these are the big accounts), the B accounts are to be visited every other Monday (half of them will be visited on the first and third Mondays and the other half on the second and fourth Mondays), and finally the C accounts to be called on monthly are shared equally between the four Mondays. This procedure is repeated for every other day of the working week. The work is in this way spread as evenly as possible over the whole twenty days of the cycle.

F

The problem of adapting this procedure to industrial marketing includes the following:

1   There may be certain customers who are so important that they *must* be called on at the time which suits their convenience. For example, it may be that the representative has been trying to meet the commercial director of an important customer, and when the chance comes it is not to be missed.
2   The representative may be called away on a 'fire alarm' call, a message that a customer has a problem requiring immediate attention. Such factors as these confuse the sales task in industrial marketing.

Flexible planning

It may, however, be possible to produce a *preferred* call pattern to cover the basic fairly regular work, leaving some time for 'specials' and accepting the need to depart from the pattern temporarily when pressures dictate and revert to it when the pressures subside. 'Preferences' may also be varied according to the changing probability of particular customers placing contracts.

In the first instance it will be necessary to estimate the proportion of time which is required for those valuable 'special' accounts and for problems which require priority attention. To measure this will require some records to be kept for a trial period. The sales manager must then consider, in the light of the tasks which he wishes the sales force to undertake, whether this is the right proportion. It may be too low if he wishes them to spend more time nursing the 'specials' or it may be too high and he will seek ways of relieving the salesmen of some of this load so that they may spend more time on, for example, prospecting.

The problems of fire alarm and similar calls may be eased by analysis. For example, in one company analysis showed that the main reason why a representative was interrupted in his routine calls was to attend to technical problems, and that in well over two-thirds of the cases his action on arrival at the customer's plant was to phone head office for a technical service engineer. In general, a telephone call to the customer would have revealed the nature of the inquiry, the technical help could have arrived more quickly, and the routine calls would have suffered less interruption.

It should be noted that in territories with an efficient plan, the representative will often be in the near vicinity of a customer requiring special attention within a few days, and may thus by arrangement call on him with minimum interference with regular calls. There may also be a case for considering whether the area sales manager should not follow up some of these special calls when the representative is not in the vicinity.

The remaining accounts may be classified into two or three groups, according to the frequency with which routine calls should be made, for example:

A (medium accounts)	Four-weekly
B (smaller accounts)	Quarterly
C (very small)	Only if these can be fitted into spare time when the representative is in the vicinity or in response to an inquiry.

Analysis of salesmen's records, or special studies, will have revealed the extent to which, on average, time must be devoted to these priority 'special' claims. Suppose it is found that 40 per cent of the time must be devoted to them. This means that in a period of four five-day weeks, eight days will be required for specials and some allowance (say 2 days), must be made for time in the office. The remaining ten days will be available for systematic calling. The salesman does not, of course, know in advance which days will be required for 'specials', but he estimates that in most weeks he will have $2\frac{1}{2}$ days available for regular calls.

The calls can then be identified by setting out A and B accounts on a map, using different coloured pins. If it is desired that the salesman travels around his territory each four weeks, the territory is divided into four areas (each representing one of his weeks for systematic calling) and each area into twelve groupings of customers to represent one quarter's load. The actual day on which each customer-grouping is visited is not necessarily a predetermined part of the plan; it can be scheduled nearer the time to fit in with the requirements of the 'specials'. Time allowed to cover each group of customers can well err on the side of generosity. The margin uncommitted can then be used for prospecting and for the C accounts.

Another alternative which has been tried is for the representative to spend one week on routine calls and the second on the priorities. This is suited to circumstances where, once interest is aroused in a prospect company, several subsequent calls are necessary to complete the deal. The free week is thus spent on developing the leads produced in the routine calls.

A simple scheme is to recognise that 80 per cent of business comes from a few key accounts, to allow prior time for these and build other calls around them. It will still be necessary to develop an organised frequency for the 'others'.

When schemes such as this are being introduced for the first time, it is best to experiment in one territory; it is rare to get the plan just right first time. The actual detailed planning is left to the salesman concerned, in order to promote flexibility. The sales manager would receive a regular forecast of calls to be made.

This planning procedure will show whether the territory size is appropriate for the representative. If all accounts cannot be called on with proper frequency, then it is a sign that the work-load may be too heavy for one representative and either the territory size must be reduced or the smaller accounts dropped or visited less often. Alternatively, it may show that the territory is too small and too much time is spent on visiting C accounts. Once the system is operating, it is not uncommon for a salesman making regular calls to find a buyer saying: 'I thought you'd be around about now. I've got this matter I've kept to discuss with you.' The salesman will also have less of his spare time occupied with *ad hoc* planning.

Finally, a cautionary but true story told by a sales manager who thought all his salesmen were diligently occupied—until he stopped at a petrol-filling station and the man who filled his tank was a member of his own sales force.

The second element in the formula on page 145 was the proportion of calls which are current prospects. This issue is more important in some types of business than in others. Larger accounts must usually be visited consistently, but various methods have been adopted to make other calls more productive. The identification of leads by formal market research together with support from mail shots or advertising may help to use sales time more effectively. The use of a junior representative for prospecting can sometimes make senior time more productive. The collection of information on one visit can help choose the time for the next which more closely matches customer buying plans.

Selling by telephone

With the increase in the cost of personal calls by sales staff, more attention is now being given to the systematic use of contact by telephone. The sales force have always used the telephone to fix appointments, make supplementary contact and follow up on matters arising out of calls.

There appears now to be the gradual development of sales systems incorporating a major role for a sales staff specialising in selling by 'phone. Most such systems in the industrial field relate to simple-to-understand products, low on complexity and risk. The telephone staff work with and back up the regular sales force. Telephone calling can raise the frequency of customer contact, deal quickly and promptly with routine orders and release the professional sales representative both to give time to those prospects and customers who need special attention and to maintain some personal contact with the others.

Introducing such schemes is not easy. Special staff need to be recruited for the work and given proper training. The regular sales staff need to be brought into the development programme so that both sales forces—field and 'phone—work harmoniously together.

As with any other important innovation, test the new system in one area before general introduction.

The problem of small accounts

One source of dispute in many companies is whether or not small accounts should continue to be visited by salesmen. The argument is that small accounts, even if not economical at the present time, may one day grow into big profitable accounts. This problem can be approached by examining the economics of calling. In this discussion data used approximates to current levels, but inflation soon makes such figures obsolete. The calculations below should be regarded as illustrating the principle involved, and the examples reworked at current prices.

What is the cost of an individual call? Suppose that in a particular company a representative costs in all (salary, commission, superannuation and expenses) £10,000 to keep on the road. After deducting holidays, Bank holidays, sick leave and time necessary in the office for conferences and administration, he may be making calls on customers for 225 days in the year. If he is averaging two calls per day, giving some 450 calls per year on average, each call costs £22.

Assuming that it is necessary to call on a small account four times per year to keep it active, then the account costs £88 annually to service. If the contribution (and the word contribution, rather than profit, is the right one to use for marginal accounts) which the supplier earns on goods sold is 50 per cent, then he must expect to receive £176 worth, i.e. twice £88, of business each year from the company concerned to break even. The value of this business will then cover the cost of calling—but no more. The £176 provides £88 to cover incremental production and related costs and £88 to cover the cost of the representative's call.

Clearly there is no point in calling on a company simply in order to break even, so the executive will set a higher minimum level. He might very well decide not to call regularly on a customer who was unlikely to place at least £300 of business with his company annually. This does not necessarily mean that this level will be obtained every year, but that it can reasonably be expected taking one year with another.

The simplicity of this analysis has, of course, to be modified in a particular case. If a company producing products of low differentiation seeks about one-third of the market for its products, any company averaging £1500 of purchases in its class of goods is worth regular attention. The total amount of business which a prospect company places and the average share are not always sufficient criteria. Even if 33 per cent is the share of the overall market a supplier holds, there will be some buyers from whom it can expect a much higher share of the business on average, and others from whom it will expect less. This can be taken into account in planning calls and modified from time to time as circumstances change. There will also be occasions when the representative, after visiting the specials and A and B accounts in an area, will have time to visit the only other accounts locally, even though they are small. The opportunity cost is nil, because otherwise the time would have been unused.

It may be necessary to take a firm line with the subeconomic accounts and reduce them to the level of C accounts. It is true that one or two of these will grow, but to visit regularly many such accounts against the day when one may grow incurs a loss which the company has to carry today. Perhaps the few with a high probability of growth may be exceptions. If these outlays are to be genuinely recovered in the future, the losses of today must be recouped with compound interest. Finally, the possibility of keeping in touch in other ways (telephone, for example) and reducing the call frequency should be examined. Often a careful survey of all possible customers, present and prospective, in a territory may reveal conscientious calling on some small and uneconomic accounts, but omission of some which offer more potential. More complex models can take account of the probability of obtaining orders from particular customers and their probable volume.

Costs per £100 of turnover or (better still if practical) contribution are key yardsticks in assessing performance. As a measure of efficiency, it has the limitation of any other average. Average cost can be low because the territory is being 'creamed' and some worthwhile but small accounts are not being properly covered. Average contribution can be high for the same reason. The real test is the marginal one: the smallest group of accounts regularly visited should be economic when cost and return are compared, and those accounts which are not called upon should be subeconomic by the same yardstick. If there are accounts not being visited which could potentially yield a worthwhile contribution on this basis, then it is of advantage for them to be visited even though the turnover/cost ratio for that group of accounts will be below average. If in reducing time spent on subeconomic accounts the salesman directs his attention to these better accounts, a double benefit is achieved.

Records and returns

The concept of control in the industrial sales force, particularly with the senior representative, is one to be used with discretion. The objective must be to create a team relationship in which the enthusiasm of the sales manager communicates itself to the salesman and the systematic search for economic sales becomes a joint effort.

This does not mean that the sales manager does not require information and does not follow up the salesman's progress to commend achievement and amend weakness. It does mean that he tries to involve the salesman in the process of examining problems and to decide by joint collaboration the means of solving these problems. In the last resort, the sales manager may have to take more drastic action; he may, for example, have to install plans and procedures which are not well received to begin with, but (except in real emergency) this should follow a period in which the salesmen have had explained to them the nature of the problems and are given an opportunity to discuss and put forward their own proposals, and to comment on those of others. The examination and consideration of these comments must be real and not a façade—this is easily detectable and results in harm not benefit.

Filling forms (apart from a claim for expenses) is not popular with anyone, and salesmen are no exception. The best salesman is not necessarily the best at making returns. Yet the information is needed for marketing action, for sales force planning and for the salesman's own information. Returns should be collected only on information required for action which cannot reasonably be secured otherwise. Call reports, plans for forthcoming calls, and customer reports are the chief information required from salesmen. Where calls follow a regular pattern and there are a number each day—say four or more—it may be possible to present the form in such a way that much of the required information can be completed by a tick in the appropriate box. Details of companies seen, people met, sales achieved will have to be written in if required, and fuller supporting information supplied on those few calls that really justify it. Where calls are less frequent and each account more important, then more detailed reports will be required indicating matters discussed, sales made, customer's buying and other plans, competitive action, reasons for failure to get an order, and the follow-up programme. The representative must be guided to provide material relevant to decision-making and planning.

When a prospect is called on for the first time, a special customer report giving much fuller information about his company is required, and is to be subsequently updated systematically. Information of this sort is transferred to a customer record in the office to provide a comprehensive picture. Many salesmen also find it worth keeping their own record cards, which include not only details of past calls and commercial details to be followed up, but details about the interests, attitudes and prejudice of the decision-makers he meets. Consulting these documents before the next call enables him to plan the call properly: the objective of the call, who he seeks to see, what points he wants to make, what objections and complaints to prepare for, and how to match what he says to the man he is meeting. Some companies also require completion of a regular intelligence report at monthly or quarterly intervals.

Even when the salesmen's job cannot be planned in much detail, it is still worth, over a period of, say, six months, preparing an analysis of calls made in relation to business received or potential from different sizes of accounts, to see if the overall pattern of calls is consistent with the importance of different customers.

Assessing results

Records are, in fact, the only basis other than personal contact on which the sales manager can assess the performance of a representative in those circumstances in which the link between the individual's efforts and sales achieved is not a close one in the short term. Particularly when a salesman is building a new territory, or developing a market for a new product, the results of his efforts in terms of turnover may not appear for some time.

Analysis of records provides much information which can be used in evaluating salesmen and permit counselling to improve performances. Some of the factors commonly examined are discussed below, and in most companies standards of performance become established. These standards will require adjustment to allow for differences in the products sold, territory differences, and customer differences. The number of calls made is one common test, and allowance must be made here for different distances between customers in various parts of the country, and for differing times required with particular customers. This variations are inevitable, but big differences and trends require examination.

The average success rate and average sale per call are sometimes useful indications of performance. Too high a figure may be as significant as a too low one. It may be that a salesman's territory is too big; he can then concentrate on the bigger and better accounts and leave somewhat smaller (but still potentially profitable accounts) un-exploited. If several salesmen are doing this, then a reapportionment of territories and the employment of additional salesmen may be justified. Before taking this action, the sales manager will explore the potential among the small customers to ensure that the extra business will cover the cost. He will be examining the relationship between ac-counts called on and the total worthwhile accounts—a study of value in itself.

Often where sales are in large 'lumps' special analyses may be made to assess the share of each major buyer's business which the company is achieving. Big contracts will be the focus of multi-level selling by a number of staff and there will be special reviews of factors influencing success and failure.

Quotas, where feasible, are part of the armoury of assessing a sales-man. These, however, judge him on short-term results, and should therefore be used cautiously where this is not appropriate. Quotas for this purpose commonly include a moderate incentive element, sufficient to imply full extension on the part of the salesman. Setting industrial quotas is not easy and usually involves a study of area potential—with particular reference to major accounts—and a com-parison with past sales. Where incentive payments are related to quotas, these will commonly begin at something less than 100 per cent of quota. It goes without saying that the quota cannot be settled with-out full consideration of the views of the salesman concerned.

Where the salesman has other objectives to achieve, performance will also need to be assessed against these. They can include such tests as new accounts opened and level of expenses in relation to business produced.

The importance of training in salesmanship to promote productivity has already been mentioned. More industrial salesmen could be pro-vided with efficient visual aids to support their presentation. A few managers plan a proper presentation kit for each man, at least in res-pect of those lines which are being most strongly pushed at any time. A good folder of well-mounted photographs, case histories and other material, with notes to remind the salesman of the product benefits and answers to objections, can help gain and hold the prospect's interest and provide visual support for the salesman's verbal presentation.

Desk-top projectors with moving films can add punch to a presentation by showing equipment actually operating. Sales manuals are also not always provided to representatives in industrial selling, yet most companies who use them have found them a valuable tool. There are different ideas about what should go into the manual, but the following is an illustration:

1   Background information about company policy.
2   Methods of making presentations, dealing with common objections and closing sales.
3   Information on customer benefits from company products.
4   Information on competitors' products, prices and policies.
5   Reference material.

If the customer is really important, there must be a group presentation, which requires specially prepared aids and can well be rehearsed in advance, with a critical group of executives playing the role of buyers.

12 ANCILLARY SERVICE

In marketing in general, but in industrial marketing in particular, the customer's need to 'solve problems' is not always met completely by the product purchased. There are associated problems to be solved before the full benefit of the product is realised in terms of extra sales, higher productivity or other criteria. Additional assistance by way of ancillary service may be required. This ancillary service may be supplied from one of three sources: within the customer firm, from a third party (for example a specialist firm) or by the supplier himself. In many circumstances it can be in the interest of the supplier to provide these services.

There are, of course, transactions in which service is the 'thing' sold: its role is the same as that of the tangible product which is the core of many other sales. Circumstances in which this is so are many: the services of banking, travel, management consultancy, insurance, are but a few examples. The ancillary services discussed in this chapter are not at the core of the transaction but of a supplementary nature whereby the benefits provided by the product are enlarged and made effective. The guiding economic principle of ancillary service as a marketing tool is that the supplier who thus improves the value of the product to the customer in turn benefits directly or indirectly through extra sales, better prices or lower marketing or other costs. In some industries service has become a key factor in long-term competition, and the cost of providing those services is more than offset by the net returns received.

Most services impinge on the customer/supplier relationship in one or more of three ways:

1 *Transaction services* Services that facilitate the transaction between customer and supplier.
2 *Application services* Services that increase the benefit of the product to the customer, e.g. raising the efficiency with which the product is used or bringing it into effective operation at an earlier date than would otherwise be the case.
3 *Background services* Assisting the customer in some way unrelated to specific transactions.

Ancillary service is often part of an ongoing relationship with customers, which operates before, during, and after sales, welding together separate deals into a continuous relationship.

Transaction services

Three services which commonly facilitate the sale are:

1 *Delivery.*
2 *Finance.*
3 Technical advice relating to product specification and selection.

The third item in this list is conveniently considered in the context of application service, discussed later in this chapter.

Delivery

Major aspects of delivery relate to speed, punctuality and form.

Speedy delivery is the ability to meet requests for delivery at an early date. Ability to do this may depend upon the size of stocks held by the supplier concerned and whether they are held conveniently to the purchaser. Holding stocks is expensive and the decision on quantities to be stocked depends upon the frequency of demand for early delivery, the lead time and the importance that customers place upon this factor. Systematic contact with customers can sometimes reduce the number of 'urgent' requests.

In many routine products, stocks will be on hand at the time of the order or a further supply will commonly be scheduled for early production. Where economies of long runs are not great, smaller stocks will generally be carried, but where long runs are clearly more economical, then the economic solution will be to carry more stock rather than be forced into emergency short runs.

Good organisation is important. Frequently, a review of stock levels will show that some lines are overstocked, and others persistently understocked. If the proportions are adjusted, if better forecasts are introduced of short-run demand by, perhaps, exponential smoothing techniques, and if production schedules are carefully planned, delivery problems may be eased. In addition, communication with the sales force may require attention. Embarrassment and bad feeling can result when representatives make delivery promises which cannot be implemented. Even if there is no firm promise of delivery by a certain date, departure from past practice may cause consternation and difficulty when the purchaser has had no intimation of it.

Nevertheless, when all is said and done, there is a balance to be struck between the cost of carrying stocks of finished goods and the danger of losing an order for a product, perhaps related orders on other products, perhaps even a customer. Policy depends on the importance of these matters to the customers and the value of the business of the customer concerned.

When *punctual delivery* to a customer's schedule is important, close working with the customer can result in a supplier-customer 'team' planned as a unity so that the production by the supplier is tied in closely with the requirements of the customer, to the benefit of both. This can reduce the total stock needed, with consequent saving.

A related problem arises when the runs are short and the product is to some degree adapted to the requirements of individual customers. For example, if glass containers are being produced, many customers will have, for promotional or other reasons, special requirements. Customers' demand will have to meet different deadlines, which are known by the sales or marketing departments but not always by the production department. In order to match output to customer requirements under these conditions it may be an advantage for scheduling of production to be a marketing department responsibility. The lines of communication are shortened and the marketing department, aware of both customer priorities and of production limitations, carries full responsibility for meshing output with demand. Finally in view of the way in which industrial disputes have often interrupted production and delivery, the importance of good relations with production and maintenance employees must be stressed.

The form of delivery including the type of packaging is also sometimes an issue. Conditions of transit, storage and usage have to be ascertained to ensure that the packaging will be such that the product is in good condition on arrival. This will have to take account of handling and storage facilities which the customer is likely to have, and local weather conditions, pests and perils of pilferage. Some goods may be delivered direct to a customer's production line and the planning problem is to minimise packaging and to harmonise suppliers' and customers' loading and unloading arrangement and equipment so that a streamlined and economic operation takes place: the supplier is virtually an extension of the customer's production line.

Finance

Another factor often important in completing a deal. Most firms provide some credit to customers although at time of writing high interest rates make this an expensive service. There is also a danger of bad debts arising if the amount of credit advanced and the period of repayment go beyond reasonable levels. The individual supplier may therefore have to set limits on the credit he is prepared to offer, otherwise the cost can exceed the benefit and the supplier himself may run out of ready cash with detriment to his business as a whole—perhaps even bankruptcy. Some suppliers, aware of the limitations of what they can do themselves, have provided the customer with information on national and international sources of funds (for example in relation to major construction works in overseas countries). Others have developed special relationships with some finance institution and a few big firms have developed their own credit subsidiary (for example in connection with agricultural machinery). Leasing may be offered as an alternative to outright purchase. In most countries there are special governmental facilities for the provision of credit for exports. Suppliers to benevolent and religious organisations have advised customers on fund-raising activities for such purposes as the finance of the restoration of historic buildings.

Application services

Companies provide many different advisory services for prospects and customers to help specify the most suitable grade or model of a product for specific application and to provide fullest value in use. Technical service is the popular term but there is in fact a wide range of services offered. Some are not technical in the narrow sense: examples include the design of customers' equipment by electronic manufacturers, of retail packaging by packaging manufacturers, and the analysis of office systems by suppliers of equipment.

These services do not end with the transaction but continue afterwards, when appropriate, as part of the continuous relationship. They are often provided without special charge when the business which will be generated seems likely to be sufficient to cover the cost. In some industries this is the normal practice which the supplier cannot but follow.

A supplier of lubricants may willingly survey the plant of a company, identify all the points which should be lubricated and present a report recommending lubricant grades of his own brand as appropriate and prescribing the frequency of lubrication. Such a survey at infrequent intervals may be inexpensive in relation to the potential business and part of the sales function. Not all companies may want such service; bigger firms may have their own specialist staff and in some lines of business reasons of security may limit the extent to which a customer will permit a representative of a supplier to have access to the information which he requires.

Although treating such pre-sales service as a normal sales overhead and not charging for it separately is common, nevertheless the policy of free surveys and advice can become expensive if a sufficiently high volume of business does not follow. Sometimes care in making an advance appreciation of inquiries may eliminate a proportion of those which have a low probability of developing into business. Where the survey is extensive, it may be possible after limited preliminary work to discuss progress with the prospect and at this stage form a view of the possibility of business resulting, and perhaps even obtain a commitment that an order will be placed. There are some industries where it is possible to make a charge for surveys and others where after a preliminary study more advanced planning work is at the customer's expense.

Background services

This is a less common class of services where the supplier assists customers in some way not closely linked to their characteristic business relationship. Most examples involve the provision of general management or other advice which benefits the customer in his business, thus a firm of agricultural suppliers may help farmers in this way. The benefits to the supplier firm, such as they are, flow from the goodwill generated from the greater prosperity of customers providing more business. It may however be more realistic to regard this as justifiable on social rather than business grounds.

An extreme example (which perhaps stretches this concept) is discussed by de Monthoux and Persson [36] who describe how four countries (France, Britain, USA and Sweden) competed for 'one of the biggest arms transactions ever' when Belgium, Denmark, Holland and Norway planned to exchange their Starfighter combat aircraft for a modern plane. Compensations outside the deal were offered to the future buyers: such compensations included, for example, part production of the aircraft in buying countries, construction of an airport, a water purification scheme and other forms of large financial, industrial and technological support. Such offers were made not only by potential contractors but some also came from sub-contractors.

The continuing relationship

After-sales service, whether expressly agreed by contract or implied because of the reputation and image of the company, can often be identified and costed in relation to each unit of product or each particular contract. In some industries, the service requirement is trivial and can be met by good technical literature and a well-informed representative, apart from the occasional problem which requires attention from a specialist. In other industries the requirement for service is widespread, because of the lack of the required specialised knowledge among customers. The needs will often tend to be highest among products which are technically complex and new, with fast-growing demand, so that there is widespread ignorance in the customer firms and little expertise to alleviate this. Under such circumstances, technical service can be of tremendous value in the marketing strategy, and a link which the customer will be reluctant to break because of the possible loss to him. A continuing relationship is thus forged.

The market may be segmented by the need for service. Some parts of the market—perhaps the larger firms or those concerned with technical products themselves—may have no need for service although they may appreciate occasional consultation with a respected specialist.

Where the volume and type of post-sales service required differs from customer to customer, the costs involved can sometimes be charged back to the customer directly or reflected in his individual price. At the minimum, it is necessary to check that each customer or group of customers makes sufficient contribution to cover the costs incurred.

Where, however, the need for technical backing is pervasive and service costs on average only a small proportion of the value of the business flowing from it, then it will not be charged separately, but will be 'free'. It helps to cement relations between the supplier and the customer and will often give the supplier access to decision-makers in the customer firm whom it might otherwise be difficult to contact. Under these circumstances, it can help to cut down the cost of obtaining repeat orders. The customer's staff becomes familiar with this supplier's products and will tend to be influenced by this knowledge when preparing designs and specifications. The supplier will be aware of the customer's developing plans and will be able to anticipate his needs and have new products well forward in development when the need becomes apparent.

What sort of supplementary services should be offered? The range is tremendous.

The provision of maintenance and spares is a widespread requirement. Maintenance provided under some form of express or implied warranty, including the meeting of justifiable complaints, is a cost which a company must be prepared to bear.

Some large companies find it difficult to ensure that maintenance charges cover expenses. To overcome the difficulty, company policy may seek to avoid business which involves maintenance and may try to leave this to intermediate manufacturers or distributors. Spares are normally profitable and sometimes very much so, as demand is not very sensitive to price. Spares can, however, often involve considerable costs in stock-holding, clerical work, packing and carriage which should be fully recognised.

Systems selling

The development of services to back up the transaction has led in some industries to the concept of systems selling. Systems selling seeks to perform a complete function for the customer and to provide everything necessary to perform that function. Thus a scientific instrument manufacturer concerned with process control in the paper industry would provide a complete package of computer, instrumentation, process model, computer programs, staff training and maintenance. A packaging manufacturer would design not only the package but develop the product to be packaged, develop the promotional programme, design the package, and test market product and pack. It can be argued that this approach carries marketing to its logical conclusion since it focuses not on the product but on the end of purpose which motivates the transaction.

Technical service and the sales force

Technical service is an arm of marketing and must be closely integrated for the best results. Where the service requirement is not of too sophisticated a nature, it may well be possible to leave the sales engineer or equivalent to carry out the bulk of the work. This is particularly appropriate for pre-purchase service. Where, however, technical service is highly complex, it may well be better to limit the technical role of the salesman and support him with specialised technicians. In some instances a variety of specialisations may be needed to provide what is required. The relationship between the technical adviser and the negotiating salesman must be very close, and the lines of communication and organisation should be designed to facilitate this. It is possible to envisage a situation in which there are non-technical salesmen selling standard products, and specialists selling more complex products; from this it is a short step to the point where the sales team consists of non-technical salesmen working with service representatives responsible for maintenance and similar after-sales service.

The evaluation of technical service

Simon [35] suggests that all technical product service can be broken into the following ingredients:

1   *Anticipation* Prediction of customers' needs for technical product and provision for these predicted needs.
2   *Accuracy in problem definition* The determination with the customer of the precise problem on which the service organisation is to work.
3   *Completeness* The scope, range or number of technical services provided for customers.
4   *Responsiveness* The speed with which the service organisation responds to emergency situations.
5   *Problem-solving efficiency* The time necessary to achieve a technically correct solution of the problem which permits the customer to accomplish what he expected with the aid of the service rendered him.

He recommends that to evaluate the efficiency and aptness of the technical service, results under these headings should be assessed.

Certainly, the importance of service in industrial markets is often high. The failure to consider it which has sometimes occurred has probably resulted from the earlier emphasis given to consumer marketing, in which this aspect is often of less importance. Service may deserve more management attention than it is sometimes given, to ensure that it is correctly focused on appropriate objectives and that it is on a sound economic basis.

13 PLANNED ADVERTISING

The traditional definition of advertising describes it as communication by an identified sponsor through a paid impersonal medium. As sometimes interpreted, it is by no means clear whether this usage would include direct-mail advertising. It is, however, convenient to include direct mail in this chapter, and to consider both display advertising in journals and mail advertising together.

The role of advertising

While the role of advertising in industrial markets is less striking than it is in consumer markets, and advertising budgets are, on the whole, lower as a percentage of turnover, it is by no means unimportant. It is one link in the chain of effective marketing, and if the advertising link is weak the total marketing effort will suffer.

One way of looking at the role of industrial advertising is to regard its prime purpose as a method of making the sales force more effective and more economical. In this way it reduces selling costs and boosts turnover. To achieve this, advertising has to be woven into the complex pattern of communications methods in general use in industrial markets; this requires close cooperation between the advertising agency and the marketing company to ensure that there is a comprehensive overall design in the approach to marketing communication. Display advertising must tie in with mail shots, exhibitions, seminars, the literature which the company uses and the presentations of the salesman.

This general task is effected in a number of ways. Frequently, advertising prepares the ground before a call. It briefs the buyer and other executives whom the salesman will meet so that they are aware of the company, its reputation, its products, its product features, its technical service or any other points which they must know. The salesman then finds he is starting an interview with a man who is already aware, interested and, if the advertising has been good enough, somewhat inclined to deal with him.

Advertising also helps to convey a message in depth to a prospect company. The decision-making network is complex and normally the salesman will not be regularly in touch with more than two executives. The rest of the network may be hard and expensive to reach, and indeed even to identify. An important task of advertising is to contact others on the network and move them to a fuller appreciation that this is the right product to buy and the right company to buy it from.

Where the market for a product is widespread and many companies make a small volume of purchases, the salesman's calls on them will be infrequent—perhaps once or twice a year. The 'gap' between calls must be filled, and this is a role which advertising can play.

Advertising also may have the responsibility of generating 'leads' which can make the work of the sales force more effective. This is particularly valuable when much of the sales force's work is in searching out new prospects, because the product is one which is bought infrequently. In some exceptional circumstances, where the sale is by post, advertising has the entire responsibility for making this sale. It is also used to support the work of distributors and intermediate manufacturers and to motivate them to greater selling effort.

No review of what advertising has to offer is complete without reference to its contribution to projecting the company image. This is a function which extends beyond that of directly assisting the making of sales. It is considered more fully in Chapter 14.

In general it may be said that the marketing executive tries to use advertising when it is the most economical way of undertaking a particular part of the total communication function. It is not easy to assess when this applies, and as a practical matter it is very hard to give more than general suggestions.

Managers sometimes see the problem of advertising expenditure as a question of whether to spend extra money on advertising or to use that money to employ another representative. This is often the wrong way of looking at the problem. The sales force and advertising are part of a unified package of communication and the decision is how big is the total package to be. There is no point in selling the buyer on a product unless others in the company are prepared to accept his recommendation. Similarly, there is little point in trying to persuade a customer to purchase a particular textile yarn unless the consumer is willing to accept and perhaps even prefer it to others.

Advertising objectives

By the time that the advertising is being planned, the marketing man's thinking should have developed through a number of prior stages. He has first settled his overall approach to the market, he has determined the general nature of his communication strategy within his overall marketing plan, and now he comes to the specific question of determining the role of advertising. A common difficulty that advertising agencies in this field have to face is that advertisers come to them without having gone through this initial process. The broad marketing goals which are to be supported by advertising should have been decided; the task of developing goals for advertising which are as precise and quantified as possible follows from this.

The advertising brief must therefore specify:

The broad marketing goals.
The nature and size of the target audience.
The role of that audience in the purchase process.
The change in knowledge and attitudes sought.

There may well be several groups of people who will be targets for the campaign. Each group can involve different objectives, different advertisements and different media. Thus a company might specify its objectives as follows:

1   To inform 100 top executives in industry X that the company is a reliable and trustworthy source of supply.
2   To inform 1000 design engineers in that industry that a new product of the company is suited to a particular application.
3   To stress to 1000 buyers that the price has been reduced and delivery is prompt.

In practice this degree of precision is hard to achieve. Nevertheless, unless the purpose of the advertising is defined in terms which have a reasonable degree of precision, the advertising effort may well be dissipated and of little value.

The advertising approach

At this stage, responsibility is shifting on to the shoulders of the advertising specialist who is being briefed, although the process of briefing is in the nature of a dialogue in which an exchange of views promotes clarity and greater understanding on both sides about what is sought and what is feasible. The 'raw' message has to be turned first into a general approach and then into copy. Media have also to be selected. While it is convenient and necessary to look at these steps individually, there is of course a process of feedback by which thinking on one aspect affects thinking on another.

The approach is the general basic idea about the way in which the chosen message may be put over effectively and convincingly. It may be desirable to put the message as a straight exposition of the merits of the company, by way of testimonials from satisfied users. Applications' information may be put over by a case-history approach (telling how others have successfully used the product) or by question-and-answer approach which involves the reader by requiring him to respond, mentally at least. To the purchasing officer a message about price change may well be put over 'straight'. Service may require different handling, for example by showing that the company has a technical service representative available in every industrial city.

Some of these approaches may be more effectively interpreted at an exhibition, by issuing a Press release or by a mail shot. Even then display advertising in support of the main effort is common.

The creation of effective copy is described in specialist texts. This matter is, of course, complicated by the difficulty of testing whether or not the copy has been effective. The copy itself should always be based on what interests the target reader, in relation to the product or service offered. Like the salesman, the advertising man talks in terms of customer benefits. This is an obvious guideline—yet it is easy to forget.

In technical and industrial advertising, the primary arguments are almost invariably on a rational level, supported by factual evidence.

Different classes of decision-makers have different interests, and each message may require a different medium and separate tailoring to a particular audience. Before settling down to the development of copy, the advertising man will spend a great deal of time on the basic problem of understanding the product and what it does, and on thinking through the likely reaction of his different target audiences.

As in most advertising, the first task of the copy is to attract the right readers. Individuals who may only be flicking through a journal need to be impelled to study a particular advertisement. The target audience is picked out by the headline or illustration of the advertisement. Each relevant reader must react as if, at the back of his mind, a voice was saying 'This is something I should look at'. Messner [37] says 'A good industrial advertisement has about it an air of *promise* for the reader', and he gives the following advice on the headline:

'To do its job well, a headline should:

1 Seek out the kind of readers which you would like to read your advertisement.
2 Encourage them to read further in the copy.
3 Inspire belief.
4 Communicate an understandable message.'

From there on, the copy must pick up and intensify interest. If the product has well-defined advantages, this is not a big problem. When, however, the product is much the same as other products on the market, the good copywriter must take more obvious facts and bring them to life in a manner which adds interest, impact and credibility. Enlivening the advertisement with linked emotion and human interest can reinforce even industrial advertising.

This is a real challenge to the copywriter's abilities. His objective may be to *maintain* rather than create goodwill and a positive awareness. Under such circumstances an indirect approach may be used—for example, by highlighting service or dramatic examples of product application. Finally, the general tone of the advertisement and its layout will have an effect, over time, on the way in which the reader may think about the company.

Normally, a company's specific advertisements are part of a larger campaign. Advertisements may well appear in a series in the same journal, and they strengthen each other if there is a family likeness and a unifying theme to consolidate impact. For example, a campaign to show the versatility of a product may feature in successive advertisements a series of dramatic instances in which the product has been used in an unexpected and intruiging way.

Frequency and size of advertisement is a difficult problem, and at this stage the advertising man has little more than rule-of-thumb judgment to guide him. Is it better to have a quarter-page advertisement every month, half a page every two months, or a full page every four months? The valid answer, 'Whichever does the job better', is not often helpful as a guide to action. A common view is that size is important, and the advertisement should be large enough to make an impact or even to dominate the medium. To some extent it depends on the journal concerned. Some journals are studied with loving care, filed as a source of reference, and even the smaller advertisements noted by relevant readers. Others are read more casually and the probability of being noticed will depend very much on the size and location of the advertisement. Similarly with repetition; this reminds and builds up.

Media selection

Industrial advertising uses many different media. The object it to find a channel which goes to the target audience and is likely to combine the appropriate emphasis and acceptability with economy. Sometimes the choice is at first sight surprising, but the varied problems of industrial marketing require an equally wide range of answers. Television, for example, is not an obvious selection for industrial goods. It has, of course, a place in 'back-selling' campaigns for influencing consumers. Sometimes it has been used for the direct promotion of goods to decision-makers in industrial markets, for example, a new type of copying equipment which would interest very many companies, each perhaps with several buying points, and the total number of people who could influence buying decisions very great indeed. Because the product could be demonstrated on television, the message could be transmitted with a credibility and impact which other media would find hard to match.

The same medium has been used in a somewhat different way for the sale to farmers of fertilisers, seeds and other requirements. For these, the advertisers selected a television station which served an area with a strong agricultural bias, and chose a suitable time for promotion. Here it was considered economic to use television selectively to contact a moderately large specialised audience at times when the target audience viewed.

Industrial advertising is also carried in the 'quality' daily and weekly Press and journals. Some of this is 'image' projection, but there are frequently advertisements more directly concerned with developing short-term sales. These are generally products of a non-technical nature which would be of interest to a wide range of industries; in particular they are often items of direct interest to the administrative and commercial staff.

A quick look at this Press reveals advertisements for automatic tea and coffee units, towel services, leasing of motor vehicles, and secretarial, financial and commercial services of all types. These advertisements aim to appeal to various levels of management in business, Government and elsewhere. Some industrial advertising uses posters as a medium—for example, posters outside agricultural shows promoting goods to farmers. One company used advertisements in London underground trains to promote drain-cleaning services to businessmen.

More important in most industrial advertising, however, is the wide range of trade and technical journals and the main problem of media planning is concerned with deciding which of these to use and to what extent.

Discussion of trade and technical media has developed its own language. The prime distinction is between 'vertical' and 'horizontal' media. A vertical medium penetrates different levels in a particular industry; for example, *British Printer* is read by many different executives in the printing industry, whereas *Modern Purchasing* for purchasing officers across a wide range of different industries is horizontal.

Life being what it is, media do not always fit neatly into these classes. When considering journals reaching a specific industry—particularly a large and growing industry such as electronics or chemicals—there are some which penetrate to many different executives in one sector of the industry, others which reach one class of executive across the industry (that is to say, they are vertical or horizontal within the industry). Some media are L-shaped (part vertical and part horizontal) and others overflow from one industry into another.

Another important distinction is between journals which are issued free to a controlled circulation and those which have a paid, but unrestricted circulation. The former are distributed only to certain categories of eligible executives. The entire income is from advertising. The object is to ensure that the circulation of the journal is directed to a particular professional or industrial audience. In this they differ from the general run of journals sold to any subscriber.

To achieve his objectives of selecting media to reach the right audience with the right quality of impact, the media planner needs to know the profile of the target audience and to choose media whose readership matches this profile. One general problem is the lack of a clear and standardised nomenclature for different executive functions in business. This makes both definition and matching of the audience profile difficult. Data about the audience for different trade, technical and professional journals is therefore important and the supply of information is increasing in many countries.

Circulation figures usually come first. In some twenty countries Audit Bureau of Circulation (representing agencies, advertisers and media) now set standards of definition for measurement of circulation and other data and disseminate verified information.

The British ABC, for example, provides the following:

1   *Paid journals*: normal rates, reduced rates, unpaid

2   *Controlled circulation journals* (copies sent free and post free) to specific interest groups:

Individually requested
Company requested
Non-requested

3   *Society or association members*:

Optional
Non-optional

Circulation is minimal information: readership is different and information on the total number and type of readers is better for media selection by advertisers. Media data forms which provide this information are becoming more widely used, especially in the USA and the UK. There is of course no obligation for publishers to provide this information.

For media planning what is more useful are studies which focus on different categories of executive identifying the journals they read. There are few such studies as yet, but the numbers are slowly increasing, mainly as a result of pressure from advertising agencies.

There are other considerations as well as readership figures which must be taken into account when selecting media. One is the quality of the journal: some are more authoritative than others, and this may be reflected in the reader's attitude to the advertisements. Some are studied closely by readers, while others are read in a more relaxed mood. Some journals are normally filed and kept for future reference by the executives who read them, and advertising may have a longer-term value. To assess the journals in this way, the media planner can study their content and reinforce his views by inquiry among readers.

Finally, the facilities which the journal offers may influence the decision. The availability of colour, the willingness to accept inserts and whether or not there are reader reply cards at the end can be relevant. There are occasions when there is no journal which serves the particular audience. In that case the advertiser must create his own medium. This is one reason for the development of direct mail and the house journal.

Direct mail

This is a valuable medium for the industrial advertiser, and its popularity is high. The term is self-explanatory: it is the sending by post of promotional material direct to customers' and prospects' staff. It is an extremely flexible medium, since in addition to national campaigns it is possible with careful planning to carry out local campaigns which tie in closely with the salesman's calls or the work of a local distributor. However, most executives receive a great deal of direct mail, so most mail 'shots' face keen competition and the problem of making them effective can be serious.

A key factor in successful direct mail is an up-to-date list of the people who are the targets for promotions. Mailing lists for a market which is being entered can often be purchased from specialist suppliers, at least as a first step. However, a company with a regular interest in a particular market will normally maintain its own list. This may begin with a purchased list, but this is developed and kept up-to-date from such sources as directories, association membership lists, exhibit visitors, salesmen's feedback of staff changes, inquiries received, and mail returned undelivered. The records must be classified by industry, function and other relevant categories so that addressees with particular interests can be identified and appropriate material sent to them. Their time and the advertiser's money is then not wasted on irrelevant mail shots. The maintenance of the mailing list is a substantial and important job, requiring the continuous attention of reliable staff. The problem of list maintenance requires careful thought at the time the list is first established.

The list should be as far as possible a list of people's names. How then to deal with a report that there is a new Purchasing Manager at XYZ Limited? Inserting the firm's name before the respondent's on the address list can ease the problem.

The cost of direct mail is often more expensive than that of an insertion in a journal with a comparable readership. There is not only the initial preparation of the material, but also the printing of the literature and the actual mail cost. Having met this cost, there is still the possibility that the shot, although addressed to the individual technician, purchasing officer or other executive by name, may still be unread or may never reach its target because it is intercepted by a subordinate or thrown away unopened. People who receive a large amount of literature in this way sometimes seem to develop some sixth sense for mail advertising material!

Direct mail requires at least as much care in writing as any other advertising. Effectiveness is usually increased by starting any covering letter with 'Dear ————' and addressing the individual by name. With large-scale mailing lists the cost of entering each individual name is high, and the marketing executive must weigh the extra cost against the effect on response rates.

Much direct mail is concerned with developing leads, and the system for recording and acting on these leads must be carefully planned. Direct mail is, of course, also used for keeping customers briefed: sending out literature of all sorts, catalogues, servicing information, suggestions on applications and uses. The pressure of direct mail is growing and the competition in an executive's in-tray can be intense.

New ideas are therefore at a premium, and the advertiser is continually seeking new forms of presentation which will catch the executive's attention and encourage him to read on. These include pamphlets mailed under 'first-day' covers with new postage stamps, three-dimensional devices, and samples. Yet still the search for originality continues. Commonly there will be series of shots (analogous to series of advertisements in a journal) in order to make the fullest impact at the right time.

The assessment of advertising effectiveness is discussed more fully later in this chapter. Mail advertising aiming to produce inquiries does, however, have the advantage that it may be possible to test response to different variations of a message before embarking on a large-scale campaign. Some regular users of mail advertising have carried out small sample experiments of this nature and assessed relative effectiveness of different copy from inquiries received; they have found that useful comparisons are possible. The 'samples' for such experiments must be chosen according to the basic rules of sampling. There are also certain operating considerations which need attention, such as the need to conform to postal regulations.

Setting the advertising budget

Against this background, the advertiser is forced to decide how much to spend on the budget for media advertising. Methods of making this decision vary from those which are easy to apply but difficult, perhaps impossible, to justify on logical grounds, to those founded on a sound theoretical basis but difficult, and sometimes impossible, to apply in practice because of the problem of making the necessary estimates.

In the first category are a number of rule-of-thumb formulae. These are:

1   Allocate a percentage of past sales.

2   Allocate a percentage of profit.
3   Allocate a percentage of expected sales.

The actual percentage chosen may be derived from past company practice or by examining what competitors are doing. The logical deficiencies of such approaches are easy to see. The sum calculated is an appropriation but not a budget in a managerial sense. It is not based on any consideration of the relationship between the amount of expenditure and the expected returns which will flow from that expenditure. The best arguments that can be advanced are that its regular use provides some relationship with past experience, and if the company has been intelligent in its approach to the market it may have approximated to a reasonable figure. If competitors' figures are looked to for a guide, it ensures that the company does not fall behind in its relative expenditure (although it is not always easy to obtain information about the relative advertising expenditure of competitors, and when it is obtained it is often not a comparable basis).

Any historic relationship between advertising expenditure and turnover, even if it were correct in the past, is not necessarily the right figure for the future. Changes in the rate of innovation in the industry leading to more new products can lead to a change in the need for advertising. If a company sets out to expand its sales by seeking greater market penetration, entering new markets, or developing new applications, then this will affect the role of advertising.

Faced with this difficulty, some companies seem to have given up any idea of a logical approach to the advertising budget, and the amount is determined by no clear method. Others have attempted to move towards a method which has the merit of logic—the task method.

In this method, the company works from the amount of advertising needed to the estimate of what the budget should be. That is to say, the logical flow of thought is as in Exhibit 13. In this way, the amount to be spent on advertising flows in a logical manner from the task of advertising in the total marketing programme. In developing the advertising budget by this method it is necessary to assess how frequently to insert advertisements and in what media or determine how many mail shots are necessary in order to achieve the advertising objectives.

Yet when it comes down to it, this difficulty cannot be avoided. The percentage share methods are ways of closing one's eyes to the problem. It seems far better to face the basic issues and, with an awareness of the limitations of what is being done, nevertheless use all possible skill and judgment in trying to arrive at an answer which is cap-

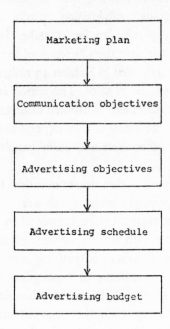

EXHIBIT 13 Setting the advertising budget

able of reasonable justifications. As advertising expenditure is commonly a small part of turnover in industrial markets, an honest and intelligent endeavour to apply the task method can result in a guesstimate which may be described as of the right order of magnitude.

When companies have been using some type of percentage method it is still possible to examine the question: 'How is the task for advertising next year changing and how is the budget requirement changing as a result?' It may appear to be more feasible to give an answer to this question than to derive a budget by the pure task method described in the last paragraph, and it avoids the need to present to the board a detailed forecast of the forthcoming year's expenditure. The board itself may find this reasoning which starts from an established level of expenditure easier to understand and accept. Finally of course the budget must be reasonably consistent with total company resources.

G

Assessing the effectiveness of advertising

At the back of all the discussion on advertising there remains yet one more hard to answer question: 'How beneficial is the advertising which has been put out?' This question has not been answered with complete satisfaction even in consumer advertising, where appropriations running into millions of pounds can be at stake. Indeed, researchers have often preferred to measure the efficiency of the communication by criteria such as those indicated in Exhibit 13 rather than attempt to judge the effect on the volume of sales. The reason is that, even if specific results can perhaps be reasonably attributed to advertising in mass consumer markets, in industrial markets they depend not only on advertising, but also on many other communication variables as well.

There is much to be said for the view that communication results are the appropriate measure. Exceptionally where goods are sold entirely by advertising, the results can reasonably be examined by comparing cost of advertising expenditure with volume of sales generated. This however is uncommon. In most instances advertising is one part of the job. It may be most valuable to maintain a warm goodwill towards a product among purchasing officers, but if in fact the salesman fails to call on those particular officers, then the goodwill may be wasted. Advertising may have carried out its role well in the chain of persuasive communication, but sales may not have been consummated.

Where a principal function of the advertising is to generate sales leads, replies received may be a preliminary basis for assessment of results. It is necessary to take account of the value of replies, and the real test should be the sales generated by the leads received.

However, if there is a long gap between the date of the original inquiry and the placing of an order, as there is in many industries, then the assessment is long-delayed and less reliable. In these circumstances the salesman who follows up the inquiry is often asked to report on the quality of the lead. Is the inquirer a genuine prospect? Is business likely to result in the short term? In the long term?

The need for a systematic procedure for following worthwhile enquiries relatively soon after they are received hardly needs stressing. An efficient system of recording and control is necessary to ensure that this in fact happens.

Ideally, advertising should have specific quantitative objectives which are capable of being measured by market research. For example, it might be decided that in order to generate a sufficient volume of demand for a building product the aim should be to make 75 per cent of the architects in Southern England and London aware of its special qualities. Prior to the campaign, a survey shows that only 10 per cent of them are aware of this information. After the preliminary campaign, (or at some convenient point in it) further market research is carried out to measure progress towards the target.

While this is the ideal, the cost of market research can sometimes seem disproportionate to the advertising expenditure. The choice then is either to carry out the market research anyway, for if the company does not have it (even at a comparatively high price) the marketing plan may be damaged by inefficient or misdirected advertising, or to use informal methods to assess how the advertising is going over. The latter can often give useful indications when the cost of research seems too high. Information is sometimes obtained through salesmen, provided it is made clear to them that it is the customer's view that is wanted, not the representative's own, and that what the company wants to know is whether the advertising message has got through and not whether the prospect thought it was a good advertisement. This can be backed up by information received at trade exhibitions, comments in the Press, and information from distributors. Even competitors' reactions may be illuminating.

In the United States, research on industrial advertising in a formal way is more common, though far from universal. One of the best-known services is the Starch service (by Daniel Starch and Staff) in which a sample of readers of some of the larger-circulation industrial journals are asked whether they have:

1   'Noted' the advertisement, i.e. remembered having seen it.
2   'Seen-associated'—whether they remembered seeing the advertisement *and* associated it with the advertiser (or brand).
3   'Read most', i.e. read more than 50 per cent of the advertisement.

In Britain some work is done by publishers sending out to subscribers copies of a recent issue of a journal, and asking them to indicate which advertisements they remember reading. This method is obviously much less satisfactory than the full personal interview approach. Even, however, with the most conscientious of methods the respondent may well have great difficulty in giving an accurate answer to a question like 'Did you read more than half this advertisement?'

The advertising agency

In view of the range of possible ways available for communicating to the market in industrial products, the advertising agency in this field must be prepared to take a correspondingly wide view of its function, and to offer a wide range of services to its clients. It has to plan a related sequence of messages blending both personal and impersonal communication. Thus it must work very closely with the client and be well briefed on his sales and service operations, as well as more customary information. It must ensure that the timing of the advertisements is appropriate and must be ready as a normal service to provide related material to assist in face-to-face selling and to brief the sales force on the many marketing communication tools which are in use.

Traditionally, the advertising agency has lived from commission received from the media. Agencies evolved from the function of agents who sold advertising space for newspapers on a commission basis. Gradually, they found that the best way of selling space was by helping the buyer of the space to decide what to put in it! Nevertheless, agencies still substantially retain the system by which the remuneration comes from the medium-owners as commission, and not from the client who is their true employer and to whom the agencies' loyalty should be directed.

The commission system is subject to some criticism in relation to consumer advertising and it seems to create difficulties in industrial markets. The advertiser may require help mainly with items which do not involve booking space in media, and the biggest item in the communications budget may be exhibitions or direct advertising. The percentage received from the media on space booked in a small firm's industrial advertising campaign may be very low in relation to the effort the agency may have put into it. Commission in industrial advertising has sometimes been modified by using one of two other methods:

1 Agreeing a service fee for the work to be done.
2 Guaranteeing the agency a certain level of payment. If this is not achieved through commission, then the balance is made up by the advertiser.

Making the most of advertising

When a campaign is carried out, its benefit can often be enhanced through other channels. Its value should be brought home to the sales force, and material in the campaign can often be adapted for use by the salesman in making a presentation to a customer. Distributors also should be kept fully briefed and supplied with copies of advertisements. Reprints can be used as mail shots. Publishers usually provide reprints on reasonable terms, providing inquiry is made in advance of publication. Publishers and advertisers have a common interest in working together in this way.

14 PRINT, PROMOTION AND PRESS RELATIONS

This chapter brings together a range of communication methods which are of considerable importance in marketing industrial products, and have not been covered earlier. Some of them are complex in the range of alternatives which they offer and the purposes they can serve. If the executive is looking at his whole communication problem, he will probably readily identify his need for print, although there is room for imagination and ingenuity in deciding in detail what form it shall take. With promotion and public relations, it is often more difficult to decide what exactly their role shall be, and to assess their effectiveness.

The forms of print

This term is used for all the literature produced by, or specifically for, a company, thus distinguishing it from advertising in media owned by third parties, such as the trade and technical Press.

This material may be sent to BPIs by mail, but much goes through other channels: it is a tool of the salesman in making a presentation, is distributed at exhibitions, and will be passed on by distributors and agents. The term 'direct advertising' is sometimes used to cover this entire field.

Literature is essential in most industrial marketing situations, yet it has not been much discussed by writers on marketing, perhaps because until recently most of them have been more concerned with consumer markets. Frequently a marketing man who has clearly understood what he is trying to achieve in terms of the communication grid described earlier will have little difficulty in deciding what literature is necessary. 'When you have your task defined, print needs fall into place', said one specialist in this field.

The process of analysis by which this point is reached must be painstaking, for it requires considerable attention to detail. Lack of the right literature at the right time can mean a sale missed, and, since good literature does much of its work when the salesman is not around, his firm may not know until it is too late and perhaps not even then. The literature must thus be suited to its purposes and well designed. Its quality must be influenced by the standing of the company which issues it and the status of the proposed recipient. Distribution also deserves thought at the very beginning to ensure that the literature is effectively used. The sight of quantities of obsolescent material being thrown away is only too common.

The range of possibilities is extensive. With display advertising, the advertiser is constrained by the need to fit the requirements of the medium, but with print he is creating his own medium and the only constraints are those of effectiveness and cost. This, of course, makes classification difficult. The following breakdown is convenient, but much of the material has more than one function.

Persuasive   Material under this heading serves the prime purpose of directly creating favourable attitudes towards the company and what it has to offer. It includes such items as personalised letters, printed and illustrated letters, leaflets, folders, booklets and business reply cards.

Informative   This includes reference material such as catalogues, price lists, spare-parts lists and wall charts, technical and other aids to using and maintaining the product, and a wide range of other material including external house journals, letters and posters.

Reminders   Calendars, blotters, notebooks and diaries are intended to serve the primary purpose of keeping the supplier's name and business in mind, and perhaps to remind of address and 'phone number. Again they must be apt to the proposed user.

Utilitarian   This includes labels, letterheads, envelopes and business cards and similar material. Even these items contribute to the 'image' of the company.

Where there are a very large number of people slightly involved in the buying decision, it is often desirable to have a small and informative leaflet which can be given away liberally. Such a leaflet will be inexpensive and not too technical, but it can still be well designed. It is an easy way of putting in the picture many people whose individual influence may be small but collective impact can matter. It ensures that discussion at all levels in the prospect company is better informed, and reduces the possibility that adverse eddies of opinion may develop. It seeks to leave a favourable impression of the supplier, his products, his service and his general reliability.

A leaflet of this type is by no means sufficient for the BPIs more closely concerned with the product purchase decision. Fuller literature is necessary. Commonly there is a need for two classes of document, sometimes more. The man who is concerned with commercial policy requires literature which puts over the story of the company which is supplying the product and shows how the decision will bring commercial gains. This document will stress broader advantages (such as cost saving, extra sales, better employee relations, and Government investment grants) which will accrue from a proposed purchase and will provide factual evidence and accounting or statistical calculation. It may also emphasise the commercial reliability of the supplier, if this may not be well appreciated by the customer.

The technical man will benefit from a different class of literature, explaining how the product works, its technical characteristics and applications, helping him to satisfy himself that it is fit for his purpose. These documents have a workman-like air. Drawings and diagrams could be of the 'blueprint' type probing the inner workings of the product and giving details of laboratory and field tests. It should aim to help the technician decide on the product and select a model which will suit his purpose. This class includes individual data sheets.

It is likely to be an advantage to produce different literature for different industries. In some instances suppliers have found it economical and efficient to produce a brochure solely for executives of one major company which represent substantial potential business, showing how a basic material could be used in the prospect's own products. The quality of the literature (paper, size, style, design) must be appropriate. The actual writing is often difficult since it may need to communicate technical material in layman's language, and the technical specialist may need to cooperate with the skilled writer.

The job of this class of literature is to aid the salesman and to be a silent salesman when he is not around. The target decision-maker can browse over it at his leisure, he can talk about it with colleagues and the literature can penetrate through to people whom the salesman has never met. Often the buyer or the works manager has made a favourable decision, but then has to recommend that decision to a committee or superior for approval. The literature gives him the tools to back his case. It strengthens the salesman's approach and helps reduce the time required to achieve a sale.

Reference material

'Reference material' is a convenient expression for that literature which the buyer and others in his organisation keep for consultation when a need for a purchase is identified within the company. The executive's files and shelves are an extension of his own memory, and up-to-date material in a form which is easy to locate adds memorability to the products.

Commonly used items include the catalogue (or its equivalent), price lists, spares lists and data sheets. These are designed to be efficient tools.

For many products, the catalogue is extremely important and companies are taking great care to make them simple and speedy to use. This involves improving the clarity of type and headings, good indexing at the front and other facilities such as thumb indexing and colour-coding page edges. Some companies are experimenting with unorthodox methods of locating entries, for example by recording details on edge-punched cards for quick and easy tracing. Focusing more on benefits in the accompanying text may be justified.

Technical and instructional handbooks must be provided when the nature of the product requires it. These may describe installation, operation and repair and maintenance. They may need to be durable enough to stand constant use, perhaps in the works under arduous conditions. In some departments, the collection of shelves of technical literature seems to become a sort of status symbol with some executives. To these may be added training material for customers' production, maintenance and sales staff.

The size of any document which is to be filed and kept for a period of time or included in a folder to be sent to a client or senior executive must conform to the practice of the industry concerned. In some industries specialist agencies now offer to provide buying firms with a filing system containing the literature of suppliers and to keep this up to date on payment of a rental. The supplier of the literature is also charged a fee for inclusion in these records.

The house journal is often used to advantage. The range of possibilities is very wide, depending upon the purpose which the journal is designed to achieve and the audience which it is to serve. Leaving aside the internal house journal of staff news—irrelevant for this purpose—one finds prestige-type journals (of which the reviews of major banks are an example) which have no immediate selling purpose but maintain the standing of the organisation concerned. Others are addressed to maintenance men and have a content of lighter material plus a core of useful advice. Journals may be addressed to technologists, and the content suitably matched to the readership. Again, the aim is to provide a useful and respected publication with only indirect promotion of the company, and that primarily through items with interest value. The major part of the material may be about scientific and technological developments. The costs of such journals show great variation.

The value of calendars and diaries is difficult to assess. No one seems really to know exactly what benefit they achieve, or even if they are retained by the original addressees or passed on either to junior staff members or the addressee's family. In theory, they keep the supplier's name in front of the recipient, but a man who receives three or four diaries rarely uses more than one. Including reference material of particular interest to him which is not conveniently accessible elsewhere may encourage the addressee to retain a diary. Calendars present a similar challenge.

Aspects of promotion

The word 'promotion' is widely used and seems to have a variety of meanings. The term is used here to cover any method of putting over a message which goes beyond the use of media and personal representation and backs them up with an attention-drawing 'boost'.

The most common method under this heading is the exhibition, which can be a major trade exhibition or a special exhibition organised by the supplier himself or on his behalf. Personal observation is one of the ways in which people obtain information, and the exhibition provides a suitable opportunity to see products and sometimes to see them in action. BPIs who the salesman would not normally meet may visit the stand, and the number of useful contacts in one day may be high. This is a great advantage in some markets.

The trade exhibition is, however, often a source of much heart-searching. It can be the biggest item in the industrial communication budget (apart from personal representation).

Some companies are carrying out research to assess the value of attendance at an exhibition, but the results do not yet seem to help settle the issue. Sometimes it appears that the majority of 'new' contacts at the exhibition represent unimportant executives in present customer firms, or casually interested inquirers representing little, if anything, in the way of business. Other inquirers may already be known to the company's sales force. Some companies report receiving a useful volume of business at the exhibition, but are uncertain whether or not most of this would in any case have been picked up when the salesman next called. More attention is being directed at determining the type and number of visitors to the exhibition and noting the stands which they visited. Companies putting on exhibits keep as full a check as is possible of callers at their stand, and the possibility of ABC audits of attendance is envisaged.

A major influence in deciding whether or not to attend is concern about what competitors may be doing. The fear is that if the company does not attend and the competitor does, then this gives the competitor a chance to cultivate the company's present customers, and perhaps gain the orders which are now due or at least establish a bridgehead for the future. The result is that attendance seems sometimes to be contagious—on one occasion all the companies making a certain product attend, the next none of them!

Certainly, companies appear keen to find out whether competitors propose to be at particular exhibitions. Overseas exhibitions are not quite the same, and a well-attended exhibition overseas may provide a good entry into an export market.

Once a decision has been made to attend an exhibition, then it is necessary to extract every ounce of benefit from the heavy cost involved. Planning must start well in advance. The stand itself must attract, and much thought and cost is given to this. Customers and potential customers must be invited and often entertained as well, although exhibitors try to keep entertainment costs in proportion. The public relations staff must see that the Press is kept well informed and well catered for by information, photographs, samples and other relevant material. The stand must be well staffed, properly supplied with literature and care taken to ensure that serious inquirers are given all possible assistance, and that proper follow-up by the sales staff takes place afterwards.

Some companies avoid the national trade exhibitions and stage their own exhibitions, perhaps on coincident dates to catch the same audience. Their products do not then have to compete with those of competitors. It is, however, necessary to generate an audience for the show, since it cannot rely upon the audience which is automatically generated by the trade show. This means that customers must be circulated by mail and the exhibition also advertised in trade journals. In some way, prospects not on the company's mailing list but who might attend the national show must be reached.

Another alternative for the smaller-size product is a travelling exhibition—perhaps in a specially built caravan or in a room rented in each locality, or a distributor's showroom. This permits a wider range of customers' staff to attend and will also attract people from smaller companies and institutions who may not travel to a national exhibition.

Rather similar is a procedure by which executives of prospect companies are invited to attend 'open days' at suppliers' works. This is particularly suitable when the product is such that the chance to see it operating may make all the difference in securing business. These occasions can be given a very high status, and directors or other very senior executives may well be interested in coming. Such an audience is given VIP treatment and may be brought by special plane or other special transport to heighten the intensity of the occasion. To have a 'captive' audience at this level is often of great value for capital equipment. Even though the cost per guest appears high, it can pay off. All the details need careful planning, and again the contact must be followed up in order that other levels of influence in the customer's company also receive the necessary attention. Selection of the right audience to attend is vital or the outlay can be wasted.

Sometimes it is possible to go one step further, and stage a visit by prospective buyers to a previous customer's works to see a product actually in use. Naturally, the customer will be concerned at guarding what he considers to be his trade secrets from people who may be competitors, and this can sometimes be a complete bar to this approach. Some companies have found that with suitable precautions this type of promotion has been possible and successful. Ingenuity can find other variations on this theme. One company held an 'at home' on the product—the product in this instance being a ship! Such occasions as these are of interest to the trade and perhaps also to the general business Press.

Film The use of film and video-tape is becoming more common recently and has advantages under appropriate circumstances. For moving machinery, construction plant, surgical instruments and similar products the film can show both process and product in an easily understood and effective manner. The cost of making films can however be quite heavy and the time span of planning may be up to a year, although in emergencies production can be quicker. The impact of this visual and aural medium can however be extremely strong.

Right at the beginning it is necessary, as with every media, to be clear on to whom the film is to be shown, the circumstances under which the showing can be achieved and the actual problem of finding or designing appropriate circumstances. Film can be used as an aid by persons outside the marketing company and can be circulated world-wide at moderate extra expense once production costs have been covered. It may be used by the salesman in a desk-top projector or shown in a large hall, and ideally the planning of a film should be linked to the specific circumstance. Other possible uses may be within companies to executives attending training programmes, by distributors to clients, or as a supplement on the exhibition stand.

When film is to be used in different countries a language problem arises. Some companies have tried to meet this problem by reducing the amount of headings visually displayed in the film and offering copies with the commentaries in appropriate languages. This is a possible way out although it presents its own problems.

PR and marketing

At this point it is convenient to recognise that the border is being crossed into the field of public relations. The subject of public relations is outside the scope of this book, and those who wish to explore it in detail should go to more specialised texts. It has, however, much of value to offer in industrial marketing and the marketing executive is interested in its effective use. The best definition is perhaps that by the Institute of Public Relations [50], which describes public relations as 'the state of mutual understanding between an organisation or individual and any groups of persons or organisations, and the extent and quality of the reputation which results.' The practice of public relations is seen by the Institute as having the primary object of assisting an 'organisation or individual to deserve, acquire and retain a good reputation' with customers, shareholders, employees, Government and the electorate. The definition identifies public relations in terms of its objective and not in terms of a particular method. It includes the projection of the corporate image of the company, and thus numbers corporate advertising, Press relations, films, exhibitions and seminars among its techniques.

In fact the chief role of the public relations adviser today may well be to act as guardian of the image of the company. The fact is that every company has an image—that is to say, a way in which the public sees it; indeed, it probably has several images which vary among its several publics. Whether these images truly reflect reality is another matter entirely, and it is this which is the concern of public relations. The image is of importance in marketing as the background against which sales are made and its effect on the authority and credence which are given to the company's sales force, literature and other promotions.

There is also sometimes a more specific contribution to be made in transmitting particular messages to particular audiences—drawing the attention of its customers to what the company has to offer through its products and services.

The hallmark of the public relations approach is indirect communication. Press relations is a case in point. One of the prime functions of many public relations men is ensuring that editors are kept informed of newsworthy matters affecting their client. The decision to publish or not to publish belongs to the editor. The final responsibility is his. The public relations adviser must, therefore, be well acquainted with the different publications and be able to advise what their editors will consider the right material for their particular readers at different times.

The appropriate trade and technical press will often be pleased to receive worthwhile information on many aspects of the company's business. The task is both to identify what is relevant and to bring it to the attention of the editor concerned by press release or any other appropriate way. New products are, almost by definition, newsworthy but so may be major contracts, the completion of large orders (particularly exports), advances in research, works and other visits by distinguished people and a range of other happenings. The experienced PR man will often see a news angle which escapes the non-specialist, and be able to identify what is likely to interest a particular relevant journal. Even for a small company, press relations will at times extend beyond the trade and technical press to the business and other national press and even to television.

To operate effectively appropriate journals read by the BPIs concerned must be identified. These should be provided with a reasonable, but not excessive, supply of material. There are some items which can be sent by press release to all journals as current news, but at the other extreme, special articles can with advantage be exclusive to one journal. Suitable articles may be under the name of a top executive—commercial or technical as befits the audience.

Public relations contribution to marketing may not end there. A company can help make itself recognised as a leader in a particular field if a senior executive writes a book which can be accepted as authoritative, thus establishing its name in that specialisation. Executives can address conferences, professional bodies or universities, and thus widen general knowledge of the area in which the company operates. An executive who is to do this can generally benefit by training in public speaking.

Seminars can gain understanding of a company's contribution to technological advance. These appeal to technicians, designers, R&D executives and others with a professional and scientific approach to their work. The seminar, usually of one but sometimes two days, consists of lectures, discussions and other material of professional interest to the audience. It must provide value in terms of ideas, and is not a selling situation. Speakers can be drawn from a variety of backgrounds: universities, scientific bodies, Government and even perhaps from competitors' staff, as well as from one's own company. The object is to draw attention to a field of interest which the company is developing and to put over the fact that the company is a progressive contributor to advance in this field. The implication is that the audience should listen to its technical representatives when they call, should read its literature and keep a sharp eye on its new products. But the seminar itself must be honest and may well be put on by a neutral body—a university, research institution or professional organisation. The basic objective is to explain technical advances in the company's field and to associate the company's name with them, perhaps even to produce a favourable predisposition towards that company.

The basic principles

The key thought in this chapter is that all these tools of communication are, so far as marketing is concerned, given point and coherence by approaching them from analysis of the buying process, content and structure, and deducing the information which is needed to gain acceptance of the merits of the supplier company and what is has to offer. This must then be followed through to make sure not only that the customer firm buys the product, but that it does in fact receive the expected benefits. Given clarity about this concept, and the necessary understanding about the customer—including perhaps his manufacturing techniques, staff organisation, market, R&D organisation, and many other details—the executive will then develop clear objectives (what is to be said to whom through what channels to what purpose) and devise planned ways of putting over the necessary messages. Even the apparently simple process of entertaining the customer's Managing Director to lunch requires more thought than is often given to it.

Summary

Whatever the media used there are certain guidelines which are common throughout. First the objectives are to be defined, that is to say what is to be said, to whom, through what channels, to what purpose. Secondly, these proposals are methods in developing a mix of communication tools planned and balanced in relation to each other. Thirdly, the total cost can be examined to see whether the expenditure seems to be appropriate in relation to the defined communication objectives.

15 PRICING IN PRACTICE

Before becoming involved in the detailed specified prices, it is necessary to decide the company's total marketing strategy for the product and the role of pricing in that strategy. If this is not done, the short-term decisions on pricing may not fit the company's long-term strategy. Rarely is the object of pricing simply to maximise short-term profits.

Examples of policy objectives in pricing are as follows (some of these will be discussed in more detail later in this and the following chapter):

1   To penetrate and pre-empt the market for a new product by charging a low price.
2   To cream the market for a new product and to obtain early profits and liquidity by charging a high price.
3   To assist in phasing out an obsolescent product by making it unattractively expensive.
4   To discourage competitors from entering the market.
5   To avoid customer and political criticism.
6   To support a company image.
7   To encourage market expansion by a low-price/high-volume policy.
8   To avoid competitive action which could lead to price warfare.

Such guidelines as these aim to be consistent with the way in which the company plans to develop long-run profitability and give a necessary background to specific price decisions.

The arithmetic of short-term pricing

It will be assumed initially that the problem is to set one basic price for the product which is to be the general level. The problems of differentials between different customers and different market segments is deferred. List prices may sometimes differ from this underlying basic price, where it is the custom of the trade concerned to allow discounts to customers. The arithmetic of pricing uses data from the company's past history and from marketing research together with personal judgment. In general the initial aim is to determine that price which will give maximum short-term contribution, and subsequently modify by additional considerations to the one deemed most appropriate to the fulfilment of the longer-term objectives.

In some form or other, the calculations bring together the following variables:

1 The prices which different customers are prepared to pay for the product (price/quantity relationship).
2 The terms on which competitors are likely to sell, taking account of their possible reaction to the price which will be determined in the present calculations [this obviously reacts on (1) above].
3 The costs of producing and marketing the product, including some estimates of competitors' costs and perhaps also customers' costs should they consider making (rather than buying) the product.

The influence of each element will first be discussed separately and then the possible procedures by which these can be harmonised in a price will be considered.

Price/demand relationship

The relationship between the price of a product and the quantity which customers will wish to buy is discussed widely in the writings of economists. Much of their analysis is built around the idea that this relationship can be characterised by a functional relationship, this is to say by a demand curve which illustrates how price and market demand interact.

In general the hypothesis is that a higher price for a product means less is sold, and conversely a lower price means more is sold. This statement is hedged with reservations. 'Other things being equal' is an important qualification. The volume of demand depends not only on price: it depends on the other aspects of the firm's marketing mix, it depends on the behaviour of competitors, changes in customer requirements, the state of the economy, and the value of money, to name a few factors.

The demand curve is a very attractive concept, but in practice the shape of the curve for a specific product is not known although interesting attempts to define such curves approximately have been made by some researchers.

It is sometimes possible to make judgment in broad terms about the sensitivity of demand to a proposed price change. Indeed, the executive has no alternative but to attempt this. Sensitivity in this context is commonly referred to as 'elasticity' of demand by economists. A product for which a price change of 1 per cent leads to a demand change (in the opposite direction of course) of more than 1 per cent is described as having relatively elastic demand; on the other hand if the demand change is *less* than 1 per cent the product is described as having a relatively inelastic demand. In between is unit elasticity.

Factors influencing elasticity

In industrial markets, demand for a class of products reacts to price change for a number of reasons:

1 If the change is substantial, intermediate manufacturers may pass the cost increase or reduction on to final consumers who may therefore reduce or increase (according to the direction of the price shift) their purchases. If the industrial product concerned was important in the intermediate manufacturer's cost structure and consumer demand relatively elastic the demand for the industrial product could be affected.

Most individual components or raw materials are a small part of the cost structure of the consumer product ultimately manufactured from them, and the cost effect on the price which the ultimate consumer pays for the end-product is proportionately generally quite small. A situation in which the effect is significant *and* consumer demand is elastic is uncommon, and for this reason industrial products mainly face inelastic demand.

2 A more substantial reason for sensitivity of demand to price in the industrial market is that the product concerned my compete with alternative products in many applications. A change in the price of copper may alter its competitive position in relation to other metals or alternative materials in particular applications. With capital equipment, price changes may affect the rate of return which can be expected on the investment involved. The gradual fall in the real price of computers has undoubtedly helped to widen their use.

3 Market reaction to a price change may take some time to show itself. A manufacturer is unlikely to undertake the re-design and re-organisation to replace (say) copper by aluminium, unless there is some evidence that an alteration in their relative prices has some durability. Even if a price alteration does lead to a change this may take some time to show its impact on demand. Previous equipment may have to be written off, existing contracts terminated, experimental work and assessment carried out to make sure that there is real benefit from change. Once the shift has gone through, a prolonged reversal of the new price relativity may be necessary before buying companies revert to their earlier buying pattern. Long-term elasticity may therefore differ from short-term elasticity.

4 When the product is one which some customers can make for themselves, a price change may react on their 'make or buy' policies.

It is worth noting that volume of demand for a product may change in response to a price change of an *alternative* product. This price change affecting the relative economics of *both* products; making one less economic and the other more economic. Thus in the example cited at (3) above a change in the price of copper reacts on the demand for aluminium.

However in industrial markets demand does not always fall when prices rise and vice-versa—at least not immediately. Sometimes when there is a change in price after a period of relative stability, buyers may conclude that the change is the beginning of a trend which will for a while persist. They may adjust their purchasing policies to the new 'trend': buying ahead on a price rise and reducing purchases on a fall.

Competition

In normal times most companies are cautious about deciding to change prices. This is partly because of the sheer mechanics of printing and amending price-lists, partly because of the fear that if the company seems to be uncertain in its pricing, then representatives will often find themselves faced with demands for price cuts. It is thus desirable that, in making a decision on price, the long-term implications should be considered, including the nature and magnitude of competitors' reactions.

The concept of competition is a very wide one. Exhibit 14 shows three half-circles. In the centre is competition from other products which are virtually identical. A firm which manufactures paint finds itself in competition with all the other manufacturers of paint, the oil company competes with all the other oil suppliers, and different makers of wire rope are in search of the same customers. As the circle widens, competition is with alternative products offering to satisfy the same need in related ways—paint against other protective coatings, oil against natural gas, wire rope against chain. Wider still, the competition may offer a rival product which is fundamentally different but provides the same ultimate benefit. Paint competes with products not requiring protection, energy with products which conserve energy or increase the efficiency of its utilisation (such as insulating materials) and wire rope for lifting purposes finds itself in competition with fork-lift trucks and conveyor systems which obviate or reduce the need for lifting within the plant. In the illustration, it is generally true that the further the competition is away from the central point of homogeneity, the longer term is the nature of the competition and the more important are the longer-run aspects of the strategy. Competitors include potential competition, such as the possibility that customers may themselves manufacture the product.

As described in Chapter 2, competitive situations are classically divided between perfect and various forms of imperfect competition. The notion of perfect competition is the rare situation at the very centre of the circle, with product undifferentiated. Real competition departs then from perfection largely by increasing the emphasis on competition through perceived product/service differences and reducing the emphasis on price.

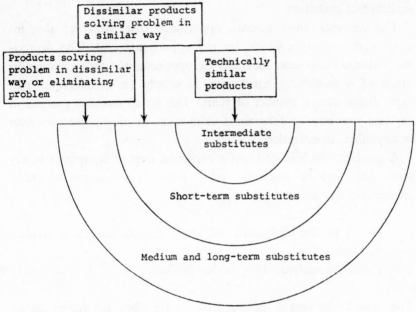

EXHIBIT 14   Circles of competition

Opportunity cost

The word 'cost' has a deceiving air of simplicity. The range of meanings which may be attached to it is very wide, and one of the most difficult problems is to define which concept of cost is relevant in a specific situation. The idea of opportunity cost is basic and fundamental. It is not a difficult concept to understand (although it can be quite tricky to apply), and every executive should be at home with the term.

Because the plant, staff and other resources of a company are limited, it follows that if they are used in one way, they cannot be used in another. Machine time and labour used for making one product cannot be used for making another; a representative calling on one customer cannot at the same time be calling on another. Thus the essence of the cost of doing one thing is that the opportunity to do something else is sacrificed and with it any associated financial contribution. The normal books of account of a company show the outlays of that company and spread them between products and periods of time; they do not show how much profit would have been made if a different 'mix' of products had been made or if the salesman had called on different customers.

The accounts cannot measure opportunity cost. Moreover, they include certain charges which are not opportunity cost. The depreciation charge in no sense measures the oppportunities for an alternative usage of a machine. Depreciation is simply an allocation of past expenditure over a number of years. The actual amounts charged in any one year may be determined more by accounting procedures than by any other consideration.

A product which is made on a particular item of equipment represents one way of obtaining value from that investment. Other alternatives are, for example:

1   To sell off the equipment and invest the net receipts in another direction
2   To use the equipment for another product.

The opportunity cost is measured by the next best net return among those alternatives which are rejected. The word 'net' implies that whichever course of action is adopted, there will generally be some income which will be received and some costs which will be incurred, and it is the difference between the two (the net return) which is relevant. For alternative (1) above, the opportunity cost is measured by the income on the reinvested funds; for (2) it is the revenue from the product less the direct costs of producing and selling the product.

The 'opportunity cost' concept implies that the manager should examine the alternatives open to him. Past outlays are not relevant to future decisions and at the date of the decision he must compare the expected returns from the various policies open to him. This guides him to the use of his resources in a way which produces the best return. Ideally all decisions should be examined in opportunity terms.

Incremental cost

Incremental cost is the answer to the question 'What costs will I incur if I decide to produce this product (or make this call or carry out any other operation) and avoid if I do not?' The incremental cost is the actual net total cost change flowing from the decision. A cost which does not change is not incremental. Usually there will also be incremental revenue to be brought into calculation. To make the point clearer, assume that the costs of an imaginary product, as conventionally estimated, consist of the following:

1   Direct materials and wages.
2   Depreciation of plant.
3   Administration, selling and other overheads.

If production is terminated it may be that the costs of direct materials and some direct operatives' wages can be avoided and are therefore incremental (if they cannot be avoided and are thus not affected by this decision, then they are not incremental). Depreciation is not an incremental cost; the plant is already bought. Overhead costs do not vary for a small change of total output, and thus involve no incremental element. The tendency is for more costs to become fixed in the short term: it is currently rarely possible to vary the direct wage bill beyond certain limits.

If a major *long-term* change is contemplated, then some of the fixed costs mentioned may become incremental. When the time comes for purchase of new equipment a different situation arises. At this time the cost of the proposed new equipment is incremental, and wages are more variable in the long run. The incremental concept also applies in relation to expected changes in revenue.

Similarly, if the cost of the call on a particular customer is under examination, the incremental concept applies. To omit one customer saves the extra travelling and out-of-pocket expenses involved, but the representative's basic salary and superannuation is not affected. If, however, the appointment of a further salesman to call on a new group of customers is contemplated all the extra costs associated with that salesman are at that stage incremental and should be evaluated against the extra return expected. Again, the accounting system does not directly provide this sort of information, but it has to be calculated to a reasonable degree of accuracy for a particular set of decisions. The word 'marginal' often applied to cost and revenue is approximately equivalent to a very small increment.

Overhead costs (mentioned above) are indirect, that is to say they cannot logically be identified with particular units of output. Any such allocation is therefore arbitrary. Direct costs are by definition traceable to particular items produced in some logical fashion and can therefore be appropriately identified with them.

Fixed and variable costs

This is a common distinction in costing for many purposes and if used with common sense a valuable one. The basis is that there are some costs which vary with the volume of output and others which are fixed (at least within a range).

Variable costs These are the costs which vary with the volume of output. Sometimes it is not an unreasonable simplification to regard the cost change as proportionate to the change in volume of output until production facilities, technological or organisational factors set a limit. On other occasions an assumption of a linear relationship between these costs and the volume of output is not appropriate, and more complicated relationships must be brought into the calculation.

Fixed costs do not change in total within a relevant range of output. Such costs may eventually change at a certain limiting level—perhaps when current machine or plant capacity is fully utilised. Whereas variable costs vary with output, fixed costs are more related to time as they depend largely on the productive capacity which management makes available in anticipation of demand within certain limits: the actual day-to-day changes in demand do not influence these costs except in a roundabout way through policy decisions. Following Barish [38] it is sometimes convenient to recognise a distinction between *pure-fixed* and *policy-fixed* costs. Pure-fixed costs 'continue to occur regardless of current managerial policy, regardless of how drastically volume may vary, regardless of whether any production takes place at all' and policy costs 'are fixed only in the sense that variations in volume or output of the existing complement of products will cause no change in these costs during the given budget or planning period in which the managerial policy has been fixed'. By these definitions the manager's salary is pure-fixed whereas the promotional outlay is policy-fixed. Some expenditure items may be a mixture of these two ingredients.

Some costs are semi-variable: primarily fixed but containing variable elements, so that as total company output expands there is some increase. By the technique of linear regression, the semi-variable costs can often be treated as though there were two parts, one part behaving as a fixed cost and the other as if it were variable. This enables the problem to be resolved for practical purposes.

More complex approaches allow for varied relationships between costs and output. The main difficulty is often not the statistical problem, but the problem of obtaining the necessary information analysed in the right way and of sufficient accuracy.

The 'full-cost' model

In practice, one of the oldest methods of determining price has been what is known as the 'full-cost approach'. In this approach direct costs are calculated, and percentage additions are made to this figure for overheads of various sorts and for profit. The percentages for overheads commonly represent the actual or expected average for the company. The calculations are something like the fictitious example shown in Table 5.

TABLE 5

Direct cost: Materials	£25 per ton of output
Labour	15
Total	40
Factory overhead (taken as 25% on direct cost)	10
Factory cost	50
Administrative and selling overhead (taken as 80% on factory cost)	40
Total cost	90
Profit (taken as 10% on total cost)	9
PRICE	£99

Variations of this approach are many, all basically requiring allocation of company overheads by a fixed rule, e.g. percentage of material cost, labour cost or total variable cost. This type of approach to pricing is very common, yet is the subject of criticism among economists and others.

The *first* criticism is that the final price in the example depends entirely on the direct cost content, and ignores customers' willingness to pay and the state of competition. What has really happened is that in the example the direct cost has been taken and increased by 147 per cent to arrive at the selling price. Whether the product is a new product with high risk but for which buyers may be expected to be willing to pay a high price, or a product in decline where the market is falling away, this procedure, applied literally, leads to a price of £99, irrespective of the demand. Yet the new product, with specialised qualities, may well earn £110 or £120 or even more. The ageing product may not sell at £99 but might sell well at £80, a price which well covers the incremental cost of £40 (assuming labour and materials to be variable costs) and makes a useful contribution towards overheads and profit. Contribution equals the difference between incremental revenue and incremental cost.

Overheads represent a large fixed element over a certain range of output, and if the ailing product provides a contribution, then there is that much less overhead to be recovered from other products and that much more available for profit.

The *second* criticism is that since the essence of an overhead cost is that it cannot be related to particular items of output, the device of allocating it in relation to the direct cost is completely arbitrary. The same argument applies to any arbitrary rule of this sort, for example allocating overheads according to volume of sales.

The *third* criticism is that however a fixed cost is allocated, its incidence per unit must depend on the number of units sold, which in turn may depend on the price. For example if actual total overheards are £216,000 and 180,000 units are sold, overheads per unit are £1.20, but if 200,000 units are sold without shifting total overheads significantly they become £1.08 per unit. Therefore, until the price is known, no forecast of sales can be made and no sensible unit cost assessed. The simple total cost formula (which implies that unit costs do not vary with the amount of throughput) thus has a built-in fallacy.

Those who make these criticisms argue that management should seek to obtain a substantial contribution to overheads and profits from those products where the market will support an appropriate price and accept a low contribution where the market will only pay a more modest one.

While the above contentions are not to be denied the arguments which see a planned full-cost approach as a handy rule-of-thumb should, however, be given their due:

1 The full-cost approach does keep before the executive the need to recover overheads and profits, an objective which has to be achieved overall if the company is to succeed.
2 It is watered down in practice: once the formula figure has been calculated, it may be possible to amend the formula price with a better understanding of the implication of such a variation. Such variations can be made either before the product is marketed or after some market reaction is received. In other words, this can be a trial price and can be adjusted by 'feedback' from the market.
3 If experience of competition and customer behaviour within the industry has shown that on average it is possible to achieve the target (including the various percentage additions), then this is some attempt at an opportunity cost, since it approximately indicates the return on alternatives. This point has not been strongly argued, but has something to commend it and might well apply to a standardised product.
4 Where there is a large number of products to be priced, and no one has any clear means to forecast market reaction to the price, this is a quick and inexpensive method of determining at least a first approximation, particularly suitable if variable costs are a large proportion of total cost.
5 The concept of a just price is still a very strong one, and there appears to be a feeling that a 'full cost' price will appeal to the Government, the buyer and the company's competitors as a reasonable and fair means of fixing a price. This is often important today.
6 In industries where customers might decide to make the product themselves (sometimes possible in industrial markets), 'full cost' indicates at what level that might occur.

These observations indicate that apparent full cost should not be dismissed out of hand, but should be used within fuller analysis.

The break-even model

A more practical approach to price determination comes about from the sensitive use of the classical break-even diagram. It has long been a useful tool in this field.

Exhibit 15 is a typical example. The product concerned has fixed costs amounting to £50,000 per annum, including such items as factory overheads, tooling-up, plant depreciation and other allocated overheads. Variable costs at the rate of £15 per ton produced are

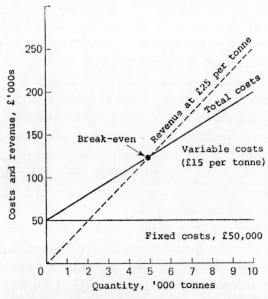

EXHIBIT 15 Traditional break-even analysis

shown in the upper section of the diagram. Semi-variables are not shown separately, and it is assumed that they have been separated into variable and fixed elements as already described. Sometimes a more detailed analysis of costs is used, but this does not affect the basic issues.

This approach asumes that variable costs per unit are the same whatever the level of output, and thus average costs will decrease throughout. Within a range, limited by present capacity, this is often a reasonable approximation.

Some adaptation is necessary if it is desired to relax this assumption. Suppose that after a certain volume of production is achieved it is necessary to add more equipment, then the fixed cost will take a 'step' up to a higher level, reflecting the cost of the addition. If employees have to work overtime to attain a certain volume of production, the variable costs per extra unit of output will increase more sharply and total costs will rise faster. Minor modifications in the diagram will allow for these variations.

If, for example, a net price of £25 per tonne is proposed for the product, it is possible to identify the break-even sales volume where costs and revenue are equal. Unlike the 'full cost' approach, the interrelationship between changes in fixed and variable costs, volume and prices can be examined.

The 'break-even' point can, of course, be calculated without reference to the diagram by a simple formula. First calculate the contribution per unit (tonne) of output: the difference between price and variable cost. In this example it equals £10 per tonne, £25 less £15. The break-even point is obtained by dividing fixed costs by the unit contribution; in the example £50,000 ÷ £10 shows that break-even is 5000 tonnes, as shown in Exhibit 15.

The break-even point depends on the size of the unit contribution in relation to fixed costs, and current thinking stresses the importance of the contribution in short-term pricing decisions. Subject to the overriding importance of company pricing and longer-term objectives. This calculation shows the volume of sales necessary to achieve a satisfactory profit after all costs (including allocated overheads) are covered. In looking at this approach remember the doubtful validity of allocating overheads as mentioned earlier in this chapter.

Improved break-even analysis

A sharper focus on contribution is obtained by modifying the traditional form of the break-even diagram so that variable costs are below and fixed costs above, as in Exhibit 16.

The illustrative figures used are the same as in Exhibit 15: variable costs are £15 per tonne, and fixed costs directly attributable to this product are £25,000. Management seeks a target contribution of £50,000 towards overheads and profits. In accordance with the argument advanced earlier, allocated overheads have *not* been included as a cost but management has set a target contribution to general overheads and profit. The total of all such contributions from all parts of the enterprise should cover all overheads and provide a satisfactory return if a firm is to continue as a self-sustaining system.

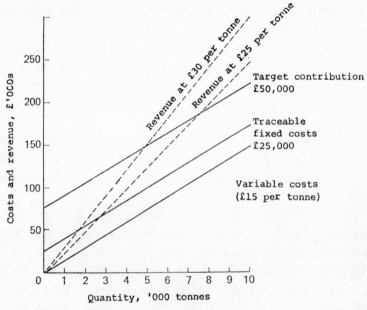

EXHIBIT 16   Modified break-even analysis

Consider first the line indicating total revenue/output relationship at a price of £25 per tonne. This naturally runs above the variable cost line of £15 per tonne. The vertical distance between these two lines is the sum available towards attributable fixed costs and as contribution to overheads and profits.

Prior to the point A_1 the product revenue covers variable costs and provides something towards fixed attributable costs: not until revenue reaches A_1 is the product contributing to general overheads. At A_2 the contribution reaches the target level set by management. A separate line indicates growth of revenue at £30 per tonne in relation to volume of sales. At B_1 in addition to covering variables revenue covers fixed attributable costs, and at B_2 target contribution will be achieved. These figures are summarised in Table 6.

The key question which at this stage remains unanswered is: 'What is the customer willing to pay?', or more precisely: 'What are different customers prepared to pay in relation to different applications?', plus the question: 'How will competitors react?'

TABLE 6 Sales volume to achieve goals at different prices

Objective	At £25 per tonne		At £30 per tonne	
	Revenue, £	Tonnes	Revenue, £	Tonnes
To cover attributable costs (£25,000)	62,500	2500	50,000	1667
To cover also target contribution (£75,000)	187,000	7500	150,000	5000

Contribution per tonne is £10 at a price of £25 per tonne and £15 at a price of £30 per tonne

It is, however, now possible to study questions on the lines: 'At a price of £25 per tonne, what is the amount we can expect to sell?', 'What is the least we are likely to sell?', and 'What is the most we are likely to sell?', and similarly for £30 (or any other price which the marketing manager considers worth examining).

These questions cannot be answered with complete certainty. Marketing and sales executives, with their knowledge of the prices of competitive products, their relative merits in different applications, and the existing ties between various buyers and sellers, can usually produce approximations. These can be explored on the diagram, or by elementary arithmetic, so that the planner knows the worst, the average and the best results which each price may produce. He then makes his decision with awareness of its implications both in terms of maximising contribution and reducing risk.

Contribution/volume ratio

Focus on contribution leads to consideration of the concept of contribution/volume (C/V) ratio. The C/V ratio indicates what proportion of each £1 of revenue is available as contribution, as illustrated in Table 7: it is obtained by dividing contribution per tonne by price per tonne.

H

TABLE 7   Contribution/volume ratio

	At £25 per tonne	At £30 per tonne
Price	£25	£30
Less Variable costs	15	15
Contribution	£10	£15
C/V ratio	0.40	0.50

The data is illustrated in Exhibit 17. Sales revenue is on the horizontal axis (note that this is revenue and not volume in tonnes), and contribution to general overheads and profit on the vertical axis.

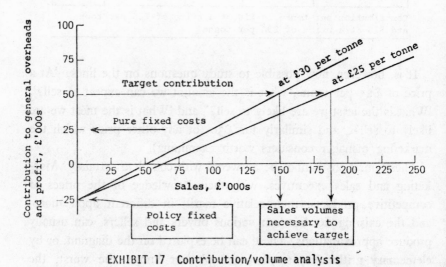

EXHIBIT 17   Contribution/volume analysis

Fixed attributable costs are measured negatively—below the horizontal line—as a first charge against the product's contribution before anything goes into the general pool. The two lines plotted across the graph show for the two different prices the total contribution generated by different sizes of revenue.

Not only does this approach focus on contribution, but it permits its relationship to fixed attributable costs to be considered, with consequent clearer thinking about them. It is also possible to set a target contribution level and identify easily what volume of sales is required at each price to achieve it. Setting this target is a management decision based on considerations of what is feasible in the market and what is desirable for the company. Again the implications of different amounts of policy-fixed expenditure may be examined.

The probability of reaching target contribution can be considered, as was done in the previous section. It also is possible to examine pricing policy for a range of related products by arriving at the average C/V ratio for the range and then carrying out the above analysis.

This approach highlights more clearly than others the interrelationship between prices, volume and fixed costs and how they affect the probability of achieving target contribution levels.

Finally, it must be emphasised that the stressing of the concept of contribution in this chapter does not diminish the marketing department's responsibility to develop annual and long-term plans which provide adequate return to cover all costs and generate profit overall.

16 SPECIAL ASPECTS OF PRICING

The previous chapter was concerned with the basic price, set in a framework of pricing objectives. General models of price determination were outlined. This approach now requires widening to build more subtlety into the analysis of pricing decisions. All the models were essentially static, yet it is an axiom of marketing that change occurs and that every effort must be made to anticipate and adapt to it. In addition, the company's problem is one of fixing a structure of prices for related products, which are often either partly competitive or partly complementary, and perhaps to set different prices for different markets.

The impact of inflation

At the time of writing double-digit inflation, i.e. a state of affairs in which prices are rising at the rate of more than 10 per cent per annum, exists in many major countries. The outcome of this is that prices quickly become out-of-date because of cost increases, calling for more frequent review than has been customary and rendering price schedules obsolete. In such circumstances Government may follow a policy of restricting price rise as part of its counter-inflation policy.

This creates special problems. Prices which take account of the historic cost of the product, i.e. the price at which materials and labour were purchased, may leave little if any, margin over replacement cost in severe inflation. Moreover increasing costs of purchased items may mean that more cash needs to be found to finance these purchases. If this cannot be recovered in current sales the company will be illiquid, seeking to borrow from the bank and other sources in very unfavourable circumstances.

Some implications are:

1　That costs must be regularly monitored to facilitate consideration of price adjustments when appropriate.

2　Credit policy, stock carrying and other aspects needing short-term financing should be reviewed.

3　Contract terms, tenders and the like should be so framed that the supplier is protected against cost increases during the period prior to fulfilment: obviously most customers would prefer a firm price, but this may be impossible.

4　Where prices are negotiated or fixed by Government and allowance for depreciation of plant and other assets is a material item in overhead costs the replacement cost should be considered as well as the historic.

5　Finally, inflation raises complex questions about the whole basis on which company profits should be assessed.

Pricing and the product life-cycle

The clearest and most effective account of the developments which take place over time is in the concept of the product life-cycle, which has been discussed in Chapter 7. Price performs a different role at different stages of the cycle, and the quality of pricing decisions can be improved by awareness of the life-cycle considerations.

When a new product is first launched, the marketing executive of an innovating company has a difficult pricing decision to make. Just how difficult it is will depend upon just how new the product is. If it is not greatly different from existing products, then the price of those products can provide a very valuable guide as to the price which is likely to be acceptable for the new product.

If the product is a more radical departure, then the problem becomes more difficult. Whatever task is to be performed by the new product is already being carried out by some other product, but in a way which is less satisfactory. Nevertheless, the costs and benefits of existing products can be compared with those of the new product. This cost comparison, together with a comparison of the benefits involved, should help to delineate a zone within which will be found the price which customers will be willing to pay.

Different market segments will, of course, differ in their reaction to price, and some assessment of these differences is required. The question 'What are the advantages of this product in different industries, for different customers and for different applications?' is often not too difficult to answer in general terms and provides a basis for judging the sensitivity of demand to price.

For the initial marketing of a product, there is usually a choice between two price policies:

1   A *skimming* (*or creaming*) *policy* which introduces a product to the market at a relatively high price, the price then being lowered progressively over the life of the product.
2   A *penetration policy*, the product being introduced at a relatively low price, which it is intended to maintain unchanged throughout much of its life.

For most industrial products, the first policy is the one commonly selected. It has a number of advantages which are very attractive in industrial marketing.

Generally, even after the most careful research, there is considerable uncertainty about the amount which customers will pay. The customers find it hard to assess what the product is worth to them, and test marketing as practised in consumer markets is hardly ever feasible.

The rate of market expansion may not depend primarily on price. Prospective customers require time to evaluate the product, train the operatives and perhaps install ancillary equipment. Thus initial demand is often small, whatever the price within wide limits. Under these circumstances, a low price offers no advantages in promoting market expansion. A higher price helps to meet the heavy initial first costs and generates the maximum short-term flow of cash. Thus the innovating company can exploit the period of monopoly which it has before competition enters the field. Initial targets are carefully selected segments where the product offers most benefits.

The skimming price can be gradually adjusted as market reactions to it are better understood. It largely avoids the danger of having to increase prices, and it is more effective for salesmen to meet buyers in circumstances of reducing, rather than of increasing, price. Moreover, the process of gradually reducing prices reflects the decline in unit costs which takes place in many products as experience and scale of production increases and probable competitive production builds up.

Penetration pricing has two major objectives: to expand the market for the new product rapidly and to deter competition. The ability to expand the market implies that it is appropriate where price elasticity is high and market expansion depends primarily on the price of the product and less upon other factors. Capacity must be available to meet this early expansion, and the case for penetration pricing is higher if the economics of the production process favour large plants and high-volume output.

The low price may act as a deterrent to competitors, although if the market is likely to be substantial and existing products made obsolete, competitors will almost certainly enter the market irrespective of price. The early penetration may, however, lead to a situation where the innovator can retain an important share of the market, either from brand loyalty and reputation or from the more efficient cultivation of the market and the close contact with decision-makers which can arise from the earlier penetration. If the product is one which competitors can easily and quickly produce, this rapid grasp of the market may well be an asset to be sought if a reasonable proportion of what is gained can be held. Conversely, if the product is protected for a while, a slowly reducing price permits each market segment to be developed in turn.

On the whole, penetration pricing is uncommon in industrial marketing, although there are a few occasions on which it has been used effectively.

In fact, it is not always an advantage to keep competition out. If the initial promotional work in expanding the market is heavy and expensive, then it may be a positive advantage for two or more firms to share the burden. Otherwise one firm may carry the cost of market development and others reap much of the benefit. For some items, customers may be reluctant to purchase the product unless there is more than one source of supply.

As the life-cycle progresses, market growth is normally assisted by product inprovement and adaptation, as well as by price reduction. The relative importance of each of these depends upon the pricing policy originally adopted.

At the same time as products tend to be improved, there is sometimes also a tendency towards standardisation. That is to say, as customers develop understanding, so there is more pressure to obtain common specifications of the products from different suppliers. Price then becomes a more important factor in the buying decision, and it becomes increasingly difficult to resist price concessions. It is sometimes possible in circumstances of price leadership to maintain prices, but a company which persists in trying to hold prices in the face of decline may expect to suffer loss of market share.

The choice then is either to move on to the next new product, or to exploit such tolerance as exists in the market. If elasticity of demand is high, the conscious lowering of price will expand sales and may improve the return on the product. If, however, elasticity is low or there are overriding longer-term considerations, then a company may prefer to price somewhat above the competitive level and aim to justify this by relying on additional service or reputation.

Market segmentation pricing

So far, discussion has assumed that at any one time one price is set for all possible customers. The demand curve can, however, be considered as representing a number of different buyers, some of whom are willing to pay more for the product than are others (see Exhibit 18). It may therefore be possible and profitable to charge several prices: a high price to those with the keenest demand, a medium price to those in the middle and so on down the scale. This policy may be crudely described as charging what the traffic will bear.

This is possible under certain circumstances only. Clearly, there must be no legal objections to this discrimination. In addition, buyers must not be expected to object or react so strongly that the suppliers concerned suffer loss of sales and profit.

Implementing this policy may have some problems. Circumstances must be such that if one customer is supplied with the product at the low price, he cannot resell to the high-price market segment. If, for example, customers in country X are charged a higher price than customers in country Y, then the difference should not be sufficient to facilitate customers in Y reselling to X. The margin between the two prices is limited by the amount of costs (such as transport) involved in transferring the product from Y to X. Services cannot be transferred, and some products can be differentiated so that the product sold to one customer is less suitable for the purposes of the other. Competition may limit the opportunities for market segmentation. A high-price market segment can be very attractive to existing or potential competitors.

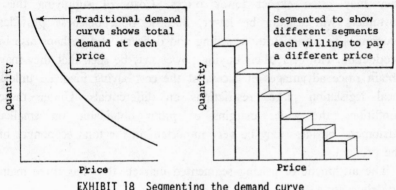

EXHIBIT 18 Segmenting the demand curve

Transport is an extreme example of price differentiation. The 'product' cannot be transferred and frequently direct costs are low and overhead costs high. Thus the objective is to follow the rule of maximising the contribution from each segment of the market separately.

This is illustrated by the international air-cargo rating system, described by Grumbridge [39], which is essentially as follows:

1   A basic rate between each pair of points per pound or per kilogram which will apply to any cargo. The tendency is for these rates to be less per mile over longer distances, because much of the cost of carrying cargo is in the handling at either end, which is constant irrespective of the distance.

2   A multitude of 'commodity rates' aimed at attracting particular flows of traffic which cannot bear the basic rate. . . .

3   Rebates for both (1) and (2) when the consignment reaches a certain size, e.g. 45 kg, because some terminal costs—documentation, accounting, etc.—are the same for all consignments. . . .

4   Minimum charges—usually set quite high—because of the heavy incidence of terminal handling and documentation costs. . . .

5   A 'volumetric' surcharge to ensure that very light but bulky cargoes pay for the space they take up in the aircraft.

6   A 'value' surcharge, so that exceptionally high-value cargo, such as gold, pays what it really can bear!

When one or two large customers dominate a market for a product, they may often expect lower prices. Costs of supplying these customers will usually be lower, because bulk business provides economies in administration, selling and delivery, and perhaps also in production. However, their buying power may be such that they may obtain price advantages in excess of the cost saving involved unless local legislation places restrictions on differentials. Under these conditions, the wider margins of profit obtainable on smaller customers' business may be very important in the total economics of the product.

The arithmetic of pricing segmented markets thus has three main guidelines for a short-term profit maximiser:

1   To charge each segment according to the sensitivity of demand to price in that segment. If demand is inelastic, the price will tend to be high (because the demand will be little greater if price is reduced); conversely, if it is elastic, the price will tend to be lower because this will expand the market. In assessing demand behaviour it is necessary to remember that demand for one supplier's product will also depend on the pricing policies of existing and potential alternative suppliers.

2   To ensure that the price to each segment makes a contribution over direct costs of the product, plus any special costs associated with that segment, e.g. special packaging costs, costs of representation, and so on.

3   To ensure that differentials are not sufficiently great to permit buyers in low-price segments to resell profitably to high-price segments (unless there are special reasons why this should be permitted).

These rules are, of course, subject to the overriding policy considerations already discussed.

Product-line pricing

The preceding section discusses price differentials related to the type of customer. This section deals with price differences between products of the same general character. In terms of demand, differences in the product line relate to products which are all expressions of the same essential concept, but differ from each other in respect of such tertiary factors as size, strength, versatility, presence or absence of supplementary features. To some extent they may be competitive, in that if the customer is buying, say, steel plate and has to choose between alternative specifications, if he chooses one grade then by the same decision he refuses another.

In a wider sense such products often support each other, for if a customer does not find a specification which matches his requirement with a sufficient degree of precision, then he may well not purchase from this supplier at all; he may buy from a rival supplier of steel plate or use another type of material.

Costs of a product line are to a degree interrelated. While each product has traceable direct costs, many overheads of administration, selling, research and development are not logically attributable to specific products but to many products jointly. Sometimes these joint cost exceed the direct costs.

Prices for the product line can be of the simple 'full cost' type described earlier. Each product has its direct cost estimated and customary additions are made for overheads and profit. The result is that prices are proportional to direct costs. A somewhat similar device is to make prices proportional to 'marginal costs', which in practice commonly means short-term variable cost.

The view taken in Chapter 16, however, was that the allocation of overheads cannot be other than arbitrary. The customer will not pay more for a product than he needs to pay, and some products cannot obtain from the market sufficient to cover the 'average' overheads for the producing company; others can receive more than this. On this principle it would be reasonable to charge what the product is worth to the buyer, and to regard those products which show insufficient contribution as candidates for withdrawal. This may, however, have to be modified to ensure price relationships between related products that buyers will regard as equitable.

Product-line pricing is, however, complicated by basic issues of complementarity and competitiveness between individual products. In some cases, the sale of one product may lead to sales of others: for example, sales of a copying machine may lead to sales of the copying medium. It may then be desirable to price the copying machine attractively and recover overheads and profit on the copying medium. Reasonable estimates should, however, be made to ensure that the overall return is satisfactory. It is necessary to make sure that the customer cannot obtain the copying medium elsewhere. Where the relationship between the sale of one product and the sale of another is less clear, it is probably wise to approach the idea that one product should subsidise the other with the utmost caution.

In consumer marketing, a range of products of different sizes are sold at the same price. This is true of some minor items like hosiery. The cost differences are small and a constant price makes selling easier. There are probably few close analogies to this in industrial marketing.

Marginal cost pricing

In some texts 'marginal costing' is used as an inclusive term for the entire concept of contribution pricing. Here it will be used in a more restricted sense to describe those circumstances in which limited quantities of the product are sold in one special segment of the market on terms which cover little more than the incremental costs associated with them. The objective is to utilize capacity which would otherwise be idle. For example, export orders are sometimes accepted on these terms. The phenomenon is most common in capital-intensive industries.

Marginal cost pricing has its place in pricing strategy as an example of the market segmentation approach already mentioned. Marginal costs are often equated with short-term variable costs, but this definition may in many practical circumstances be too narrow. For example, the marginal costs of exporting must include any special costs of clerical work, packing, insurance, freight and selling which would be avoided if the business concerned was not accepted. Sometimes, if the additional business is considerable, costs which are normally treated as fixed may vary, and these must be covered.

The danger with marginal-cost pricing is that if the volume increases, the company may find itself requiring extra capacity to meet the class of business concerned, and the returns may not be sufficient to justify the capital costs involved. It can then happen, unless management is alert, that new investment is undertaken, the cost of which cannot be recovered from the expected revenue. Marginal-cost pricing is a short-run approach to selling in minor market segments when existing capacity remains unexploited after more attractive markets are satisfied.

Tendering

Tendering raises difficult problems. In some types of industry much of the business comes as a result of tenders made to customers' specification.

Prior to the tendering stage, the shrewd supplier will have educated the specifying decision-maker in the qualities of his products so that the specification is framed in a manner consistent with his company's capabilities. He will also concentrate his attention on that part of the market where he is most likely to be successful. Preparing tenders can cost money, and sometimes a preliminary review of the situation will show that there is little or no chance of success. Under these circumstances, the expense of the tender is best saved. On other occasions, where tenders have been invited for standardised products and the specification has been somewhat different from usual standards, some suppliers have offered one of their standard products, superior to the specification. Their terms for this superior product have often been better than those of competitors who tendered only to specification and whose tenders were therefore based on the relatively high costs of a short special run.

Tendering is, in fact, a special form of segmented market; each customer is a separate segment and the competition varies from case to case. The tenderer has to assess the probability of achieving successful results at different prices.

Where a company is regularly tendering in a particular class of business and it is possible to obtain a reliable indication of the price at which contracts are placed, then this information can be used in a systematic way to give some guidance on future tenders by a simple application of probability.

The procedure consists of two main steps. First data is assembled in respect of past tenders (Table 8). This data consists of the *award prices* and the company's own estimate of the *cost* at which it could have undertaken each job. From these items of information the company estimated a price/cost ratio and builds a frequency distribution of the number of occasions at which contracts have been placed at the different price/cost ratio levels. An example is set out in Table 9. These figures are translated into percentages (in column 3), and the final column shows the number of occasions when the successful bid has been at or above the price/cost ratio shown in the left-hand column. This is used in the second part of the analysis as indicator of

TABLE 8 Analysis of past bids

Price/cost ratio	Number of occasions	Percentage of occasions	Cumulative percentage of occasions	Probability of lowest bid at or above this level
Less than 0.8	Nil	-	-	100
0.8	2	5	5	95
0.9	3	7.5	12.5	87.5
1.0	5	12.5	25	75
1.1	7	17.5	42.5	57.5
1.2	11	27.5	70	30
1.3	6	15	85	15
1.4	3	7.5	92.5	7.5
1.5	2	5	97.5	2.5
1.6	1	2.5	100	Nil
Over 1.6	Nil	-	-	-
TOTAL	40	100.0		

TABLE 9 Application of analysis to future bidding - example: cost of job £10,000, cost of bidding £100

Tender % of cost	Actual price	Profit if successful, £	Probability of success	Expected monetary value, £	Tender cost, £	Net EMV, £
0.75	7,500	-2,500	100	-2,500	-100	-2,600
0.85	8,500	-1,500	95	-1,425	-100	-1,525
0.95	9,500	- 500	87.5	- 437.5	-100	-537.5
1.05	10,500	+ 500	75	+ 375	-100	+117.5
1.15	11,500	+1,500	57.5	+ 862.5	-100	+762.5
1.25	12,500	+2,500	30	+ 750	-100	+650
1.35	13,500	+3,500	15	+ 525	-100	+425
1.45	14,500	+4,500	7.5	+ 337.5	-100	+237.5
1.55	15,500	+5,500	2.5	+ 137.5	-100	+ 37.5

the probability that bids at different prices (in relation to costs) would have been successful. In principle the larger the volume of information about a particular class of market the more reliable a guide this should be. However, it is necessary to be cautious about using data which is so far in the past that its relevance to current circumstances is doubtful.

If circumstances are such that this distribution seems at least an initial guide to what is likely to be a representative pattern, then at different tenders the probability of success can be deduced from the last column and the Expected Monetary Value (EMV) of the bid (profit $\times$ probability of success *minus* the cost of tender) calculated.

In the light of this analysis the company could consider its bid: if it sought to obtain the highest monetary value it would bid at £11,500. However if the company were short of business and no other contract was in the offing, it might bid at a lower level in order to increase the chance of success. The profit actually obtained on this bid if successful at this price is £1500 less tendering cost of £100 equalling £1400 net.

The analysis is only a guide: if it were known that at a particular time competitors were heavily committed or, on the other hand, were short of work, then it is legitimate to revise this pattern in the light of this knowledge and raise or lower probability estimates as the case may be.

There may also be circumstances in which the company bidding may see, for reasons of its own, advantages in success which are not covered in the normal cost calculations: for example the gaining of experience, obtaining its first contract with a potentially important customer, or an urgent need for business to fill a temporary shortage. In such cases the calculation in terms of expected monetary value can be modified to take account of these benefits ascertained.

17 CHANNELS OF DISTRIBUTION

Many manufacturers negotiate and sell direct to their industrial customers at least in the home market. There are however some circumstances in which intermediaries (brokers, agents and distributors) are employed.

Basic concepts

The intermediary is a link in the chain of negotiations by which the manufacturer-supplier is joined to the manufacturer-customer. For the present purpose the intermediary is deemed not to perform any significant manufacturing operation on the product but may provide ancillary services such as installation, maintenance and repair. Sometimes the relationship between an important supplier and an intermediate manufacturer may be analogous.

Relationship and coordination between successive members in a channel over a period of years may be the result of:

1 Deliberate and conscious action by some influential member(s) of the channel. For example, individual suppliers may adopt a positive policy to influence decisions of subsequent members, e.g. distributors, and thus harmonise their interests and promote effective linkage through to the user.

2 Pressures of economic and social factors on channel members so that they find it to their advantage to trade with or through each other: such factors can mould channels over a long period and sometimes the patterns they produce can persist through inertia after the reasons for which they arose have ceased to be relevant.

3   Action by bodies established by Government or international agencies.

The relative importance of (1), (2) and (3) vary from one circumstance to another. Where (1) is the significant feature channels can be described as 'guided' (since the supplier uses his financial and other influence to promote a certain type of behaviour but cannot insist on it). This chapter is primarily about guided channels.

Traditionally, many agricultural products and other raw materials have passed through natural channels. More recently Governments operating through marketing boards have become more active.

One writer (Revzan [40]) argues that in industrial marketing: 'Generally, the following factors will be of some help in understanding the high significance of direct channels:

1   The small number of potential users for certain types of industrial goods, requiring very close and continuous contact by the manufacturer of no potential or actual sales opportunities are to be overlooked.
2   A large average unit sale which requires long periods of time for completion of negotiations. [Visualise for example, the time periods involved in the sale of jet planes to airline companies, or complete, streamlined trains to the railroads. (*Footnote from the original source.*)]
3   Concentration of actual and potential customers in very compact geographic areas, thus permitting intensive use of a relatively small sales force.
4   The need for considerable technical advice and assistance in making the initial sales, and in the continuous post-sales servicing period.
5   The need for providing key executives on the selling side to match the organisational levels of the buyers.
6   The impact of reciprocity in making industrial goods sales.
7   The impact of the greater incidence of integration among industrial goods sellers and buyers.
8   The length of time required to introduce buyers either to new uses of existing products, or to revolutionary types of new products (such as electronic computers).

On the other hand, there are many factors which underlie the use of many types of merchant and/or agent middlemen in semi-direct and indirect channels:

1 The need for specialised knowledge of and contact with specific markets on a widely distributed geographical basis, thus involving a relatively large force of marketing representatives.
2 The inability of many manufacturers, because of financial and manpower reasons, to perform any or all of the marketing task for their product line.
3 The frequent need for guaranteeing products which originate from relatively unknown manufacturing sources.
4 The existence of a 'thin' market in the geographic and sales sense. In order to spread the costs of the channel under such conditions, the use of wholesale middlemen handling competing and/or non-competing lines of products may well be the only satisfactory solution.
5 The existence of a large, widespread market in which customers place frequent orders consisting of many items needing rapid delivery service.
6 The existence of well-known, standardised products requiring less technical and intensive sales arrangements.
7 The existence of large numbers of small buyers who frequently require financial assistance in making purchases.

While there are in different industries and countries many intermediaries with various titles, most of them can be fitted into the following classification (a more detailed classification is provided in Revzan's book):

Broker—whose relationship with his principal is the subject of what is legally a separate agreement on each occasion (although the same standard contract may be adopted). He sells on behalf of any principal, often on percentage commission, usually in a relatively passive role, taking what the market will offer.

Agent—who has a longer term relationship with, and sells on behalf of, a principal. The agent does not own the goods he sells, but is generally expected to take a more active role in seeking and serving customers.

Distributor—who buys from the supplier and then resells to user, intermediate manufacturer, or some other distributor.

The agent may carry lines for several manufacturers but often these are not in competition with each other. He is, in fact, a close substitute for the company's own salesman. He may hold stock on consignment and his prime justification is the ability to carry out the selling process at low cost because he is offering a wider range of products to the same group of customers. The agent's income is from the commission on the sales he makes. A firm entering an overseas market for the first time will often operate through an agent in the market concerned. Some countries have special legislation to defend the rights of such agents.

The distributor is independent, buying and selling on his own behalf and making his profit from the mark-up. He is, however, financially responsible for his own stock, although this responsibility is in practice sometimes softened by the manufacturer, who will offer longer credit terms, willingness to take back obsolete stock and some protection against the impact of price changes. In fact, the distinction between the agent and the distributor in practical terms, can become blurred. Discussion below focuses on the work of the distributor, but much of what is said applies with modification to the agent. One distinction, sometimes of importance, is that resale price maintenance legislation may forbid manufacturers to prescribe the price at which the distributor sells, but leaves him free to control the price at which his agent sells.

Key roles of the intermediary

Transport A classic role is that of breaking bulk. Where items are bought by many customers in small quantities, it is cheaper to transport the goods to convenient centres and from these distribute in small lots. The existence of agricultural and builders' merchants is related to this cause.

Stock-holding Stocks can be held by at least three different interests; the manufacturer, the intermediary or the customer. Stock-holding by the customer of reserve supplies of spares and small items in irregular demand is generally less economical than stock-holding by an intermediary who deals with a number of customers and can average out their demand variations. As he is nearer the customers, his stock can be drawn upon by them more speedily than by obtaining the goods from the manufacturer. The existence of this stock can be a two-edged sword, as the manufacturer can lose touch with what is happening to user demand until he receives an order from the distributor which, if ill-considered, could exaggerate the change in final demand. The relationship with the distributor requires some consideration of the ways in which accurate information can be provided.

Representation and communication   Sometimes because of the small size of the business between one individual supplier and each individual customer, the cost of a salesman calling direct from the manufacturer on each customer can be disproportionate to the business generated. Both distributor and agent normally carry a number of manufacturers' products, and this can keep average costs down by spreading the cost over all these lines. In both cases they may also be able to take advantage of local knowledge and existing customer loyalties to sell more effectively.

Choice, display and customer convenience   There are some lines in which the intermediary offers the convenience of choice so that the purchaser can compare products offered by different manufacturers more economically and conveniently than if he had to deal with and evaluate separately the offerings of each directly. He may also appreciate the advantage of seeing the goods displayed, and of local facilities for installation and maintenance.

The original manufacturer has, however, some special problems in dealing with the distributor. First, there can be a conflict of interest. The distributor and manufacturer are each interested in his own business and his own profits, and these interests will not automatically coincide. The distributor's interest in making profitable sales implies that he will sell one manufacturer's products as willingly as he will sell the competitor's models of the same product. Loss of control by the original manufacturer follows, and introduces complexities in planning his marketing. He is therefore faced with the need to obtain results by developing arrangements which, while providing profitable business for his own company, will recognise the distributor's legitimate interest in developing his own profits, to the benefit of both parties. The object is to create an alliance between a team of distributors and the manufacturing company which is fruitful for all the parties concerned.

Supplier/distributor relationships

The first decision then is whether or not to use distributors, and the answer will in many cases be obvious—pre-empted by economics and customer habits. In other cases the decision will be less clear-cut and there may be a case for leaving certain parts of the market to the distributor and handling the rest direct, in accordance with the principles already discussed. The split of the market may be decided on the basis of the following variables:

1   *Region*   Areas of low demand may be handed to the distributor rather than dealt with by the manufacturer himself. The distributor handling other products and having special local knowledge may operate more effectively than the manufacturer.

2   *Customers*   This policy may be further modified, perhaps by reserving to the distributor customers whose business is below a certain annual volume and to the manufacturer those above. This involves certain problems, as individual customers' turnover increases or diminishes. Certain national accounts may commonly be reserved to the manufacturer.

3   *Types of product*   Simpler products and smaller sales will go through distributors, with the more complex technical products being handled by the manufacturer's salesman, perhaps with some commission to the distributor where he plays a part in generating a sale.

4   *Size of order*   Orders below a certain size are reserved to the distributor, those above it to the manufacturer (with perhaps an intermediate common zone).

Defining the distributor's market is not straightforward. Naturally, it is desired to be as simple as possible, but it is not always possible to be both simple and acceptable to both parties.

The manufacturer may adopt a policy of selling to all distributors, subject to the usual considerations of credit-worthiness; this is common in distributing many minor products to the building industry. Alternatively, he may operate a policy which involves a preferential arrangement with some distributors. In return for the preference shown, the distributor may be expected to cooperate in the overall marketing plans of the manufacturer. Preferential arrangements can vary from complete exclusivity, under which each distributor has sole rights for a particular part of the market, to distributors who are limited in number but do not have completely exclusive rights. It may be a scheme under which some distributors are 'approved' to work in close cooperation with the manufacturer, who gives them particular backing, while still being prepared to supply other distributors.

In choosing which of these principles to adopt, the manufacturer will have to be fully aware of marketing motivation affecting the product concerned. If for example the product is to be sold through all suitable outlets, it is assumed that the potential user of a product in wide demand will be motivated to ask for it and that the supplier's brand will be acceptable, perhaps even preferred or insisted upon. The important marketing function of the distributor is that of stocking the product. The process of 'back-selling' operates to produce customer inquiry, and this needs the support of widespread distribution and availability. Sometimes the product can be treated like a fast-selling consumer good. Point-of-sale display of promotional material or of the product may be backed by premium offers, couponing or competitions.

Thus the supplier's salesman will seek to ensure that all distributors are stocking the product and that the stock is maintained at reasonable levels. Advertising, public relations and promotion will seek to keep the name of this product not only before the customer but before the staff of the distributor, so that they are well informed about the product and firm in their selling of it. The object is to concentrate the selling efforts on the product of the manufacturer concerned. His salesman when he calls on the distributor will try to ensure that everything that can be done is done to move the product out. Such factors as clarity of packing so that the storeman can quickly identify type and size of product, good literature for the use of the staff and customers of the store are imperative.

If some preferential arrangement is adopted, then the supplier/distributor relationship becomes closer. In choosing a distributor who is to represent him, the manufacturer will check the quality of product knowledge among the sales and technical staff concerned and will, if it can be arranged, provide formal training relevant to his product line. He will cooperate to provide literature benefiting both parties and offer a wide range of advice to make sure that the business of the distributors is growing and profitable. He may provide finance or management consultancy service. The manufacturer's own sales staff may at times undertake selling to distributor's customers on behalf of the distributor. This would be appropriate on a short-term basis, when a new market is being opened or a new product introduced.

The closest relationship is the one of exclusivity in which the manufacturer has handed over certain business within a particular area to one distributor with the assurance that no other distributor in the same area will be appointed to handle these products. This, of course, puts the distributor in a favoured position if the product is a good one which can expect to meet a ready market reaction. The manufacturer should choose such a distributor with particular care and ensure that his staff has, or can reasonably soon obtain, sufficient expertise (technical, selling and executive) the quality and reputation of the management is such that the market can be developed fully and efficiently.

The distributor may well cooperate with the manufacturer on stock planning to ensure that sufficient stocks will be carried. In addition, the manufacturer may offer, and expect the distributor's personnel to attend, training programmes to ensure that the standard of competence and knowledge of his products is maintained and developed. Some manufacturers will go to great lengths to help distributors, making available all manner of management services on subsidised terms or free of charge. Where they have not considered existing distributors efficient, or where there has not been a distributor network in existence, a company may recruit promising applicants, train them, back them with finance and thus produce good-quality distributors.

Exclusive distribution generally requires that a distributor will agree to meet specified obligations concerning stock, and training of some specialised staff, and will cooperate willingly in developing the market. Cooperative advertising and other cooperative ventures to enlarge the market may be developed, each party paying part of the cost. Ideally, before appointing the dealer, checks may very well be carried out among customers to ascertain what qualities they look for when deciding to deal with a distributor, how much importance do they attach to quick delivery, good advice and other factors, and what reputation has the distributor amongst possible customers.

The distributor may be asked to accept an obligation not to stock directly competing products. Sometimes this may be an unreasonable requirement, when competitors' brands are well known, sought after and conveniently purchased and sold in conjunction with other products. In these circumstances, perhaps the distributor may handle these products but will cooperate in pushing those which are the subject of the distributorship. He may also be asked to provide inventory, sales and other market intelligence at appropriate intervals.

The supplier may accept obligations to leave certain classes of business with the agent, train his staff, provide promotional material, advise on inventory and short-term (sometimes long-term) feedback.

The idea that the representatives who work with the distributors should be a separate section of the sales force has much to commend it. The problems of the distributor are sufficiently different to require specialised attention and knowledge, and this is one way in which these can be provided.

One interesting use of distributors in Britain is the authorised industrial distributor in the electronic equipment field. The number of small users for electronic products is many and varied—laboratories, industrial users, educational establishments and others.

Manufacturers 'authorise' distributors for particular areas of the country. Within this area orders received are dealt with on the following basis:

Small orders—handled by the distributor.
Intermediate orders—handled either by the manufacturer or the distributor.
Large orders—handled by the manufacturer.

It should be noted that under this arrangement a 'small order' received by the manufacturer will be transferred to the distributor, and vice versa for the large orders.

In the intermediate zone, orders may be handled by either party, but if one of them is unable to give prompt attention to an order, for example because the goods are out of stock, it will be transferred to the other. The size range covered by the terms 'small', 'intermediate' or 'large' will, of course, be specified in the agreement between the distributor and the manufacturer. In general, manufacturers agree to the distributor stocking competitors' products, as the well-balanced product line is the attraction to the buyer.

18 ORGANISATION AND MARKETING

Any discussion of the organisation of firms and of the departments that compose them is complicated by the fact that there are two major directions from which these issues may be approached. The earlier 'classical' approach envisaged a company as an organisation divided into sections, each section consisted of a group of employees, and the company as a whole was a hierarchy of sections. At the apex was the chief executive, and immediately under him was a number of sections, each headed by a senior manager. In turn each of these senior managers had a layer of sections subordinate to him, and so on down through the company. The system of relationships could be set out in an organisation chart. Each individual would be aware of his place in the system, to whom he reported and who reported to him. The head of each section had work delegated to him by a superior, and in turn could delegate to his subordinates.

The organisation chart is certainly often a convenient way of depicting the most important formal relationships in a company. Nevertheless critics have stressed the limitations of the classical approach. It appeared often to regard people as passive instruments behaving mechanistically, and not as human beings with motivations of their own. It did not give attention to the informal groups which develop in a firm. The formal organisational structure and autocratic management which it facilitated seemed often to create frustration among workers and prevent job satisfaction. The approach seemed not to encourage the sense of common purpose and shared values which are helpful if individuals are to work together. More recent writers give much more weight to alternative approaches which stressed the benefits of less rigid approaches with participative management styles, where individuals could communicate laterally as well as vertically and where more decision-making was shifted to lower levels of the organisation.

The company context

Marketing is not the concern of the marketing department alone, for the marketing approach seeks to achieve a company-wide focus on the market. Looking first at its formal location three possible interpretations of the department's authority have been identified by Kotler [41]:

1 The conventional company: organised by major functions (marketing, engineering, production, finance and personnel). Marketing carries responsibility for its own sub-functions (sales, advertising, market research). However, other functions also carry related sub-functions which impinge on the customer, as follows:

   Finance: credit.
   Engineering: R&D.
   Personnel: public relations, purchasing.
   Production: physical distribution.

2 The effective marketing department: still based on the principle of major functions, as before, but *all* customer impinging sub-functions are taken over by marketing and are not left with other main functional departments.

3 The marketing company: carries the leadership role of marketing to its limits as all *major* functions of the firm have been subordinated to the marketing department.

Whatever the ultimate logic of the third interpretation, it is rare indeed that it is formally applied to marketing industrial goods (although some service agencies, such as advertising, approach this type of structure). This in fact may not be a disadvantage. To attempt to restructure an existing organisation to conform to the third interpretation may cause harm through the internal stress it generates which exceeds any benefit which can reasonably be anticipated. It may be better to be satisfied with a less thoroughly marketing oriented structure if informal understandings can produce a company wide marketing attitude. Indeed some, often smaller, firms appear to approach the third classification without marketing as a separate department.

The marketing department generally have responsibility for or substantial influence on all customer and market impinging activities, and makes its own particular contribution, derived from its understanding of long-term environmental trends, to the development of the firm's strategic policy.

The corporate attitude can be influenced towards marketing in many ways. Informal methods include the facilitating of social contacts between the staff of marketing and that of other departments, involving them together in planning teams and committee work, offering full cooperation with and consulting other departments on policy and operations which affect them and taking account of their views. The company training system can also help through introductory sessions on marketing in induction courses, and special seminars or short courses on marketing for non-marketing departments.

If carried through with skill and attention to detail, the marketing plan, for which his department is responsible can also underpin the marketing manager's role in corporate leadership. The plan, with its sales goals and clear indications of what is necessary to achieve these goals and harmonise the entire firm to the process, gives authority, not only in its preparation but also as marketing carries out its role as watchdog on the plan, monitor of the environment and source of contingent guidance or corrective action to offset shortfalls.

The marketing manager

The marketing manager (using that term to designate the top executive of the marketing department, whether he is in fact called manager or director) thus has not only a departmental responsibility, but also the duty of developing the marketing attitude throughout the whole company. This task is most heavy when the department is newly established. There is much misunderstanding about the nature of marketing, and some existing departmental heads may see the new department as derogating from their authority. In fact the contrary is the case, for through the marketing plan the marketing department provides a framework which should improve the commercial effectiveness of all sections of the company.

Formal authority not being itself a sufficient basis for developing a different company attitude, the new marketing manager who expects a ready acceptance of his views is often disappointed. Even those executives originally responsible for making the appointment have sometimes been found not to have appreciated fully the implications of their decision, and one of the early needs is to obtain understanding and acceptance by top management of the full implications of the marketing approach. New attitudes cannot be developed amongst subordinates solely by issuing orders. An important quality of the executive selected for this post when it is first created is the ability to command sufficient personal acceptance to clear these hurdles.

The new marketing manager must have the skills of management in its fullest sense. He cannot, for example, hope to carry weight in discussions with the finance officer, unless well informed about the financial and accounting concepts of managerial significance. He should have some insight into basic statistical concepts. He must be versed in the principles of management and skilled in their application. His own department must be run crisply and efficiently. He will find that a leadership role among his colleagues in the company is not his inalienable right, but must be won by his abilities in practice, by the cogency and skill with which his own ideas are presented. Because the formal structure of the company is unlikely to move towards Stage 3 he must use informal contacts to achieve his purpose.

Departmental organisation

Within the department, one would commonly expect to find in a conventional company responsibility for such activities as:

1 Market research and forecasting.
2 Marketing planning.
3 Selling and sales organisation.
4 Advertising, publicity and promotion.
5 Distributor relations.
6 Service.
7 Physical distribution sometimes.

Scheduling the exact content of these items is not attempted here, because of the inevitable variation. Each is discussed in its appropriate chapter. Moreover, when the detailed content is examined it becomes more difficult to say where precisely marketing responsibility begins and ends. The criterion of quick coordination and communication is one which should be given much weight in relation to those matters which particularly affect competitive advantage at the time the sale is closed. If an early delivery date is the key, then production scheduling authority may well be with the marketing department; if minor price variation is the nub, then sufficient authority must be with marketing and so on. The ideal would be so to decentralise these decisions that they are made as close to the customer as possible, but there is difficulty in following this through because of the wider implications which such decisions may have and the difficulty of ensuring that the sales staff concerned fully understand and work in accordance with current policy.

Within the department, the basic organisational design is concerned with the reconciliation of three pressures:

1 The pressure to organise by function, because this gives functional economies of scale.
2 The pressure to organise by products because of the natural technical and economic requirements of the productive process with which marketing must coordinate.
3 The pressure to organise by customer or market segments in order to best meet differing needs.

In the simplest of cases there is no problem.

Where there is one major product or a group of naturally related products sold to many customers, the natural organisation is the very simple functional basis illustrated in Exhibit 19. Here each of the main functions is separately responsible to the marketing manager, and all work on any one function is grouped together. Sometimes two or more functions may be linked, for example, marketing research reporting to marketing planning.

The planning section is an important part of the marketing department. It is initially responsible for developing the overall marketing plan, including special projects such as the launch of new products. It has to work closely with marketing research, which provides the external information on which the plan is based. It needs strong links and good relations with all major departments of the firm.

In many companies, the sales section has more staff than the rest of the marketing department together, and the sales manager is a powerful and influential figure. His post is an important one, but his

EXHIBIT 19 Functional organisation of the marketing department

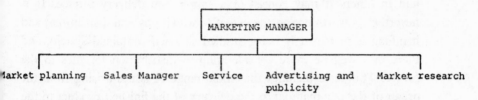

influence can lead to a department concentrating on the short-term sales volume and losing sight of the goal of long-term profitability. Today's problems are pressing; they arrive as letters, memoranda and telephone calls demanding immediate answer. Long-term problems may seem to lack the same imperative demand for action. Unless the responsibility for looking ahead is clearly specified, it can fail to receive the attention it deserves.

Ancillary service is frequently responsible to the sales manager, but may be a separate section within the marketing department when the emphasis is on post-sale service such as repair and maintenance.

The marketing research department may well have functions wider than its name implies. It can operate to assist not only as a provider of information but as a diagnostic aid in the analysis of marketing problems, the identification of the information needed and the development of strategy.

Depending on the volume of work to be done, the advertising, promotion and publicity department may place its media advertising through an agency, reserving to itself responsibility for some or all of the company's literature and mail shots. Practice varies. Where the company decides to accept responsibility for literature, it must employ an experienced writer, either full-time, or perhaps part-time if someone suitable can be found on this basis. A production department will also be needed; some of the work may be contracted out, but bigger departments may prefer to do most themselves. Public relations and press relations may be associated with advertising or directly responsible to a higher level. If it is within the publicity section, the PR man may need a flexible relationship, with authority to consult senior executives, up to managing director, when matters of sufficient consequence arise.

Physical distribution is a specialised area, varying from industry to industry; in some companies it is highly complex, with goods being transported by pipeline, canal, express freight train and road vehicles, and in others it may consist of a simple van delivery service. It is nevertheless worth noting the extent to which physical distribution and handling is increasingly being studied as a self-contained system, and there may well be more consideration to distribution logistics in the future. This term includes the whole range of issues arising from the origin of the raw material to the delivery of the finished product to the end-user (including transport, handling, storage, packing, documentation, insurance, finance, losses in transit and management of the system).

Alternative forms

In order to deal with the problems of reconciling function, products and customers' problems in the organisational structure and to knit together diverse departments, the post of product manager has been created in some industrial marketing departments. The product manager is given responsibility for overseeing a group of products. His task is to ensure that new applications and product variations are developed and integrated marketing plans devised. He recommends these plans to the marketing manager for submission to appropriate Board or other committees for sanction. After approval he monitors them and uses his influence to see that these plans are conscientiously implemented. His job is to persuade and he is not normally given line authority, although his role in planning gives weight to his representations. He keeps check on the profitability of his products and ensures that plans throughout the company are attuned to the market in all aspects from production to delivery.

Clearly this is not an easy job to fit into some traditional organisations. The product manager must, for example, liaise with the sales department to ensure that the sales force has all necessary aids, calls on the right customers, spends an appropriate amount of time on his products and stress the right points in their presentations. In doing this he could conflict with the authority of the sales manager over his sales staff or develop into a sort of supernumerary salesman concentrating on a few major accounts. He must also cooperate with production on questions of job priorities, run length and inventory, and with finance on credit and costing. Yet the idea of having one focus for information, planning and oversight of marketing action is an attractive one. It corrects the difficulty which can arise of there being no one in the company who has a complete view of what is happening to a particular product class, and who is able to form an opinion as to why it is happening and what action is necessary. It seems to work best where there is a clear need for this task because of the variations in products and where a tradition of tolerant management permits.

Another alternative is to appoint market managers to oversee actions aimed at specific markets. Their function is to integrate across products. This is a less common solution which perhaps deserves more attention.

Some companies as they grow replace the functional organisation by a decentralised system in which the marketing department is divided into sections each concerned with part of the company's business. The sections are commonly differentiated by reference either to particular groups of products or to particular markets. Commonly some specialised functions may remain centralised as a common service to all, but where a particularly heavy requirement exists a section may require its own staff, for example, its own sales or service staff.

Exhibit 20 fits to either type of specialisation, although they involve different approaches, one emphasising the bringing together of staff concerned with the same product group, the other bringing together staff concerned with the same markets. A product structure is probably more common, but again market structure perhaps deserves more consideration.

Carried further this leads to the total organisation becoming market centred as discussed later in this chapter.

I

EXHIBIT 20 Sectional organisation of the marketing department

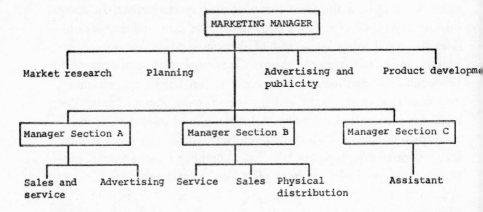

Product planning

One particular function over which there can be dispute is the location of the product planning section in the company as a whole. In consumer marketing it is commonly in the marketing department. This gives the marketing department decisive influence over what is to be produced and the detail of the product.

Clearly the views of marketing should have full impact. In consumer markets most product changes flow from an evolutionary adaptation to customer and market pressures, with fundamental research only a factor in a small proportion of the changes, except in such areas as pharmaceuticals. The emphasis is more in development than research. Moreover, promotional costs are often a much greater factor in consumer marketing.

Given the company has determined explicitly or implicitly a particular corporate strategy, the question 'What products will potential customers need in a few years' time?' must determine the general direction of research and development, and the question 'What product detail is appropriate for today's customers?' is the specification of current products. These questions are ones which the marketing department must answer, and it must give guidance at an early stage —even before research has gone ahead.

The problem then is whether the answers given by the marketing department can most effectively be integrated with the company as a whole by placing product planning within that department, or by setting it up separately, directly responsible at top level within the company to appropriate marketing oriented leadership. Its major proposals might be reported to an interdepartmental committee, and much of its details controlled by project groups as proposed in Chapter 7.

The solution will depend upon a number of considerations. Features which would encourage the location of product planning in the marketing department include:

1   High cost and risk in marketing the finished product.
2   Rapid change in the market.
3   Importance of features of the product.
4   Assurance that R&D will have a high probability of devising the types of product normally required.
5   Ample opportunity to expand in present markets.
6   Low probability of marketable ideas being generated by other departments, for example R&D, as a by-product of other work.

Where the opposite emphasis is present, it is more difficult to resist the arguments for a central product planning department independent of other major departments. Finally, much would depend upon the individual knowledge and qualities of the marketing director concerned. His need for objectivity is very important, as the area of new products is one in which objectivity can be difficult to achieve. Even if product planning is a separate department, the marketing planning section will have special responsibility for giving attention to this subject.

Supplementing these basic sections, some companies have found it desirable to have other sections for special purposes. Market development is an example. This is a separate section to negotiate with substantial customers when marketing new products or entering new markets. Market development has more authority to agree prices or enter into long-term commitments than has the regular sales force.

Establishing a marketing department

When a company is establishing a marketing approach and a marketing department for the first time, it is faced with the problem of changing from the present structure to a new one with minimum disruption of existing staff relationships. The sales manager has ranked at the level of other departmental heads, and will not relish the prospect of a marketing manager above him.

The change from existing organisation may then take place in several steps phased over a period, the company having clearly in mind the ultimate structure which it seeks to create.

If the sales manager is a suitable individual for appointment to marketing manager, the process of adjustment is easier. It can be a logical step in his career; he knows the company and its customers and may be willing to learn the new skills and develop new attitudes to take his place as a key man in the company's top management. His claim deserves careful consideration.

If he is not so inclined, the alternative is to bring in a man from outside, who may be a good marketing man but will have to learn about the company, its products and its customers. One solution which has been adopted is to appoint a marketing manager at the same level as the existing sales manager. His job is then to focus on the planning, profitability and long-term aspects of the marketing role, until such time as it may be expedient to take the further step in sharply defining the marketing organisation. Marketing research will inevitably come into prominence in the company as the planning procedure develops.

The total firm and its environment

The earlier paragraphs of this chapter discussed the place of marketing in the firm. But marketing in its widest sense involves the total relationship between the firm and the outside world. It has been argued that the form of organisation of the firm itself must also suit environmental characteristics.

Traditional organisational patterns are often functional but Hanan [42] suggests that a market-centred organisation can sometimes be more effective: in this system 'major markets become the centres around which its divisions are built', A market is a group of customer needs, thus an electronics firm may focus around such areas as: instrumentation and control, home entertainment industries and computer manufacturers. The style has its disadvantages and Hanan argues that five particular instances favour 'market-centring'. He identifies these as situations :

1 'When market leadership is threatened by a competitor who has achieved sufficient product parity to deprive the leader of price superiority.'
2 'When new product famine has afflicted the product development function.'
3 'When a product manufacturer desires either to diversify into high margin services . . . or to market systems.'
4 'When a manufacturer . . . shifts his marketing strategy to feature the financial benefits of customer profit improvement.'
5 'When a marketer desires to attract a more entrepreneurial type of manager.'

This is, of course, not the only organisational approach worth examining. The idea of a matrix system, where an individual has a dual responsibility (perhaps one product-oriented, the other function-oriented) may also prove to have marketing effectiveness.

Formality and informality

No discussion of the adaptation of the firm's fit to its environment would be complete without considering some recent writings on organisational and managerial styles. An environment can be relatively stable and predictable (when there is little change) or fast moving and hard to forecast. Some recent writers have argued that the more environmental change is rapid and uncertain, the more advantageous it is to the firm to:

1 Have a participative management style (rather than an authoritarian style).
2 Have a wider span of control with fewer layers of authority (rather than the reverse).
3 Have a low reliance on formal rules.
4 Have a longer time horizon amongst managers and professionals.

This is summed up in the following comments (Lawrence and Lorsch [43]):

'an organisation dealing with a rapidly changing environment . . . must be capable of creative and flexible problem-solving to discover potential opportunities for conducting more favourable transactions. Here again that unit will thrive which relies not on rules but on a more complex and flatter communication network which serves to stimulate new ideas. Such a unit would be oriented to a longer time perspective. It would thus be matched with the features of its environment as it works at solving the problem of defining and continually redefining the terms of its environmental transactions.'

These matters deserve more consideration than is possible here, but there is an increasing volume of research supporting these hypotheses.

The venture team

From this philosophy, has developed the 'venture team', an interesting organisational innovation for the particular purpose of fitting the company's organisation to the purpose of developing new products, especially those which represent signficant innovations. The team is separate from the operating organisation lest established structures and staff should inhibit its operation. It is (according to Hill and Hlavacek [25]) a multidisciplinary team with a diffuse authority within the team and unstructured relationships. The 'spirit of entrepreneurship was most effectively heightened by financial arrangements which permitted venture team members to share in the profits of the venture'. The team has wide discretion and reports to a senior level in the organisation.

19 CORPORATE STRATEGY

At first sight a chapter on corporate strategy may seem out of place in a text on marketing. There is however a good reason for its inclusion. Marketing begins when the corporate strategy of the firm is determined and cannot be expected to achieve its maximum contribution unless that strategy is thought through. The definition of marketing recommended in Chapter 1 was that it was concerned with the interaction between the firm and the world outside. Corporate strategy is concerned with the same question, but with emphasis on the very long term during which fundamental changes could be made to the essential nature of the firm's business. Marketing is concerned with the somewhat shorter term in which the general nature of the firm's generic product, its principal technology and its class of market mission are not substantially varied although individual products, operations and customers may well change.

Both sets of decisions flow from analysis and anticipation of what is happening 'out there' beyond the formal limits of the organisation concerned, and consideration of what action is feasible to fulfil the company's objectives within the limitations of the resources which it has or might obtain. In some industrial markets in which product development may take twenty years or so to bring to fruition, or customers may take a decade or more in the buying decision process and may be as large as a national government, marketing and corporate strategy merge to a considerable extent.

The periods for which business decisions are made can be classified into three:

1   *The strategic period* This is the longest and is the period for which quantitative forecasting is of least value because the uncertainties involved create a wide margin of error.

2   *The mid-term period*   The nearer period of time, such as
is commonly covered by the 5 to 10 year forecast of financial returns, the expected limits of error not being so great as to destroy
the value of the forecast.

3   *The operating period*   The short-term decision-making period
which characterises the regular cycle of operations throughout
the company.

In the strategic period, the concepts of corporate strategy and of marketing converge and become indistinguishable. The strategic decisions
control the marketing policy which is followed in the mid-term period,
and this in turn is the framework for the marketing plan and the individual managerial operating decisions (see Exhibit 1).

The rise of corporate strategy

Factors which have brought corporate strategy to the fore are from
two main sources. One is the time and cost involved in creating the
complex of fixed assets and corporate skills which make up the modern
business. Buildings, plant and other expensive equipment must be
matched to each other to create a cohesive unit fitted to the market
purposes which they are to serve. They must be backed by qualified staff
(executives, sales representatives, research and development scientists)
and skilled operatives. Once these assets and skills are established they
substantially determine which market opportunities the company is
equipped to exploit and which it is better advised to leave alone, although good strategy seeks to incorporate a sufficient measure of
flexibility and adaptability. It follows therefore that rational management seeks to look well ahead so that it can consciously develop an
organisation equipped to adapt to and prosper in the unfolding business environment. The other major source of pressures to change and
adapt is the rise and fall of substantial markets. The causes are
various and are discussed below. (Students find the word PEST provides
a helpful mnemonic.)

Political and legal factors operating in many ways: changes in tariffs
have opened markets to some suppliers and threatened others with new
competition. Legislation seeking to protect workers, consumers and

society at large has had similar effect. Governments have acted in ways which have benefited some firms but distressed others.

Economic forces have been at work on a wide front. The rise of living standards, faster in some countries than others, has caused differential demand growth for consumer goods and services and reacted on the demand for industrial goods. Most dramatic was the change in prices of primary products in 1973/4 which may have a long-term affect on the relative usage of some industrial products, and may stimulate study of recycling and usage efficiency.

Social pressures Concern with the environment has an impact on firms whose products and processes affect the air, water or countryside either as causes or cures; the unhappy growth of urban terrorism has led to the development of services and products to protect, prevent and counteract. A host of influences derived from changing norms and habits have directly or indirectly affected industrial markets.

Technological change has led to the decline of some markets and the growth of others; the chemical industry has developed materials which can provide alternatives to existing products in many industries; and has gone on to provide alternatives to its own alternatives. Manufacturers in many fields must continually ask themselves whether a chemical industry product may provide a better means of satisfying the customer in such fields as textiles, packaging and building materials. Electronics has reacted on communication, office organisation, instrumentation and control with similar effect.

Developments such as these can damage and destroy the traditional market on which a company's prosperity has been built. The company may then find itself with its past markets disappearing and an array of resources—using that word as a short description not only of its physical assets but also for the skills of its managerial staff, specialists and operatives—which are ill suited to compete in any other market. The best operating decisions on product planning, salesmanship and promotion may well be limited in what they can do to relieve the gloom, as the root of the problem lies in an earlier failure to adopt a suitable approach to the changing outside world.

I*

The broad trends which bring about such situations have sometimes been visible years in advance, not especially to the statistician, market researcher and economist, but to any perceptive businessman who reads, absorbs and thinks about the contents of the leading daily and weekly press, and of the more serious television programmes. If a company appreciates the broad significance of these trends in time, it can seek out other suitable areas of market opportunity to which it can adapt and from which it can profit. Yet despite this possibility, there have been companies making such products as, for example, small arms and motor cycles which have left it over-late to adapt.

The strategic approach

Corporate strategy seeks to anticipate such developments, so that the firm can modify its business in good time to move out of areas of business with poorer prospects into others with better. It is a positive approach to the achievement of organisational goals.

Change may close some doors, but can also open others, and a company in no way threatened but infused with an entrepreneurial spirit, may well wish to address itself to the question: 'Can we do better by identifying, and setting out to adapt to fit the new market opportunities of the future?'

Strategy seeks to lay down guidelines designed to achieve the maximum possible match between today's long-term decision and the firm's anticipated future environment. The many decisions made every day in a firm each affect some detail of its assets, competences and philosophy. Their collective effect over a period of years is to reconstruct it. Unless constrained by some wider approach, it will be sheer chance if the company achieves a structural pattern which is suited to take advantage of the unfolding environment.

The dominating principle of corporate strategy is that company top management should study the trends apparent today, in order to identify the emerging risks and opportunities of the future. After a systematic analysis of the assets and competences of the company, decisions are made determining how the company might adapt to fit best to new horizons.

In practice, much strategic thinking is less formal than the approach described here. A firm's development may be more by evolution and adaptation in response to circumstances than by a grand strategic plan. Nevertheless, this formal process gives a basis with which less rigorous analyses may be compared.

Fundamental objectives

If one were to ask a businessman to state the fundamental purpose of his company his answer is traditionally expected to be 'To make as much money as possible' or 'To maximise profits.' Such replies focus on the economic objectives of the business and offer these formulae as a first approximation to them.

Although a complete set of objectives of the company will include certain non-economic purposes, it is useful to look carefully at the economic objectives. Most businessmen, if pressed, would probably seek to qualify this traditional view. A typical comment might be: 'In the long term of course—I don't mean you charge as much as you can today and end up with no customers next year', or perhaps a suggestion that the objective is 'To maximise the long-term return on equity'.

It is certainly a common assumption that it is the intention of management to seek some such objective. Nevertheless, this view must often be subject to a very qualified interpretation.

Even if the interest of the equity shareholders were the prime concern, all major management decisions are made with some degree of uncertainty as to their outcome. Because of this element of risk, some writers have emphasised the overriding importance of survival. This may well lead a company to decisions which do not offer the maximum probable return but to prefer a course of action which offers somewhat less but with greater certainty as to its achievement. The executive of a company which has been selling electronic equipment for defence purposes may have observed that a change of Government policy could lead to the termination of major contracts and imperil company prospects. The company may, therefore, prefer a more flexible and low-risk strategy and seek to expand non-defence markets for its products, even though this may reduce probable profits at least for some years. Some balance has to be struck between expected profit and the risk involved in attaining this profit.

It is, however, less clear to what extent the policy of a company should be directed to seeking the maximum benefit for the share-

holders. There are many voices which argue that this is only one responsibility, and the ordinary shareholder himself is not particularly
active in seeking to defend his interest. 'It is only after a disaster has
happened that the shareholder's voice is normally heard', says one
writer (Shonfield [44]).

Trade unions press the interest of their members. Employees certainly have an interest in the wellbeing of the firm in which they work.
Quite apart from the unions' own bargaining power, the law in different
countries increasingly insists on the employee's right to be consulted
on major company decisions affecting employment prospects and sometimes requires worker participation on the Board.

A company is under pressure from many other groups seeking to
protect some interest or other. Government and semi-Government
agencies concerned with prices, restrictive practices, monopolies and
other matters have been established in many countries to safeguard
the public interest, described with varying degrees of precision.

Andrews [45] argues that the personal preference of senior executives can modify company objectives. Top executives are also normally
employees. They are not necessarily personally committed to a profit
maximisation objective but may prefer other goals for the firm which
suit their own personal motivations: they might favour sales maximisation for example once a certain minimum level of profit has been
reached. One executive may drive to expand the business whilst another
may prefer a quieter existence avoiding sharp competition. Certainly,
executives will have difficulty in running a business with objectives
seriously conflicting with their own personal dispositions. Nevertheless
the possibility of a takeover has proved on occasion wonderfully stimu-
lating to a self-satisfied management.

It is assumed however that business organisations will have important economic objectives. The emphasis of these objectives will depend
on individual circumstances. Proprietors hoping to sell a small firm
may seek dramatic short-term results. Entrepreneurial individuals
initiating a new firm may accept high risk as a necessary accompani-
ment of rapid growth: they may have much to gain and little to lose.
A well-established company may seek moderate rates of profit and
risk, and adopt a flexible pattern of resource allocation by broadening
its markets or entering different industries.

These objectives will be amplified by others reflecting the interests, philosophy and ethical attitudes of the proprietors or top executives of the company. There are well-known firms in which these considerations have carried great weight: a classic example is the dedication of the late Lord Thomson of Fleet to *The Times* newspaper.

Much of the earlier writing on this subject largely assumed that the businesses were in general owned by private individuals as shareholders, and that their policies were largely determined by a small number of executives who could choose, subject to the law of the land, what these policies should be. In many countries today major businesses are state-owned or substantially state-influenced. Their management can be under pressure to give less weight to traditional commercial criteria, and more to such criteria as keeping market prices down, keeping people employed and other policies deemed to foster national goals (and, perhaps, win support for the Government of the day?).

With all these factors at work it is hardly surprising that a statement by a board of its formal objectives does not automatically result in a company pursuing those objectives. What actually happens reflects a compromise between varying interests: these compromises may take place at different levels in the company and thus operational objectives can drift away from those the Board has attempted to legitimate.

Specific objectives

At this stage, from the fundamental objectives, a set of more specific business objectives is prepared. These traditionally would indicate if formally spelt out:

1   *Commercial objectives* Typically target return on investment linked to growth rate desired and risk level acceptable.
2   *Ethical and social objectives* or constraints.
3   *Personal objectives* of those who control the company.
4   *Basis of growth* including reference to special skills, knowledge or facilities which are the basis of the policy.

The long-term period was defined as the period within which useful forecasts of financial results are normally feasible. In the strategic period these forecasts are less satisfactory.

Ansoff [46] stresses this difficulty and suggests that instead characteristics of the firm contributing to long-term commercial success be measured: these include sales growth (relative to industry) and other measures related to the external position, internal position and flexibility of the firm.

Strategic guidelines

The executive is now faced with aspirations (what it is hoped to achieve), expectations (what is likely to be achieved with present policy) and resources (a heritage from the past, probably fitted to current markets). The key problem is to decide in what lines of business the company is most likely to achieve its aspirations (or something not too far removed from them). From this decision flow the strategic guidelines which disseminated through the firm will guide management at all levels on how they should adapt progressively in the following years. The dividing line between objectives and these guidelines is apt to be rather fuzzy but the following are typical issues which need to be resolved:

1   The market opportunities to be met, the classes of product mission to be filled, and the markets to be served, perhaps also the principal technology to be exploited. The company may not wish to put 'all its eggs in one basket' but prefer to have some degree of flexibility (e.g. through diversification) in order to reduce the risks involved in dependence on too narrow a base. This may be regarded as specifying in broad terms the general nature of the company's future business.
2   The process by which (1) is to be achieved, e.g. by growth from within, or by takeover and divestment; the actual process will depend to some degree on opportunities but the company's general attitude can be clarified and such steps as are reasonable put in train to produce the results sought.
3   The character of the competition to be offered in the different area, its intensity (offensive, defensive) and quality (whether on the basis of technological advance, price, service, for example).
4   The competences which are to be particularly developed, weaknesses to be remedied and strengths to be utilised (this if seriously

carried out will mean a very thorough and by no means easy study of the company, its fixed and other assets, the skills of those who work there, the quality of its organisation and the ability of the management in all functional areas).

Basically, the search is for a 'common thread' (Ansoff [46]) around which different activities of a company are harmonised, giving point and coherence to those activities and directing them towards the desired level of results and pattern of business.

The search process

Thus it will be desired to specify whether the product mission (the class of needs to be satisfied) is to be varied and whether the groups of customers to be served is to be varied. The natural starting point is to examine the probable results to be obtained from remaining in the company's present business, and to compare this with the aspirations (or tentative objectives) which have been specified. Perhaps the company's objectives may be satisfied by selling the same class of goods (including the natural development of other products consistent with the same overall purpose) to the same class of customers.

Suppose, however, that a review of trends indicates to the company's executive that this is unlikely to achieve its reasonable hopes for the future. Take, for example, the company manufacturing steam locomotives which saw that its natural market was likely to be lost to electric or diesel-electric traction, and that steam could not challenge this competition successfully. The executive will therefore search more widely beyond the limits of the present market.

The search process involves a systematic check of possible opportunities in different industries: it seems natural having examined first the firm's present business, to study next, related businesses and perhaps then to extend the search to examine conglomerate possibilities.

There are three possibilities. *First*, the executive might say: 'We are in the business of providing traction for rail and similar types of transport. Let us therefore set to and develop into a *new technology* and manufacture electric and diesel-electric locomotives.' However, after taking a good hard look at the implications of this decision, the executive might have further thoughts.

It might take the *second* line of approach and argue 'To develop that totally different type of technology in a reasonable span of years so that we can compete effectively with existing manufacturers looks a pretty tough job. Let us therefore find a new *market* opportunity for a different class of product using our present technology.' Both approaches are forms of related or concentric diversification.

The first approach stays with the present product mission and plans to change the technology. The second stays with the technology and plans to change the product mission. Both policies involve using in part existing company competences and in part developing new ones.

If examination of the two foregoing possibilities fails to produce an acceptable opportunity, then the company may examine the *third* difficult possibility of conglomerate diversification, moving both to new markets and to new technologies. This step is one which usually requires a high order of management skill, and it could be argued that in the conglomerate it is this skill which is a link relating the new development to the original base from which the company is moving. The purpose still remains the search for an appropriate market opportunity, to which the company can be adapted.

The resource inventory

Success in corporate strategy depends upon choosing a market matched to the company's feasible pattern of resources, a term which here includes not only its balance-sheet assets, but also the less tangible company skills, 'know-how' and experience. A necessary stage is therefore the preparation of an inventory of company resources: in particular, it is desired to identify those resources which the company has which are uncommon—differentiated or specialised resources. The company may be able to achieve a competitive advantage by turning them to account, and markets in which they can be utilised deserve careful scrutiny. Table 10 makes clear what is implied by such an inventory (Kline [47]).

The analysis thus covers the facilities and equipment which are possessed, the experience available, the suitability of the organisation for various purposes and the ability of management. This is obviously a lengthy process which requires impartial assessment. Success in a particular business depends in the long run on whether a company's

pattern of resources can be made appropriate to its market—
'appropriate', that is to say, as compared with competitors, for the
higher the qualities of competitors' assets and skills and the more
closely they match to the market opportunities, the higher will be the
standard by which the company should judge itself.

LE 10 Inventory of company resources

nancial strength	Money available or obtainable for financing research and development, plant construction, inventory, receivables, working capital, and operating losses in the early stages of commercial operation.
w material reserves	Ownership of or preferential access to, natural resources such as minerals and ores, brine deposits, natural gas, forests.
ysical plant	Manufacturing plant, research and testing facilities, warehouses, branch offices, trucks, tankers, etc.
cation	Situation of plant or other physical facilities with relation to markets, raw materials or utilities.
tents	Ownership or control of technical monopoly through patents.
blic acceptance	Brand preference, market contracts and other public support built up by successful performance in the past.
ecialised experience	Unique or uncommon knowledge of manufacturing, distribution, scientific fields, or managerial techniques.
rsonnel	Payroll of skilled labour, salesmen, engineers, or other workers with definite specialised abilities.
nagement	Professional skill, experience, ambition and will for growth of the company's leadership.

As each possible business is studied, the analyst will be attempting to
answer the following questions:

1 What are the trends in the business being studied?
2 What are the requirements for success in it?
3 How far do competitors match these requirements?
4 Is it possible that my company's present pattern of skills and
   assets can be developed to match these requirements as well as,
   or better than, competitors?
5 Can we therefore expect to compete successfully, and what competitive policy would achieve success?
6 By what steps can we proceed from our present pattern of resources to the required pattern?

Having identified promising business areas, the analyst seeks to forecast the expected level of success and compare this with the companies' aspirations. In principle the process continues until the aspirations are reasonably satisfied or perhaps revised to a more realistic level.

In determining this relationship, the company will have considered how far it can build on present resources, and by what competitive policies success in its chosen mission/market relationship is likely to be achieved. A company strong on R&D may seek to succeed by technical leadership. Another less strong in this aspect, perhaps smaller and with lower administrative costs, may prefer the role of a follower. It may leave major innovation to others and be content to come in later with minor variations built on the benefits of observing their experience. One company may take over an existing company in its planned area, while another may spread out from its present base.

Where a company is extending into new fields, there is often an advantage if this leads to the further exploitation of those *distinctive* resources which are not widely available in other companies. This gives a competitive advantage, and there may be economies from fuller utilisation of those resources and sometimes from a better balance between different skills or assets.

Conversely, there is always some degree of risk when a company leans too heavily on one resource, whether it be a market, a product, a skill, a person or an idea. Individual markets, products, skills, people and ideas are perishable and there is a need, therefore, to balance the advantages of exploiting the special qualities of a company to their fullest extent and the risk of building too heavily upon a narrow base.

Tests of strategy

Developed fully, the strategy now sets out the company's intended 'business' and the means by which its seeks success. Communicated to all managerial levels, it indicates what strengths are to be developed, what weaknesses are to be remedied and in what manner. Thus plans and operating decisions are developed in a manner which gradually brings the company into the relationship with the emerging pattern of market opportunities which analysis has shown to offer the highest prospect of success.

The following tests of the appropriateness of a strategy have been recommended by Andrews [45]:

1 Is the strategy identifiable and has it been made clear either in words or practice?

2 Does the strategy fully exploit domestic and international environmental opportunity?

3 Is the strategy consistent with corporate competence and resources, both present and projected?

4 Are the major provisions of strategy and the programme of major policies of which it is comprised internally consistent?

5 Is the chosen level of risk feasible in economic and personal terms?

6 Is the strategy appropriate to the personal values and aspirations of the key managers?

7 Is the strategy appropriate to the desired level of contribution to society?

8 Does the strategy constitute a clear stimulus to organisational effort and commitment?

9 Are there early indications of the responsiveness of markets and market segments to the strategy?

BIBLIOGRAPHY

1   H. W. Dickinson, *Matthew Boulton*, Cambridge University Press (1937).

2   A. R. Prest and D. J. Coppock, *The UK economy: a manual of applied economics*. Weidenfeld & Nisolson (Fourth edition, 1972).

3   E. M. Rogers and F. F. Shoemaker, *Communication of innovations*, Collier Macmillan (1971).

4   P. Gisser, *Launching the new industrial project*, American Management Association (1972).

5   B. Achilladelis *et al.*, *Project Sappho*, University of Sussex Science Policy Research Unit (1972).

6   National Economic Development Office, '*Handbook for marketing machinery prepared for the Machine Tools EDC*, HMSO (1970).

7   H. Hakansson and C. Östberg, *Industrial Marketing an Organizational Problem*, 4th Annual Workshop on Research in Marketing, The Marketing Institute (1975).

8   Y. Wind and R. Cardozo, 'Industrial market segmentation', *Industrial Marketing Management*, No. 3 (1974).

9   R. E. Frank *et al.*, *Market segmentation*, Prentice-Hall (1972).

10 P. J. Robinson *et al.*, *Industrial buying and creative marketing*, Allyn & Bacon (1967).

11 J. Thompson, *Organisations in action*, 1967. (*Copyright material used by permission of McGraw-Hill.*)

12 J. G. March and H. A. Simon, *Organisations*, John Wiley (1958).

13 S. Becker and L. Whisler, 'The innovative organisation', *Journal of Business* (*University of Chicago*), 40 (4), (1967).

14   R. W. Hill, *Marketing technological products to industry*, Pergamon Press (1972).

15   K. Lawyer, *Product characteristics as a function in marketing* (1967—unpublished).

16   P. J. Donnely and R. Holton, 'A note on product differentiation and entertainment expense allowance in the United States', *Journal of Industrial Economics* (March 1962).

17   NIAA Industrial Advertising Research Institute, Report No. 9, *Motives in industrial buying*, IARI (1959).

18   B. White, *Market planning*, unpublished paper presented to a seminar on Industrial Marketing, Central London Polytechnic (1968).

19   J. McFarlane-Smith, 'Interviewing techniques', *IMRA Journal* (August 1974).

20   A. Wilson, *The assessment of industrial markets*, Associated Business Programmes (1973).

21   A. E. Ansell, 'Industrial group discussions', *IMRA Journal* (May 1974).

22   D. J. Luck *et al.*, *Marketing research*, Prentice Hall (Third edition, 1970).

23   Industrial Marketing Research Association, *European guide to marketing consultancy*, IMRA (1975).

24   I. Maclean, 'Calculating the technical/economic change function', *IMRA Journal* (November 1972).

25   R. M. Hill and J. Hlavacek, 'The venture team: a new concept in marketing organisation, *Journal of Marketing (USA).* (July 1972).

26   C. Freeman, *The economics of industrial innovation*, Penguin (1974).

27   C. Shannon and W. Weaver, *The mathematical theory of communication*, University of Illinois Press (1949).

28   R. H. Colley, *Defining advertising goals for measuring advertising support*, Association of National Advertisers (1961).

29   E. Gunther, 'Evaluating corporate image measurements: a review of techniques', *Proceedings of the Fifth Annual Conference of the Advertising Research Foundation Incorporated* (1959).

30   T. Levitt, *Industrial purchasing behavior*, Division of Research,

Graduate School of Business Administration, Harvard
University (1965).

31 E. W. Duck, 'The integration of R&D and commercial functions', *in* A. Keynes (Editor), *Economics of research and development*, Central London Polytechnic (1967).

32 'Search for the perfect package', *Dunn Review* (November
1963).

33 D. N. Chorafas, *Sales engineering: the marketing of technological products*, Cassell (1967).

34 J. O'Shaughnessy, *Evaluate your sales force*, Management Publications *for* British Institute of Management (1971).

35 L. S. Simon, 'Measuring the impact of technical services',
Journal of Market Research (February 1965).

36 D. G. Monthoux and B. Persson, *The Eurofighter troika—a joint
venture case of complex systems industrial marketing*, 4th Annual
Workshop on Research in Marketing, The Marketing Institute
(1975).

37 F. R. Messner, *Industrial Advertising* (1963). (*Copyright
material used by permission of McGraw-Hill.*)

38 N. N. Barish, *Economic analysis* (1962). (*Copyright material
used by permission of McGraw-Hill*).

39 J. L. Grumbridge, *Marketing management in air transport*,
Allen & Unwin (1966).

40 D. A. Revzan, *Wholesaling in marketing organisations*, John
Wiley (1961).

41 P. Kotler, *Marketing management: analysis, planning and control*, Prentice Hall (Second edition, 1972).

42 M. Hanan, *'Reorganise your company around its markets'*,
Harvard Business Review (November/December 1974).

43 P. R. Lawrence and J. W. Lorsch, *Developing Organisations:
diagnosis and action*, Addison Wesley (1969).

44 A. Schonfield, *Modern capitalism*, Oxford University Press for
the Royal Institute of International Affairs (1965).

45 K. Andrews, *The concept of corporate strategy*, Dow-Jones/
Irwin (1974).

46 H. I. Ansoff, *Corporate strategy*, Penguin (1968).

47 C. H. Kline, 'The strategy of product policy', *Harvard Business
Review* (July–August, 1955).

48 Booz, Allen & Hamilton, Inc., *Management of new products* (1968).

49 P. J. Harrison and S. F. Pearce, 'The use of trend curves as an aid to market forecasting,' *Proceedings of the Sixth EVAF Conference,* European Association for Marketing Research (1971).

50 Institute of Public Relations, *Working definition,* unpublished (1975).

51 E. J. McCarthy, *Managerial marketing: perspectives and viewpoints,* Irwin (Revised edition, 1964).

INDEX